E-commerce: Principles, Technologies and Business Applications

E-commerce: Principles, Technologies and Business Applications

Edited by
Nathalie Porter

Larsen & Keller
www.larsen-keller.com

E-commerce: Principles, Technologies and Business Applications
Edited by Nathalie Porter
ISBN: 978-1-63549-053-4 (Hardback)

© 2017 Larsen & Keller

 Larsen & Keller

Published by Larsen and Keller Education,
5 Penn Plaza,
19th Floor,
New York, NY 10001, USA

Cataloging-in-Publication Data

E-commerce : principles, technologies and business applications / edited by Nathalie Porter.
   p. cm.
Includes bibliographical references and index.
ISBN 978-1-63549-053-4
1. Electronic commerce. 2. Commerce. I. Porter, Nathalie.
HF5548.32 .E26 2017
658.872--dc23

The publisher's policy is to use permanent paper from mills that operate a sustainable forestry policy. Furthermore, the publisher ensures that the text paper and cover boards used have met acceptable environmental accreditation standards.

Printed and bound in the United States of America.

For more information regarding Larsen and Keller Education and its products, please visit the publisher's website www.larsen-keller.com

Table of Contents

Preface

E-commerce is a rapidly evolving new field. It has changed the way we view business and Internet use. With the emergence of e-commerce, the traditional way business and trade works is being challenged and new and innovative ways are being added every day. As social media is developing very fast, the utilization of these resources to advertise, promote, trade and perform other business related activities through e-commerce is expanding. This book will give thorough insights into the growing field of e-commerce. It will explain in detail the new methods and uses of Internet in business and e-commerce. While understanding the long-term perspectives of the topics, this text makes an effort in highlighting their impact as a modern tool for the growth of the discipline. The book is meant for students who are looking for an elaborate reference text on this field.

Given below is the chapter wise description of the book:

Chapter 1- The trade and business performed through digital networks such as Internet and social networks is termed as e-commerce. Technologies used in e-commerce are online marketplaces, e-services and electronic business. This chapter is an overview of the subject matter incorporating all the major aspects of e-commerce.

Chapter 2- Businesses develop business models in order to achieve their targets and goals. The business models used in e-commerce are omnichannel, business-to-business, consumer-to-business, customer to customer and public eProcurement. As business to business is a situation where a commercial interaction occurs between two businesses and consumer to business is a business model where businesses consume values created by customers.

Chapter 3- Shopping cart software, jigshop, inventory management software and track and trace are the softwares used in e-commerce. The systems used for tracking orders, sales and deliveries are known as inventory management software whereas the process of determining the location of an item or property is track and trace. The topics discussed in the section are of great importance to broaden the existing knowledge on various e-commerce softwares.

Chapter 4- Mobile commerce is an emerging field of study. Mobile commerce is worth billions, with Asia representing almost half of the market. Some of the services of mobile commerce discussed in this chapter are mobile ticketing, mobile banking, mobile payment and mobile marketing. The topics discussed in the chapter are of great importance to broaden the existing knowledge on mobile commerce.

Chapter 5- Online banking helps the customer of any bank manage financial transactions through the bank's website. Online advertising on the other hand are the advertisements used on the Internet to promote marketing messages to consumers. Some of the applications of E-commerce discussed in the text are online banking, online auction, online advertising, electronic publishing and net market.

Chapter 6- The chapter on open source e-commerce offers an insightful focus, keeping in mind the complex subject matter. Various free and open-source software are available online that help to maintain store inventory and other databases. OsCommerce, drupal commerce, magenoto, nopCommerce, spree commerce and woocommerce are some softwares related to open source E-commerce.

Chapter 7- Websites that operate on darknets or the deep web are known as a darknet market. Darknet markets basically function as black-markets and they deal in illicit substances such as drugs, weapons and steroids. This chapter incorporates the types of darknet markets which are as agora, evolution and Silk Road.

Chapter 8- The systems used to settle financial transactions such as the transfer of money are known as payment system. A number of electronic payment systems have emerged such as debit cards, credit cards, direct credits and Internet banking. The various electronic payment systems discussed in this section are digital wallets, giropay, Google wallet and comparison of payment systems.

Indeed, my job was extremely crucial and challenging as I had to ensure that every chapter is informative and structured in a student-friendly manner. I am thankful for the support provided by my family and colleagues during the completion of this book.

Editor

Introduction to E-commerce

The trade and business performed through digital networks such as Internet and social networks is termed as e-commerce. Technologies used in e-commerce are online marketplaces, e-services and electronic business. This chapter is an overview of the subject matter incorporating all the major aspects of e-commerce.

Electronic Business

Electronic business, or e-business, is the application of information and communication technologies (ICT) in support of all the activities of business. Commerce constitutes the exchange of products and services between businesses, groups and individuals and can be seen as one of the essential activities of any business. Electronic commerce focuses on the use of ICT to enable the external activities and relationships of the business with individuals, groups and other businesses or e business refers to business with help of internet i.e. doing business with the help of internet network. The term "e-business" was coined by IBM's marketing and Internet team in 1996.

History

In 1998, IBM, with its agency Ogilvy & Mather, began to use its foundation in IT solutions and expertise to market itself as a leader of conducting business on the Internet through the term "e-business." Then CEO Louis V. Gerstner, Jr. was prepared to invest $1 billion to market this new brand.

After conducting worldwide market research in October 1997, IBM began with an eight-page piece in the *Wall Street Journal* that would introduce the concept of "e-business" and advertise IBM's expertise in the new field. IBM decided *not* to trademark the term "e-business" in the hopes that other companies would use the term and create an entire new industry. However, this proved to be too successful and by 2000, to differentiate itself, IBM launched a $300 million campaign about its "e-business infrastructure" capabilities. Since that time, the terms, "e-business" and "e-commerce" have been loosely interchangeable and have become a part of the common vernacular.

Business Model

When organizations go online, they have to decide which e-business models best suit their goals. A business model is defined as the organization of product, service and information flows, and the source of revenues and benefits for suppliers and customers. The concept of e-business model is the same but used in the online presence.

Revenue Model

A key component of the business model is the revenue model, which is a framework for generating revenues. It identifies which revenue source to pursue, what value to offer, how to price the value, and who pays for the value. It is a key component of a company's business model. It primarily identifies what product or service will be created in order to generate revenues and the ways in which the product or service will be sold.

Without a well defined revenue model, that is, a clear plan of how to generate revenues, new businesses will more likely struggle due to costs which they will not be able to sustain. By having a clear revenue model, a business can focus on a target audience, fund development plans for a product or service, establish marketing plans, begin a line of credit and raise capital.

E-commerce

E-commerce (short for "electronic commerce") is trading in products or services using computer networks, such as the Internet. Electronic commerce draws on technologies such as mobile commerce, electronic funds transfer, supply chain management, Internet marketing, online transaction processing, electronic data interchange (EDI), inventory management systems, and automated data collection systems. Modern electronic commerce typically uses the World Wide Web for at least one part of the transaction's life cycle, although it may also use other technologies such as e-mail.

Concerns

While much has been written of the economic advantages of Internet-enabled commerce, there is also evidence that some aspects of the internet such as maps and location-aware services may serve to reinforce economic inequality and the digital divide. Electronic commerce may be responsible for consolidation and the decline of mom-and-pop, brick and mortar businesses resulting in increases in income inequality. Author Andrew Keen, a long-time critic of the social transformations caused by the Internet, has recently focused on the economic effects of consolidation from Internet businesses. Keen cites a 2013 Institute for Local Self-Reliance report saying brick-and-mortar retailers employ 47 people for every $10 million in sales, while Amazon employs only 14. Similarly, the 700-employee room rental start-up Airbnb was valued at $10 billion in 2014, about half as much as Hilton Hotels, which employs 152,000 people. And car-sharing Internet startup Uber employs 1,000 full-time employees and is valued at $18.2 billion, about the same valuation as Avis and Hertz combined, which together employ almost 60,000 people.

Security

E-Business systems naturally have greater security risks than traditional business systems, therefore it is important for e-business systems to be fully protected against these risks. A far greater number of people have access to e-businesses through the internet than would have access to a traditional business. Customers, suppliers, employees, and numerous other people use any particular e-business system daily and expect their confidential information to stay secure. Hackers are one of the great threats to the security of e-businesses. Some common security concerns for e-Businesses include keeping business and customer information private and confidential, authenticity of data, and data integrity. Some of the methods of protecting e-business security and keeping information secure include physical security measures as well as data storage, data transmission, anti-virus software, firewalls, and encryption to list a few.

Privacy and Confidentiality

Confidentiality is the extent to which businesses makes personal information available to other businesses and individuals. With any business, confidential information must remain secure and only be accessible to the intended recipient. However, this becomes even more difficult when dealing with e-businesses specifically. To keep such information secure means protecting any electronic records and files from unauthorized access, as well as ensuring safe transmission and data storage of such information. Tools such as encryption and firewalls manage this specific concern within e-business.

Authenticity

E-business transactions pose greater challenges for establishing authenticity due to the ease with which electronic information may be altered and copied. Both parties in an e-business transaction want to have the assurance that the other party is who they claim to be, especially when a customer places an order and then submits a payment electronically. One common way to ensure this is to limit access to a network or trusted parties by using a virtual private network (VPN) technology. The establishment of authenticity is even greater when a combination of techniques are used, and such techniques involve checking "something you know" (i.e. password or PIN), "something you need " (i.e. credit card), or "something you are" (i.e. digital signatures or voice recognition methods). Many times in e-business, however, "something you are" is pretty strongly verified by checking the purchaser's "something you have" (i.e. credit card) and "something you know" (i.e. card number).

Data Integrity

Data integrity answers the question "Can the information be changed or corrupted in any way?" This leads to the assurance that the message received is identical to the message sent. A business needs to be confident that data is not changed in transit, whether deliberately or by accident. To help with data integrity, firewalls protect stored data against unauthorized access, while simply backing up data allows recovery should the data or equipment be damaged.

Non-repudiation

This concern deals with the existence of proof in a transaction. A business must have assurance that the receiving party or purchaser cannot deny that a transaction has occurred, and this means having sufficient evidence to prove the transaction. One way to address non-repudiation is using digital signatures. A digital signature not only ensures that a message or document has been electronically signed by the person, but since a digital signature can only be created by one person, it also ensures that this person cannot later deny that they provided their signature.

Access Control

When certain electronic resources and information is limited to only a few authorized individuals, a business and its customers must have the assurance that no one else can access the systems or information. Fortunately, there are a variety of techniques to address this concern including firewalls, access privileges, user identification and authentication techniques (such as passwords and digital certificates), Virtual Private Networks (VPN), and much more.

Availability

This concern is specifically pertinent to a business' customers as certain information must be available when customers need it. Messages must be delivered in a reliable and timely fashion, and information must be stored and retrieved as required. Because availability of service is important for all e-business websites, steps must be taken to prevent disruption of service by events such as power outages and damage to physical infrastructure. Examples to address this include data backup, fire-suppression systems, Uninterrupted Power Supply (UPS) systems, virus protection, as well as making sure that there is sufficient capacity to handle the demands posed by heavy network traffic.

Cost

The business internet which supports e-business has a cost to maintain of about $2 trillion in outsourced IT dollars just in the United States alone. With each website custom crafted and maintained in code, the maintenance burden is enormous. In the twenty-first century, look for new businesses that will help standardize the look and feel of the internet presence of a business to be more uniform in nature to help reduce the cost of maintenance. Expect maintenance by graphical software tools instead of directly by code as a key business proposition that will revolutionize the internet once again.

Security Solutions

When it comes to security solutions, sustainable electronic business requires support for data integrity, strong authentication, and privacy.

Access and Data Integrity

There are several different ways to prevent access to the data that is kept online. One way is to use anti-virus software. This is something that most people use to protect their networks regardless of the data they have. E-businesses should use this because they can then be sure that the information sent and received to their system is clean. A second way to protect the data is to use firewalls and network protection. A firewall is used to restrict access to private networks, as well as public networks that a company may use. The firewall also has the ability to log attempts into the network and provide warnings as it is happening. They are very beneficial to keep third-parties out of the network. Businesses that use Wi-Fi need to consider different forms of protection because these networks are easier for someone to access. They should look into protected access, virtual private networks, or internet protocol security. Another option they have is an intrusion detection system. This system alerts when there are possible intrusions. Some companies set up traps or "hot spots" to attract people and are then able to know when someone is trying to hack into that area.

Encryption

Encryption, which is actually a part of cryptography, involves transforming texts or messages into a code which is unreadable. These messages have to be decrypted in order to be understandable or usable for someone. There is a key that identifies the data to a certain person or company. With public key encryption, there are actually two keys used. One is public and one is private. The public one is used for encryption, and the private for decryption. The level of the actual encryption can be adjusted and should be based on the information. The key can be just a simple slide of letters or a completely random mix-up of letters. This is relatively easy to implement because there is software that a company can purchase. A company needs to be sure that their keys are registered with a certificate authority.

Digital Certificates

The point of a digital certificate is to identify the owner of a document. This way the receiver knows that it is an authentic document. Companies can use these certificates in several different ways. They can be used as a replacement for user names and passwords. Each employee can be given these to access the documents that they need from wherever they are. These certificates also use encryption. They are a little more complicated than normal encryption however. They actually used important information within the code. They do this in order to assure authenticity of the documents as well as confidentiality and data integrity which always accompany encryption. Digital certificates are not commonly used because they are confusing for people to implement. There can be complications when using different browsers, which means they need to use multiple certificates. The process is being adjusted so that it is easier to use.

Digital Signatures

A final way to secure information online would be to use a digital signature. If a document has a digital signature on it, no one else is able to edit the information without being detected. That way if it is edited, it may be adjusted for reliability after the fact. In order to use a digital signature, one must use a combination of cryptography and a message digest. A message digest is used to give the document a unique value. That value is then encrypted with the sender's private key.

E-commerce

Electronic commerce, commonly written as E-Commerce or eCommerce, is the trading or facilitation of trading in products or services using computer networks, such as the Internet or online social networks. Electronic commerce draws on technologies such as mobile commerce, electronic funds transfer, supply chain management, Internet marketing, online transaction processing, electronic data interchange (EDI), inventory management systems, and automated data collection systems. Modern electronic commerce typically uses the World Wide Web for at least one part of the transaction's life cycle although it may also use other technologies such as e-mail.

E-commerce businesses may employ some or all of the following:

- Online shopping web sites for retail sales direct to consumers

- Providing or participating in online marketplaces, which process third-party business-to-consumer or consumer-to-consumer sales

- Business-to-business buying and selling

- Gathering and using demographic data through web contacts and social media

- Business-to-business electronic data interchange

- Marketing to prospective and established customers by e-mail or fax (for example, with newsletters)

- Engaging in pretail for launching new products and services

- Online financial exchanges for currency exchanges or trading purposes

Timeline

A timeline for the development of e-commerce:

- 1971 or 1972: The ARPANET is used to arrange a cannabis sale between students at the Stanford Artificial Intelligence Laboratory and the Massachusetts Institute of Technology, later described as "the seminal act of e-commerce" in John Markoff's book *What the Dormouse Said.*

- 1979: Michael Aldrich demonstrates the first online shopping system.

- 1981: Thomson Holidays UK is the first business-to-business online shopping system to be installed.

- 1982: Minitel was introduced nationwide in France by France Télécom and used for online ordering.

- 1983: California State Assembly holds first hearing on "electronic commerce" in Volcano, California. Testifying are CPUC, MCI Mail, Prodigy, CompuServe, Volcano Telephone, and Pacific Telesis. (Not permitted to testify is Quantum Technology, later to become AOL.)

- 1984: Gateshead SIS/Tesco is first B2C online shopping system and Mrs Snowball, 72, is the first online home shopper

- 1984: In April 1984, CompuServe launches the Electronic Mall in the USA and Canada. It is the first comprehensive electronic commerce service.

- 1989: In May 1989, Sequoia Data Corp. Introduced Compumarket The first internet based system for e-commerce. Sellers and buyers could post items for sale and buyers could search the database and make purchases with a credit card.

- 1990: Tim Berners-Lee writes the first web browser, WorldWideWeb, using a NeXT computer.

- 1992: Book Stacks Unlimited in Cleveland opens a commercial sales website (www.books.com) selling books online with credit card processing.

- 1993: Paget Press releases edition No. 3 of the first app store, The Electronic AppWrapper

- 1994: Netscape releases the Navigator browser in October under the code name Mozilla. Netscape 1.0 is introduced in late 1994 with SSL encryption that made transactions secure.

- 1994: Ipswitch IMail Server becomes the first software available online for sale and immediate download via a partnership between Ipswitch, Inc. and Open-Market.

- 1994: "Ten Summoner's Tales" by Sting becomes the first secure online purchase through NetMarket.

- 1995: The US National Science Foundation lifts its former strict prohibition of commercial enterprise on the Internet.

- 1995: Thursday 27 April 1995, the purchase of a book by Paul Stanfield, Product Manager for CompuServe UK, from W H Smith's shop within CompuServe's UK Shopping Centre is the UK's first national online shopping service secure transaction. The shopping service at launch featured W H Smith, Tesco, Virgin Megastores/Our Price, Great Universal Stores (GUS), Interflora, Dixons Retail, Past Times, PC World (retailer) and Innovations.

- 1995: Jeff Bezos launches Amazon.com and the first commercial-free 24-hour, internet-only radio stations, Radio HK and NetRadio start broadcasting. eBay is founded by computer programmer Pierre Omidyar as AuctionWeb.

- 1996: IndiaMART B2B marketplace established in India.

- 1996: ECPlaza B2B marketplace established in Korea.

- 1998: Electronic postal stamps can be purchased and downloaded for printing from the Web.

- 1999: Alibaba Group is established in China. Business.com sold for US $7.5 million to eCompanies, which was purchased in 1997 for US $149,000. The peer-to-peer filesharing software Napster launches. ATG Stores launches to sell decorative items for the home online.

- 2000: Complete Idiot's Guide to E-commerce released on Amazon

- 2000: The dot-com bust.

- 2001: Alibaba.com achieved profitability in December 2001.

- 2002: eBay acquires PayPal for $1.5 billion. Niche retail companies Wayfair and NetShops are founded with the concept of selling products through several targeted domains, rather than a central portal.

- 2003: Amazon.com posts first yearly profit.

- 2003: Bossgoo B2B marketplace established in China.

- 2004: DHgate.com, China's first online b2b transaction platform, is established, forcing other b2b sites to move away from the "yellow pages" model.

- 2007: Business.com acquired by R.H. Donnelley for $345 million.

- 2009: Zappos.com acquired by Amazon.com for $928 million. Retail Convergence, operator of private sale website RueLaLa.com, acquired by GSI Commerce for $180 million, plus up to $170 million in earn-out payments based on performance through 2012.

- 2010: Groupon reportedly rejects a $6 billion offer from Google. Instead, the group buying websites went ahead with an IPO on 4 November 2011. It was the largest IPO since Google.

- 2014: Overstock.com processes over $1 million in Bitcoin sales. India's e-commerce industry is estimated to have grown more than 30% from 2012 to $12.6 billion in 2013. US eCommerce and Online Retail sales projected to reach $294 billion, an increase of 12 percent over 2013 and 9% of all retail sales. Alibaba Group has the largest Initial public offering ever, worth $25 billion.

- 2015: Amazon.com accounts for more than half of all ecommerce growth, selling almost 500 Million SKU's in the US.

Business Application

An example of an automated online assistant on a merchandising website.

Some common applications related to electronic commerce are:

- Document automation in supply chain and logistics

- Domestic and international payment systems

- Enterprise content management
- Group buying
- Print on demand
- Automated online assistant
- Newsgroups
- Online shopping and order tracking
- Online banking
- Online office suites
- Shopping cart software
- Teleconferencing
- Electronic tickets
- Social networking
- Instant messaging
- Pretail
- Digital Wallet

Governmental Regulation

In the United States, certain electronic commerce activities are regulated by the Federal Trade Commission (FTC). These activities include but not limit to the use of commercial e-mails, online advertising and consumer privacy. The CAN-SPAM Act of 2003 establishes national standards for direct marketing over e-mail. The Federal Trade Commission Act regulates all forms of advertising, including online advertising, and states that advertising must be truthful and non-deceptive. Using its authority under Section 5 of the FTC Act, which prohibits unfair or deceptive practices, the FTC has brought a number of cases to enforce the promises in corporate privacy statements, including promises about the security of consumers' personal information. As a result, any corporate privacy policy related to e-commerce activity may be subject to enforcement by the FTC.

The Ryan Haight Online Pharmacy Consumer Protection Act of 2008, which came into law in 2008, amends the Controlled Substances Act to address online pharmacies.

Conflict of laws in cyberspace is a major hurdle for harmonization of legal framework for e-commerce around the world. In order to give a uniformity to e-commerce law around the world, many countries adopted the UNCITRAL Model Law on Electronic Commerce (1996)

Internationally there is the International Consumer Protection and Enforcement Network (ICPEN), which was formed in 1991 from an informal network of government customer fair trade organisations. The purpose was stated as being to find ways of co-operating on tackling consumer problems connected with cross-border transactions in both goods and services, and to help ensure exchanges of information among the participants for mutual benefit and understanding. From this came Econsumer.gov, an ICPEN initiative since April 2001. It is a portal to report complaints about online and related transactions with foreign companies.

There is also Asia Pacific Economic Cooperation (APEC) was established in 1989 with the vision of achieving stability, security and prosperity for the region through free and open trade and investment. APEC has an Electronic Commerce Steering Group as well as working on common privacy regulations throughout the APEC region.

In Australia, Trade is covered under Australian Treasury Guidelines for electronic commerce, and the Australian Competition and Consumer Commission regulates and offers advice on how to deal with businesses online, and offers specific advice on what happens if things go wrong.

In the United Kingdom, The Financial Services Authority (FSA) was formerly the regulating authority for most aspects of the EU's Payment Services Directive (PSD), until its replacement in 2013 by the Prudential Regulation Authority and the Financial Conduct Authority. The UK implemented the PSD through the Payment Services Regulations 2009 (PSRs), which came into effect on 1 November 2009. The PSR affects firms providing payment services and their customers. These firms include banks, non-bank credit card issuers and non-bank merchant acquirers, e-money issuers, etc. The PSRs created a new class of regulated firms known as payment institutions (PIs), who are subject to prudential requirements. Article 87 of the PSD requires the European Commission to report on the implementation and impact of the PSD by 1 November 2012.

In India, the Information Technology Act 2000 governs the basic applicability of e-commerce.

In China, the Telecommunications Regulations of the People's Republic of China (promulgated on 25 September 2000), stipulated the Ministry of Industry and Information Technology (MIIT) as the government department regulating all telecommunications related activities, including electronic commerce. On the same day, The Administrative Measures on Internet Information Services released, is the first administrative regulation to address profit-generating activities conducted through the Internet, and lay the foundation for future regulations governing e-commerce in China. On 28 August 2004, the eleventh session of the tenth NPC Standing Committee adopted The Electronic Signature Law, which regulates data message, electronic signature authentication and legal liability issues. It is considered the first law in China's e-commerce legislation. It was a milestone in the course of improving China's electronic commerce legislation, and also marks the entering of China's rapid development stage for electronic commerce legislation.

Forms

Contemporary electronic commerce involves everything from ordering "digital" content for immediate online consumption, to ordering conventional goods and services, to "meta" services to facilitate other types of electronic commerce.

On the institutional level, big corporations and financial institutions use the internet to exchange financial data to facilitate domestic and international business. Data integrity and security are pressing issues for electronic commerce.

Aside from traditional e-Commerce, the terms m-Commerce (mobile commerce) as well (around 2013) t-Commerce have also been used.

Global Trends

In 2010, the United Kingdom had the biggest e-commerce market in the world when measured by the amount spent per capita. As of 2013, the Czech Republic was the European country where ecommerce delivers the biggest contribution to the enterprises´ total revenue. Almost a quarter (24%) of the country's total turnover is generated via the online channel.

Among emerging economies, China's e-commerce presence continues to expand every year. With 668 million internet users, China's online shopping sales reached $253 billion in the first half of 2015, accounting for 10% of total Chinese consumer retail sales in the same period. The Chinese retailers have been able to help consumers feel more comfortable shopping online. E-commerce transactions between China and other countries increased 32% to 2.3 trillion yuan ($375.8 billion) in 2012 and accounted for 9.6% of China's total international trade In 2013, Alibaba had an e-commerce market share of 80% in China. In 2014, there were 600 million Internet users in China (twice as many than in the US), making it the world's biggest online market. China is also the largest e-commerce market in the world by value of sales, with an estimated US$899 billion in 2016.

In 2013, Brazil's eCommerce was growing quickly with retail eCommerce sales expected to grow at a healthy double-digit pace through 2014. By 2016, eMarketer expected retail ecommerce sales in Brazil to reach $17.3 billion. India has an internet user base of about 243.2 million as of January 2014. Despite being third largest user base in world, the penetration of Internet is low compared to markets like the United States, United Kingdom or France but is growing at a much faster rate, adding around 6 million new entrants every month. In India, cash on delivery is the most preferred payment method, accumulating 75% of the e-retail activities.

E-Commerce has become an important tool for small and large businesses worldwide, not only to sell to customers, but also to engage them.

In 2012, ecommerce sales topped $1 trillion for the first time in history.

Mobile devices are playing an increasing role in the mix of eCommerce, this is also commonly called mobile commerce, or m-commerce. In 2014, one estimate saw purchases made on mobile devices making up 25% of the market by 2017.

For traditional businesses, one research stated that information technology and cross-border e-commerce is a good opportunity for the rapid development and growth of enterprises. Many companies have invested enormous volume of investment in mobile applications.The DeLone and McLean Model stated that 3 perspectives are contributed to a successful e-business, including information system quality, service quality and users satisfaction. There is no limit of time and space, there are more opportunities to reach out to customers around the world, and to cut down unnecessary intermediate links, thereby reducing the cost price, and can benefit from one on one large customer data analysis, to achieve a high degree of personal customization strategic plan, in order to fully enhance the core competitiveness of the products in company

Impact on Markets and Retailers

Economists have theorized that e-commerce ought to lead to intensified price competition, as it increases consumers' ability to gather information about products and prices. Research by four economists at the University of Chicago has found that the growth of online shopping has also affected industry structure in two areas that have seen significant growth in e-commerce, bookshops and travel agencies. Generally, larger firms are able to use economies of scale and offer lower prices. The lone exception to this pattern has been the very smallest category of bookseller, shops with between one and four employees, which appear to have withstood the trend. Depending on the category, e-commerce may shift the switching costs—procedural, relational, and financial—experienced by customers.

Individual or business involved in e-commerce whether buyers or sellers rely on Internet-based technology in order to accomplish their transactions. E-commerce is recognized for its ability to allow business to communicate and to form transaction anytime and anyplace. Whether an individual is in the US or overseas, business can be conducted through the internet. The power of e-commerce allows geophysical barriers to disappear, making all consumers and businesses on earth potential customers and suppliers. Thus, switching barriers and switching costs may shift. eBay is a good example of e-commerce business individuals and businesses are able to post their items and sell them around the Globe.

In e-commerce activities, supply chain and logistics are two most crucial factors need to be considered. Typically, cross-border logistics need about few weeks time round.

Based on this low efficiency of the supply chain service, customer satisfaction will be greatly reduced. Some researcher stated that combining e-commerce competence and IT setup could well enhance company's overall business worth. Other researcher stated that e-commerce need to consider the establishment of warehouse centers in foreign countries, to create high efficiency of the logistics system, not only improve customers' satisfaction, but also can improve customers' loyalty.

Impact on Supply Chain Management

For a long time, companies had been troubled by the gap between the benefits which supply chain technology has and the solutions to deliver those benefits. However, the emergence of e-commerce has provided a more practical and effective way of delivering the benefits of the new supply chain technologies.

E-commerce has the capability to integrate all inter-company and intra-company functions, meaning that the three flows (physical flow, financial flow and information flow) of the supply chain could be also affected by e-commerce. The affections on physical flows improved the way of product and inventory movement level for companies. For the information flows, e-commerce optimised the capacity of information processing than companies used to have, and for the financial flows, e-commerce allows companies to have more efficient payment and settlement solutions.

In addition, e-commerce has a more sophisticated level of impact on supply chains: Firstly, the performance gap will be eliminated since companies can identify gaps between different levels of supply chains by electronic means of solutions; Secondly, as a result of e-commerce emergence, new capabilities such implementing ERP systems, like SAP ERP, Xero, or Megaventory, have helped companies to manage operations with customers and suppliers. Yet these new capabilities are still not fully exploited. Thirdly, technology companies would keep investing on new e-commerce software solutions as they are expecting investment return. Fourthly, e-commerce would help to solve many aspects of issues that companies may feel difficult to cope with, such as political barriers or cross-country changes. Finally, e-commerce provides companies a more efficient and effective way to collaborate with each other within the supply chain.

The Social Impact of E-commerce

Along with the e-commerce and its unique charm that has appeared gradually, virtual enterprise, virtual bank, network marketing, online shopping, payment and advertising, such this new vocabulary which is unheard-of and now has become as familiar to people. This reflects that the e-commerce has huge impact on the economy and society from the other side. For instance, B2B is a rapidly growing business in the world that leads to lower cost and then improves the economic efficiency and also bring along the growth of employment.

To understand how the e-commerce has affected the society and economy, this article will mention three issues below:

1. The e-commerce has changed the relative importance of time, but as the pillars of indicator of the country's economic state that the importance of time should not be ignored.

2. The e-commerce offers the consumer or enterprise various information they need, making information into total transparency, will force enterprise no longer is able to use the mode of space or advertisement to raise their competitive edge. Moreover, in theory, perfect competition between the consumer sovereignty and industry will maximize social welfare.

3. In fact, during the economic activity in the past, large enterprise frequently has advantage of information resource, and thus at the expense of consumers. Nowadays, the transparent and real-time information protects the rights of consumers, because the consumers can use internet to pick out the portfolio to the benefit of themselves. The competitiveness of enterprises will be much more obvious than before, consequently, social welfare would be improved by the development of the e-commerce.

4. The new economy led by the e-commerce change humanistic spirit as well, but above all, is the employee loyalty. Due to the market with competition, the employee's level of professionalism becomes the crucial for enterprise in the niche market. The enterprises must pay attention to how to build up the enterprises inner culture and a set of interactive mechanisms and it is the prime problem for them. Furthermore, though the mode of e-commerce decrease the information cost and transaction cost, however, its development also makes human being are overly computer literate. In hence, emphasized more humanistic attitude to work is another project for enterprise to development. Life is the root of all and high technology are merely an assistive tool to support our quality of life.

5. Online merchants gather purchase activity and interests of their customers. This information is being used by the online marketers to promote relevant products and services. This creates an extra convenience for the online shoppers.

6. Online merchandise is searchable, which makes it more accessible to the shoppers. Many online retailers offer a review mechanism, which helps shoppers decide on the product to purchase. This is another convenience and a satisfaction improvement factor.

The e-commerce is not a kind of new industry, but it is creating a new economic model. Most of people agree that the e-commerce indeed to be important and significant for economic society in the future, but actually that is a bit of clueless feeling at the beginning, this problem is exactly prove the e-commerce is a sort of incorporeal revolution. This is due to the fact that the cost of running an e-commerce business is very low when compared with running a physical store. There is no rent to pay on expensive premises, business processes are simplified and less man-hours are required to run it smoothly. Generally speaking, as a type of business active procedure, the e-commerce is going to leading an unprecedented revolution in the world, the influence of this model far exceeded the commercial affair itself. Except the mentioned above, in the area of law, education, culture and also policy, the e-commerce will continue that rise in impact. The e-commerce is truly to take human beings into the information society.

Distribution Channels

E-commerce has grown in importance as companies have adopted pure-click and brick-and-click channel systems. We can distinguish pure-click and brick-and-click channel system adopted by companies.

- Pure-click or pure-play companies are those that have launched a website without any previous existence as a firm.

- Bricks-and-clicks companies are those existing companies that have added an online site for e-commerce.

- Click-to-brick online retailers that later open physical locations to supplement their online efforts.

Examples of New E-commerce Systems

According to eMarketer research company, "by 2017, 65.8 per cent of Britons will use smartphones".

Online Marketplace

An online marketplace (or online e-commerce marketplace) is a type of e-commerce site where product or service information is provided by multiple third parties, whereas transactions are processed by the marketplace operator. Online marketplaces are the primary type of multichannel ecommerce and can be described as a "simple and convenient portal" to streamline the production process.

In an online marketplace, consumer transactions are processed by the marketplace operator and then delivered and fulfilled by the participating retailers or wholesalers (often called drop shipping). Other capabilities might include auctioning (forward or reverse), catalogs, ordering, wanted advertisement, trading exchange functionality and capabilities like RFQ, RFI or RFP. These type of sites allow users to register and sell single items to a large number of items for a "post-selling" fee.

In general, because marketplaces aggregate products from a wide array of providers, selection is usually more wide, and availability is higher than in vendor-specific online retail stores. Also prices may be more competetive.

Since 2014, online marketplaces are abundant since organized marketplaces are sought after. Some have a wide variety of general interest products that cater to almost all the needs of the consumers, however, some are consumer specific and cater to a particular segment only. Not only is the platform for selling online, but the user interface and user experience matters. People tend to log on to online marketplaces that are organized and products are much more accessible to them.

For Services and Outsourcing

There are marketplaces for the online outsourcing of professional services like IT services, search engine optimization, marketing, crowdsourcing, and skilled crafts & trades work.

Criticism

Many service related online marketplaces have been criticized for taking jobs that would go to local industries that can't compete on price against outsourced providers.

Another criticism is that the laws and regulations surrounding online marketplaces are quite underdeveloped. As of consequence, there is a discrepancy between the responsibility, accountability and liability of the marketplace and third parties. Online marketplaces and platforms have faced much criticism in recent years for their lack of consumer protections.

E-services

The concept of e-service (short for electronic service) represents one prominent application of utilizing the use of information and communication technologies (ICTs) in different areas. However, providing an exact definition of e-service is hard to come by as researchers have been using different definitions to describe e-service. Despite these different definitions, it can be argued that they all agree about the role of technology in facilitating the delivery of services which make them more of electronic services.

It seems compelling to adopt Rowley (2006) approach who defines e-services as: "...deeds, efforts or performances whose delivery is mediated by information technology. Such e-service includes the service element of e-tailing, customer support, and service delivery". This definition reflect three main components- service provider, service receiver and the channels of service delivery (i.e., technology). For example, as concerned to public e-service, public agencies are the service provider and citizens as well as businesses are the service receiver. The channel of service delivery is the third requirement of e-service. Internet is the main channel of e-service delivery while other classic channels (e.g. telephone, call center, public kiosk, mobile phone, television) are also considered.

Definitions and Origin of the Term E-service

Since its conceptual inception in the late 1980s in Europe and formal introduction in 1993 by the US Government, the term 'E-Government' has now become one of the recognized research domains especially in the context of public policy and now has been rapidly gaining strategic importance in public sector modernization. E-service is one of the branches of this domain and its attention has also been creeping up among the practitioners and researchers.

E-service (or eservice) is a highly generic term, usually referring to 'The provision of services via the Internet (the prefix 'e' standing for 'electronic', as it does in many other usages), thus e-Service may also include e-Commerce, although it may also include non-commercial services (online), which is usually provided by the government.' (Irma Buntantan & G. David Garson, 2004: 169-170; Muhammad Rais & Nazariah, 2003: 59, 70-71).

'E-Service constitutes the online services available on the Internet, whereby a valid transaction of buying and selling (procurement) is possible, as opposed to the traditional websites, whereby only descriptive information are available, and no online transaction is made possible.' (Jeong, 2007).

Importance of E-service

Lu (2001) identifies a number of benefits for e-services, some of these are:

- Accessing a greater customer base
- Broadening market reach
- Lowering of entry barrier to new markets and cost of acquiring new customers
- Alternative communication channel to customers
- Increasing services to customers
- Enhancing perceived company image
- Gaining competitive advantages
- Potential for increasing Customer knowledge

Importance and Advantages of E-shopping

- E-shops are open 24 hours a day.

- There is no need to travel to the malls or wait at the checkout counters.

- There is usually a wide selection of goods and services.

- It is easy to compare prices and quality by using the E-shopping tool.

- Price reduction and discounts are electronically conveyed.

E-service Domain

The term 'e-service' has many applications and can be found in many disciplines. The two dominant application areas of e-services are

E-business (or e-commerce): e-services mostly provided by businesses or [NGO|non-government organizations] (NGOs) (private sector).

E-government: e-services provided by government to citizens or business (public sector is the supply side). The use and description of the e-service in this page will be limited to the context of e-government only where of the e-service is usually associated with prefix "public": Public e-services. In some cases, we will have to describe aspects that are related to both fields like some conferences or journals which cover the concept of "e-Service" in both domains of e-government and e-business.

Architecture

Depending on the types of services, there are certain functionalities required in the certain layers of e-service architectural framework, these include but are not limited to – Data layer (data sources), processing layers (customer service systems, management systems, data warehouse systems, integrated customer content systems), exchange layer (Enterprise Application Integration– EAI), interaction layer (integrating e-services), and presentation layer (customer interface through which the web pages and e-services are linked).

E-service Quality

Measuring service quality and service excellence are important in a competitive organizational environment. The SERVQUAL- service quality model is one of the widely used tools for measuring quality of the service on various aspects. The five attributes of this model are: reliability, responsiveness, assurance, tangibles, and empathy. The following table summarizes some major of these:

SERVQUAL	Kaynama & Black (2000)	Zeithaml (2002)	Janda et al. (2002)	Alawattegama & Wattegama (2008)
Reliability	Content	Access	Access	Factual information
Responsiveness	Access	Ease of navigation	Security	Business information

SERVQUAL	Kaynama & Black (2000)	Zeithaml (2002)	Janda et al. (2002)	Alawattegama & Wattegama (2008)
Assurance	Navigation	Efficiency	Sensation	General information
Tangibles	Design	Flexibility	Information/ content	Consumer- related information
Empathy	Response	Reliability		
	Background	Personalization		
	Personalization	Security/ privacy		
		Responsiveness		
		Assurance/trust		
		Site aesthetics		
		Price knowledge		

The LIRNEasia study on benchmarking national telecom regulator websites focuses on content than on accessibility and ease of use, unlike the other studies mentioned here. Websites are increasingly important portals to government agencies, especially in the context of information society reforms. Stakeholders, including businesses, investors and even the general public, are interested in information produced by these agencies, and websites can help to increase their transparency and accountability. The quality of its website also demonstrates how advanced a regulatory agency is.

E-service Cost Factor

Some major cost factors are (Lu, 2001):

- Expense of setting up applications
- Maintaining applications
- Internet connection
- Hardware/software
- Security concerns
- legal issues
- Training; and
- Rapid technology changes

Practical Examples of E-services in the Developing World

Information technology is a powerful tool for accelerating economic development. Developing countries have focused on the development of ICT during the last two decades and as a result, it has been recognized that ICT is critical to economy and is as a catalyst of economic development. So, in recent years there seems to have been efforts for providing various e-services in many developing countries since ICT is believed to offer considerable potential for the sustainable development of e-Government and as a result, e-Services.

Many government agencies in developed countries have taken progressive steps toward the web and ICT use, adding coherence to all local activities on the Internet, widening local access and skills, opening up interactive services for local debates, and increasing the participation of citizens on promotion and management of the territory(Graham and Aurigi, 1997).

But the potential for e-government in developing countries remains largely unexploited, even though. ICT is believed to offer considerable potential for the sustainable development of e-government. Different human, organizational and technological factors, issues and problems pertain in these countries, requiring focused studies and appropriate approaches. ICT, in general, is referred to as an "enabler", but on the other hand it should also be regarded as a challenge and a peril in itself. The organizations, public or private,which ignore the potential value and use of ICT may suffer pivotal competitive disadvantages. Nevertheless, some e-government initiatives have flourished in developing countries too, e.g. Brazil, India, Chile, etc. What the experience in these countries shows, is that governments in the developing world can effectively exploit and appropriate the benefits of ICT, but e-government success entails the accommodation of certain unique conditions,needs and obstacles. The adaptive challenges of e-government go far beyond technology, they call for organizational structures and skills, new forms of leadership, transformation of public-private partnerships (Allen et al., 2001).

Following are a few examples regarding e-services in some developing countries:

E-services in Rwanda

Only a decade after emerging from the fastest genocide of the 20th Century, Rwanda, a small country in Eastern Central Africa, has become one of the continent's leaders in, and model on, bridging the digital divide through e-government. Rwanda has undergone a rapid turnaround from one of the most technologically deficient countries only a decade ago to a country where legislative business is conducted online and wireless access to the Internet is available anywhere in the country. This is puzzling when viewed against the limited progress made in other comparable developing countries, especially those located in the same region, sub-Saharan Africa, where the structural and institutional constraints to e-government diffusion are similar.

E-services in South Africa

In South Africa, there continues to be high expectations of government in respect to improved delivery of service and of closer consultation with citizens. Such expectations are not unique to this country, and in this regard there is a need for governments to recognise that the implementation of e-government systems and e-services affords them the opportunity to enhance service delivery and good governance. The implementation of e-Government has been widely acclaimed in that it provides new impetus to deliver services quickly and efficiently (Evans & Yen, 2006:208). In recognition of these benefits, various arms of the South African government have embarked on a number of e-government programmes for example the Batho Pele portal,SARS e-filing, the e-Natis system, electronic processing of grant applications from remote sites, and a large number of departmental information websites. Also a number of well publicised e-government ventures such as the latter, analysts and researchers consider the state of e-government in South Africa to be at rudimentary stages. There are various factors which collectively contribute to such an assessment. Amongst these, key factors relate to a lack of a clear strategy to facilitate uptake and adoption of e-government services as well as evaluation frameworks to assess expectations of citizens who are one of the primary user groups of these services.

E-services in Malaysia

E-Services is one of the pilot projects under the Electronic Government Flagship within the Multimedia Super Corridor (MSC) initiative. With E-Services, one can now conduct transactions with Government agencies, such as the Road Transport Department (RTD) and private utility companies such as Tenaga Nasional Berhad (TNB) and Telekom Malaysia Berhad (TM) through various convenient channels such as the eServices kiosks and internet. No more queuing, traffic jams or bureaucratic hassles and one can now conduct transaction at one's own convenience. Also, Electronic Labour Exchange (ELX)is one stop-centre for labor market information, as supervised by the Ministry of Human Resource (MOHR), to enable employers and job seekers to communicate on the same platform.

e-Syariah is the seventh project under the Electronic Government flagship application of the Multimedia Super Corridor (MSC). A case management system that integrates the processes related to management of cases for the Syariah Courts.

Challenges to E-services in the Developing World

The future of e-service is bright but some challenges remain. There are some challenges in e-service, as Sheth & Sharma (2007) identify, are:

- Low penetration of ICT especially in the developing countries;

- Fraud on the internet space which is estimated around 2.8billion USD

- Privacy due the emergence of various types of spyware and security holes, and

- intrusive characteristics of the service (e.g. mobile phones based) as customers may not like to be contacted with the service providers at any time and at any place.

The first challenge and primary obstacle to the e-service platform will be penetration of the internet. In some developing countries, the access to the internet is limited and speeds are also limited. In these cases firms and customers will continue to use traditional platforms. The second issue of concern is fraud on the internet. It is anticipated that the fraud on the e-commerce internet space costs $2.8 billion. Possibility of fraud will continue to reduce the utilization of the internet. The third issue is of privacy. Due to both spyware and security holes in operating systems, there is concern that the transactions that consumers undertake have privacy limitations. For example, by stealthily following online activities, firms can develop fairly accurate descriptions of customer profiles. Possibility of privacy violations will reduce the utilizations of the internet. The final issue is that e-service can also become intrusive as they reduce time and location barriers of other forms of contract. For example, firms can contact people through mobile devices at any time and at any place. Customers do not take like the intrusive behavior and may not use the e-service platform. (Heiner and Iyer, 2007)

Major E-service Keywords

A considerable amount of research efforts already exists on the subject matter exploring different aspects of e-service and e-service delivery ; one worth noting effort is Rowley's study (2006) who did a review study on the e-service literature. The key finding of his study is that there is need to explore dimensions of e-service delivery not focusing only on service quality "In order to understand e-service experiences it is necessary to go beyond studies of e-service quality dimensions and to also take into account the inherent characteristics of e-service delivery and the factors that differentiate one service experience from another."

Some of the major keywords of e-service as found in the e-government research are as follows:

Acceptance

User acceptance of technology is defined according to Morris (1996, referred by Wu 2005, p. 1) as "the demonstrable willingness within a user group to employ information technology for the tasks it is designed to support". This definition can be brought into the context of e-service where acceptance can be defined as the users' willingness to use e-service or the willingness to decide when and how to use the e-service.

Accessibility

Users' ability to access to the e-service is important theme in the previous literature. For example, Huang (2003) finds that most of the websites in general fail to serve users with disabilities. Recommendation to improve accessibility is evident in previous literature including Jaeger (2006) who suggests the following to improve e-services' accessibility like: design for accessibility from the outset of website development, Involve users with disabilities in the testing of the site ...Focus on the benefits of an accessible Web site to all users.

Administrative Literacy

According to Grönlund et al. (2007), for a simple e-service, the needs for knowledge and skills, content and procedures are considerably less. However, in complicated services there are needed to change some prevailed skills, such as replacing verbal skills with skill in searching for information online.

Benchmarking

This theme is concerned with establishing standards for measuring e-services or the best practices within the field. This theme also includes the international benchmarking of e-government services (UN reports, EU reports); much critic has been targeting these reports being incomprehensive and useless. According to Bannister (2007) "... benchmarks are not a reliable tool for measuring real e-government progress. Furthermore, if they are poorly designed, they risk distorting government policies as countries may chase the benchmark rather than looking at real local and national needs"

Digital Divide

Digital divide is considered one of the main barriers to implementing e-services; some people do not have means to access the e-services and some others do not know how to use the technology (or the e-service). According to Helbig et al. (2009), "we suggest E-Government and the digital divide should be seen as complementary social phenomena (i.e., demand and supply). Moreover, a serious e-government digital divide is that services mostly used by social elites."

E-readiness

Most of the reports and the established criteria focus on assessing the services in terms of infrastructure and public policies ignoring the citizen participation or e-readiness. According to by Shalini (2009), "the results of the research project reveal that a high index may be only indicating that a country is e-ready in terms of ICT infrastructure and info-structure, institutions, policies, and political commitment, but it is a very poor measure of the e-readiness of citizens. To summarize the findings, it can be said that Mauritius is ready but the Mauritians are not"

E-readiness, as the Economist Intelligence Unit defines, is the measure of a country's ability to leverage digital channels for communication, commerce and government in order to further economic and social development. Implied in this measure is the extent to which the usage of communications devices and Internet services creates efficiencies for business and citizens, and the extent to which this usage is leveraged in the development of information and communications technology (ICT) industries. In general terms, the definition of e-readiness is relative,for instance depending on a country in question's priorities and perspective.

Efficiency

As opposed to effectiveness, efficiency is focused on the internal competence within the government departments when delivering e-services. There is a complaint that researchers focus more on effectiveness "There is an emerging trend seemingly moving away from the efficiency target and focusing on users and governance outcome. While the latter is worthwhile, efficiency must still remain a key priority for eGovernment given the budget constraints compounded in the future by the costs of an ageing population. Moreover, efficiency gains are those that can be most likely proven empirically through robust methodologies"

Security

Security is the most important challenge that faces the implementation of e-services because without a guarantee of privacy and security citizens will not be willing to take up e-government services. These security concerns, such as hacker attacks and the theft of credit card information, make governments hesitant to provide public online services. According to the GAO report of 2002 "security concerns present one of the toughest challenges to extending the reach of e-government.The rash of hacker attacks, Web page defacing, and credit card information being posted on electronic bulletin boards can make many federal agency officials—as well as the general public—reluctant to conduct sensitive government transactions involving personal or financial data over the Internet." By and Large, Security is one of the major challenges that faces the implementation and development of electronic services. people want to be assured that they are safe when they are conducting online services and that their information will remain secure and confidential

Stakeholders

Axelsson et al. (2009) argue that the stakeholder concept-which was originally used in private firms-, can be used in public setting and in the context of e-government. According to them, several scholars have discussed the use of the stakeholder theory in public settings. The stakeholder theory suggests that need to focus on all the involved stakeholder s when designing the e-service; not only on the government and citizens.

Usability

Compared to Accessibility, There is sufficient literature that addresses the issue of usability; researchers have developed different models and methods to measure the usability and effectiveness of eGovernment websites. However, But still there is call to improve these measures and make it more compressive

``The word usability has cropped up a few times already in this unit. In the context of biometric identification, usability referred to the smoothness of enrollment and other tasks associated with setting up an identification system. A system that produced few false matches during enrollment of applicants was described as usable. Another meaning of usability is related to the ease of use of an interface. Although this meaning of the term is often used in the context of computer interfaces, there is no reason to confine it to computers.´´

Social, Cultural and Ethical Implications of E-services

The perceived effectiveness of e-service can be influenced by public's view of the social and cultural implications of e-technologies and e-service.

Impacts on individuals' rights and privacy – as more and more companies and government agencies use technology to collect, store, and make accessible data on individuals, privacy concerns have grown. Some companies monitor their employees' computer usage patterns in order to assess individual or workgroup performance. Technological advancements are also making it much easier for businesses, government and other individuals to obtain a great deal of information about an individual without their knowledge. There is a growing concern that access to a wide range of information can be dangerous within politically corrupt government agencies.

Impact on Jobs and Workplaces - in the early days of computers, management scientists anticipated that computers would replace human decision-makers. However, despite significant technological advances, this prediction is no longer a mainstream concern. At the current time, one of the concerns associated with computer usage in any organization (including governments) is the health risk – such as injuries related to working continuously on a computer keyboard. Government agencies are expected to work with regulatory groups in order to avoid these problems.

Potential Impacts on Society – despite some economic benefits of ICT to individuals, there is evidence that the computer literacy and access gap between the haves and have-nots may be increasing. Education and information access are more than ever the keys to economic prosperity, yet access by individuals in different countries is not equal - this social inequity has become known as the digital divide.

Impact on Social Interaction – advancements in ICT and e-Technology solutions have enabled many government functions to become automated and information to be made available online. This is a concern to those who place a high value on social interaction.

Information Security - technological advancements allow government agencies to collect, store and make data available online to individuals and organizations. Citizens and businesses expect to be allowed to access data in a flexible manner (at any time and from any location). Meeting these expectations comes at a price to government agencies where it concerns managing information – more specifically, ease of access; data integrity and accuracy; capacity planning to ensure the timely delivery of data to remote (possibly mobile) sites; and managing the security of corporate and public information.

E-service Awards

The benefits of e-services in advancing businesses efficiency and in promoting good governance are huge; recognizing the importance of these benefits has resulted in number of international awards that are dedicated to recognize the best designed e-services. In the section, we will provide description of some international awards

Best Online E-service in Europe

European eGovernment Awards program started 2003 to recognize the best online public service in Europe. The aim of Awards is to encourage the deployment of e-services and to bring the attention to best practices in the field. The winners of the European eGovernment Awards were announced in the award ceremony that took place at the 5th Ministerial eGovernment Conference on 19 November 2009 (Sweden); the winners in their respective categories are:

- Category 1. eGovernment supporting the Single Market: EU-OPA, the European Order for Payment Application (Austria and Germany)

- Category 2a. eGovernment empowering citizens: Genvej (Denmark)

- Category 2b. eGovernment empowering businesses: MEPA, the Public Administration eMarketplace (Italy)

- Category 3. eGovernment enabling administrative efficiency and effectiveness: Licensing of Hunters via the "Multibanco" ATM Network (Portugal)

- Public prize: SMS Information System (Turkey)

Other Awards

Sultan Qaboos Award for excellence in eGovernance Oman(Started 2009) The award has five categories: Best eContent, Best eService, Best eProject, eEconomy, eReadiness.

eGovernment Excellence Awards Bahrain(Started 2007) The program has three categories: Government Awards: Best eContent, Best eService, Best eProject, eEconomy, eEducation, eMaturity Business Awards: Best ICT solution Provider, eEconomy,eEducation Citizen Awards: Best eContent, eCitizen.

Philippines e-Service Awards ➤ Philippines(Started 2001) Categories: Outstanding Client Application of the Year, Outstanding Customer Application of the year, Groundbreaking Technology of the Year, Most Progressive Homegrown Company of the Year.

Major Conferences Focusing on E-services

Major conferences considering e-service as one of the themes are:

- eServices in European Civil Registration conference
- Conference on e-Business, e-Services, and e-Society
- International ICST Conference on e-service
- E-service Global Sourcing Conference & Exhibition
- Annual Hawaii International Conference on Systems Sciences

- Electronic Government Conference (EGOV)

- International Conference on Electronic Government and the Information Systems Perspective (EGOVIS)

- International Conference on Theory and Practice of Electronic Governance (ICEGOV)

References

- Gerstner, L. (2002). Who says Elephants Can't Dance? Inside IBM's Historic Turnaround. pg 172. ISBN 0-06-052379-4.

- Paul Timers, (2000), Electronic Commerce - strategies & models for business-to-business trading, pp.31, John Wiley & Sons, Ltd, ISBN 0-471-72029-1.

- Jeong Chun Hai @Ibrahim. (2007). Fundamental of Development Administration. Selangor: Scholar Press. ISBN 978-967-5-04508-0.

- Enright, Allison. "Top 500 U.S. E-Retailers — U.S. e-commerce sales could top $434 billion in 2017". Internet Retailer. Retrieved 2014-05-30.

- Millward, Steven (August 18, 2016). "Asia's ecommerce spending to hit record $1 trillion this year – but most of that is China". Tech in Asia. Retrieved August 18, 2016.

- Harris, Michael (January 2, 2015). "Book review: 'The Internet Is Not the Answer' by Andrew Keen". Washington Post. Retrieved 25 January 2015.

- Duryee, Tricia (2014-03-04). "Overstock hits $1 million in sales from virtual currency". Geekwire. Retrieved 2014-05-07.

- "UNCITRAL Model Law on Electronic Commerce (1996)". UNCITRAL. 12 June 1996. Retrieved 19 August 2014.

- Steven Millward (17 September 2014). "Here are all the must-see numbers on Alibaba ahead of record-breaking IPO". Tech In Asia. Retrieved 17 September 2014.

- Head and Hands in the Cloud: Cooperative Models for Global Trade to be Murray, Kevin, RMIT University, Melbourne, Australia, 2013.

- Badger, Emily (6 February 2013). "How the Internet Reinforces Inequality in the Real World". The Atlantic. Retrieved 2013- 02-13.

- Power, Michael 'Mike' (19 April 2013). "Online highs are old as the net: the first e-commerce was a drugs deal". The Guardian. London. Retrieved 17 June 2013.

- "Online shopping: The pensioner who pioneered a home shopping revolution". BBC News. 16 September 2013.

- Ahmed, Saqib Iqbal (27 October 2009). "GSI Commerce to buy Retail Convergence for $180 mln". Reuters. Retrieved 6 April 2013.

- "'Free Shipping Day' Promotion Spurs Late-Season Online Spending Surge, Improving Season-to-Date Growth Rate to 16 Percent vs. Year Ago" Comscore, December 23, 2012.

- "Groupon's IPO biggest by U.S. Web company since Google". Reuters. 4 November 2011. Archived from the original on 13 September 2012. Retrieved 13 September 2012.

Business Models of E-commerce

Businesses develop business models in order to achieve their targets and goals. The business models used in e-commerce are omnichannel, business-to-business, consumer-to-business, customer to customer and public eProcurement. As business to business is a situation where a commercial interaction occurs between two businesses and consumer to business is a business model where businesses consume values created by customers.

Business Model

A business model is an "abstract representation of an organization, be it conceptual, textual, and/or graphical, of all core interrelated architectural, co-operational, and financial arrangements designed and developed by an organization presently and in the future, as well as all core products and/or services the organization offers, or will offer, based on these arrangements that are needed to achieve its strategic goals and objectives." This definition by Al-Debei, El-Haddadeh and Avison (2008) indicates that value proposition, value architecture (the organizational infrastructure and technological architecture that allows the movement of products, services, and information), value finance (modeling information related to total cost of ownership, pricing methods, and revenue structure), and value network articulate the primary constructs or dimensions of business models.

A business model describes the rationale of how an organization creates, delivers, and captures value, in economic, social, cultural or other contexts. The process of business model construction is part of business strategy.

In theory and practice, the term *business model* is used for a broad range of informal and formal descriptions to represent core aspects of a business, including purpose, business process, target customers, offerings, strategies, infrastructure, organizational structures, sourcing, trading practices, and operational processes and policies including culture. The literature has provided very diverse interpretations and definitions of a business model. A systematic review and analysis of manager responses to a survey defines business models as the design of organizational structures to enact a commercial opportunity. Further extensions to this design logic emphasize the use of narrative or coherence in business model descriptions as mechanisms by which entrepreneurs create extraordinarily successful growth firms.

Business models are used to describe and classify businesses, especially in an entrepreneurial setting, but they are also used by managers inside companies to explore possibilities for future development. Well-known business models can operate as "recipes" for creative managers. Business models are also referred to in some instances within the context of accounting for purposes of public reporting.

History

Over the years, business models have become much more sophisticated. The *bait and hook* business model (also referred to as the "razor and blades business model" or the "tied products business model") was introduced in the early 20th century. This involves offering a basic product at a very low cost, often at a loss (the "bait"), then charging compensatory recurring amounts for refills or associated products or services (the "hook"). Examples include: razor (bait) and blades (hook); cell phones (bait) and air time (hook); computer printers (bait) and ink cartridge refills (hook); and cameras (bait) and prints (hook). A variant of this model is Adobe, a software developer that gives away its document reader free of charge but charges several hundred dollars for its document writer.

In the 1953s, new business models came from McDonald's Restaurants and Toyota. In the 1960s, the innovators were Wal-Mart and Hypermarkets. The 1970s saw new business models from FedEx and Toys R Us; the 1980s from Blockbuster, Home Depot, Intel, and Dell Computer; the 1990s from Southwest Airlines, Netflix, eBay, Amazon. com, and Starbucks.

Today, the type of business models might depend on how technology is used. For example, entrepreneurs on the internet have also created entirely new models that depend entirely on existing or emergent technology. Using technology, businesses can reach a large number of customers with minimal costs. In addition, the rise of outsourcing and globalization has meant that business models must also account for strategic sourcing, complex supply chains and moves to collaborative, relational contracting structures.

Theoretical and Empirical Insights to Business Models

Design Logic and Narrative Coherence

Design logic views the business model as an outcome of creating new organizational structures or changing existing structures to pursue a new opportunity. Gerry George and Adam Bock (2011) conducted a comprehensive literature review and surveyed managers to understand how they perceived the components of a business model. In that analysis these authors show that there is a design logic behind how entrepreneurs and managers perceive and explain their business model. In further extensions to the design logic, George and Bock (2012) use case studies and the IBM survey data on business models in large companies, to describe how CEOs and entrepreneurs create narratives or stories in a coherent manner to move the business from one opportunity to another. They also show that when the narrative is incoherent or the components of the story are misaligned, that these businesses tend to fail. They recommend ways in which the entrepreneur or CEO can create strong narratives for change.

Complementarities of Business Models between Partnering Firms

Studying collaborative research and the accessing of external sources of technology, Hummel et al. (2010) found that in deciding on business partners, it is important to make sure that both parties' business models are complementary. For example, they found that it was important to identify the value drivers of potential partners by analyzing their business models, and that it is beneficial to find partner firms that understand key aspects of our own firm's business model.

The University of Tennessee conducted research into highly collaborative business relationships. Researchers codified their research into a sourcing business model known as Vested (also referred to as Vested Outsourcing). Vested is a hybrid sourcing business model in which buyers and suppliers in an outsourcing or business relationship focus on shared values and goals to create an arrangement that is highly collaborative and mutually beneficial to each.

Categorization of Business Models

From about 2012, some research and experimentation has theorized about a so-called "liquid business model".

V4 BM Framework

Al-Debei and Avison (2010) V⁴ BM Framework - four main dimensions encapsulating sixteen elements: Value Proposition, Value Architecture, Value Network, and Value Finance

- Value Proposition: This dimension implies that a BM should include a description of the products/services a digital organization offers, or will offer, along with their related information. Furthermore, the BM needs also to describe the value elements incorporated within the offering, as well as the nature of targeted market segment(s) along with their preferences.

- Value Architecture: portrays the concept as a holistic structural design of an organization, including its technological architecture, organizational infrastructure, and their configurations.

- Value Network: depicts the cross-company or inter-organization perspective towards the concept and has gained much attention in the BM literature.

- Value Finance: depicts information related to costing, pricing methods, and revenue structure

Shift from Pipes to Platforms

Sangeet Paul Choudary (2013) distinguishes between two broad families of business models in an article in *Wired* magazine. Choudary contrasts pipes (linear business models) with platforms (networked business models). In the case of pipes, firms create goods and services, push them out and sell them to customers. Value is produced upstream and consumed downstream. There is a linear flow, much like water flowing through a pipe. Unlike pipes, platforms do not just create and push stuff out. They allow users to create and consume value.

In an op-ed on MarketWatch, Choudary, Van Alstyne and Parker further explain how business models are moving from pipes to platforms, leading to disruption of entire industries.

Platform Business Models

There are three elements to a successful platform business model. The *Toolbox* creates connection by making it easy for others to plug into the platform. This infrastructure enables interactions between participants. The *Magnet* creates pull that attracts participants to the platform. For transaction platforms, both producers and consumers must be present to achieve critical mass. The *Matchmaker* fosters the flow of value by making connections between producers and consumers. Data is at the heart of successful matchmaking, and distinguishes platforms from other business models.

Chen (2009) stated that the business model has to take into account the capabilities of Web 2.0, such as collective intelligence, network effects, user-generated content, and the possibility of self-improving systems. He suggested that the service industry such as the airline, traffic, transportation, hotel, restaurant, information and communications technology and online gaming industries will be able to benefit in adopting business models that take into account the characteristics of Web 2.0. He also emphasized that Business Model 2.0 has to take into account not just the technology effect of Web 2.0 but also the networking effect. He gave the example of the success story of Amazon in making huge revenues each year by developing an open platform that supports a community of companies that re-use Amazon's on-demand commerce services.

Applications

Malone et al. found that some business models, as defined by them, indeed performed better than others in a dataset consisting of the largest U.S. firms, in the period 1998 through 2002, while they did not prove whether the existence of a business model mattered.

In the context of the Software-Cluster, which is funded by the German Federal Ministry of Education and Research, a business model wizard for software companies has been developed. It supports the design and analysis of software business models. The tool's underlying concept and data were published in various scientific publications.

The concept of a business model has been incorporated into certain accounting standards. For example, the International Accounting Standards Board (IASB) utilizes an "entity's business model for managing the financial assets" as a criterion for determining whether such assets should be measured at amortized cost or at fair value in its financial instruments accounting standard, IFRS 9. In their 2013 proposal for accounting for financial instruments, the Financial Accounting Standards Board also proposed a similar use of business model for classifying financial instruments. The concept of business model has also been introduced into the accounting of deferred taxes under International Financial Reporting Standards with 2010 amendments to IAS 12 addressing deferred taxes related to investment property.

Both IASB and FASB have proposed using the concept of business model in the context of reporting a lessor's lease income and lease expense within their joint project on accounting for leases. In its 2016 lease accounting model, IFRS 16, the IASB chose not to include a criterion of "stand alone utility" in its lease definition because "entities might reach different conclusions for contracts that contain the same rights of use, depending on differences between customers' resources or suppliers' business models." The concept has also been proposed as an approach for determining the measurement and classification when accounting for insurance contracts. As a result of the increasing prominence the concept of business model has received in the context of financial reporting, the European Financial Reporting Advisory Group (EFRAG), which advises the European Union on endorsement of financial reporting standards, commenced a project on the "Role of the Business Model in Financial Reporting" in 2011.

Business Model Design

Business model design refers to the activity of designing a company's business model. It is part of the business development and business strategy process and involves design methods.

Definitions of Business Model

Al-Debei and Avison (2010) define a business model as an abstract representation of an organization. This may be conceptual, textual, and/or graphical, of all core interrelated architectural, co-operational, and financial arrangements designed and developed by an organization presently and in the future, as well all core products and/or services the organization offers, or will offer, based on these arrangements that are needed to achieve its strategic goals and objectives. This definition indicates that value proposition, value architecture, value finance, and value network articulate the primary constructs or dimensions of business models.

Economic Consideration

Al-Debei and Avison (2010) consider value finance as one of the main dimensions of

BM which depicts information related to costing, pricing methods, and revenue structure. Stewart and Zhao (2000) defined the business model as "a statement of how a firm will make money and sustain its profit stream over time."

Component Consideration

Osterwalder et al. (2005) consider the Business Model as the blueprint of how a company does business. Slywotzky (1996) regards the business model as "the totality of how a company selects its customers, defines and differentiates it offerings, defines the tasks it will perform itself and those it will outsource, configures its resources, goes to market, creates utility for customers and captures profits."

Strategic Outcome

Mayo and Brown (1999) considered the business model as "the design of key interdependent systems that create and sustain a competitive business."

Definitions of Business Model Design or Development

Zott and Amit (2009) consider business model design from the perspectives of design themes and design content. Design themes refer to the system's dominant value creation drivers and design content examines in greater detail the activities to be performed, the linking and sequencing of the activities and who will perform the activities.

Design themes Emphasis of Business Model

Environment-Strategy-Structure-Operations (ESSO) Business Model Development

Developing a Framework for Business Model Development with an emphasis on Design Themes, Lim (2010) proposed the Environment-Strategy-Structure-Operations (ESSO) Business Model Development which takes into consideration the alignment of the organization's strategy with the organization's structure, operations, and the environmental factors in achieving competitive advantage in varying combination of cost, quality, time, flexibility, innovation and affective.

Design Content Emphasis of Business Model Design

Business model design includes the modeling and description of a company's:

- value propositions
- target customer segments
- distribution channels
- customer relationships

- value configurations

- core capabilities

- commercial network

- partner network

- cost structure

- revenue model

Business model design is distinct from business modeling. The former refers to defining the business logic of a company at the strategic level, whereas the latter refers to business process design at the operational level.

A business model design template can facilitate the process of designing and describing a company's business model.

Daas et al. (2012) developed a decision support system (DSS) for business model design. In their study a decision support system (DSS) is developed to help SaaS in this process, based on a design approach consisting of a design process that is guided by various design methods.

Examples of Business Models

In the early history of business models it was very typical to define business model types such as bricks-and-mortar or e-broker. However, these types usually describe only one aspect of the business (most often the revenue model). Therefore, more recent literature on business models concentrate on describing a business model as a whole, instead of only the most visible aspects.

The following examples provide an overview for various business model types that have been in discussion since the invention of term *business model*:

- Bricks and clicks business model

  Business model by which a company integrates both offline (*bricks*) and online (*clicks*) presences. One example of the bricks-and-clicks model is when a chain of stores allows the user to order products online, but lets them pick up their order at a local store.

- Collective business models

  Business system, organization or association typically composed of relatively large numbers of businesses, tradespersons or professionals in the same or related fields of endeavor, which pools resources, shares information or provides other benefits for their members. For example, a science park or high-tech campus provides shared resources (e.g. cleanrooms and other lab facilities) to the firms located on its premises, and in addition seeks to create an innovation community among these firms and their employees.

- Cutting out the middleman model

  The removal of intermediaries in a supply chain: "cutting out the middleman". Instead of going through traditional distribution channels, which had some type of intermediate (such as a distributor, wholesaler, broker, or agent), companies may now deal with every customer directly, for example via the Internet.

- Direct sales model

  Direct selling is marketing and selling products to consumers directly, away from a fixed retail location. Sales are typically made through party plan, one-to-one demonstrations, and other personal contact arrangements. A text book definition is: "The direct personal presentation, demonstration, and sale of products and services to consumers, usually in their homes or at their jobs."

- Distribution business models, various

- Value-added reseller model

  Value Added Reseller is a model where a business makes something which is resold by other businesses but with modifications which add value to the original product or service. These modifications or additions are mostly industry specific in nature and are essential for the distribution. Businesses going for a VAR model have to develop a VAR network. It is one of the latest collaborative business models which can help in faster development cycles and is adopted by many Technology companies especially software.

- Fee in, free out

  Business model which works by charging the first client a fee for a service, while offering that service free of charge to subsequent clients.

- Franchise

  Franchising is the practice of using another firm's successful business model. For the franchisor, the franchise is an alternative to building 'chain stores' to *distribute* goods and avoid investment and liability over a chain. The franchisor's success is the success of the franchisees. The franchisee is said to have a greater incentive than a direct employee because he or she has a direct stake in the business.

- Sourcing business model

  A Sourcing Business Model is a type of business model that is applied specifically to business relationships where more than one party needs to work with another party to be successful. It is the combination of two concepts: the contractual relationship framework a company uses with its supplier (transactional, relational, investment based), and the economic model used (transactional, output or outcome-based).

- Freemium business model

  Business model that works by offering basic Web services, or a basic downloadable digital product, for free, while charging a premium for advanced or special features.

- Pay what you can (PWYC) is a non-profit or for-profit business model which does not depend on set prices for its goods, but instead asks customers to pay what they feel the product or service is worth to them. It is often used as a promotional tactic, but can also be the regular method of doing business. It is a variation on the gift economy and cross-subsidization, in that it depends on reciprocity and trust to succeed.

"Pay what you want" (PWYW) is sometimes used synonymously, but "pay what you can" is often more oriented to charity or socially oriented uses, based more on *ability* to pay, while "pay what you want" is often more broadly oriented to perceived value in combination with willingness and ability to pay.

Other examples of business models are:

- Auction business model

- All-in-one business model

- Chemical Leasing

- Low-cost carrier business model

- Loyalty business models

- Monopolistic business model

- Multi-level marketing business model

- Network effects business model

- Online auction business model

- Online content business model

- Online media cooperative

- Premium business model

- Professional open-source model

- Pyramid scheme business model

- Razor and blades business model

- Servitization of products business model

- Subscription business model

Business Model Frameworks

Technology centric communities have defined "frameworks" for business modeling. These frameworks attempt to define a rigorous approach to defining business value streams. It is not clear, however, to what extent such frameworks are actually important for business planning. Business model frameworks represent the core aspect of any company; they involve "the totality of how a company selects its customers defines and differentiates its offerings, defines the tasks it will perform itself and those it will outsource, configures its resource, goes to market, creates utility for customers, and captures profits". A business framework involves internal factors (market analysis; products/services promotion; development of trust; social influence and knowledge sharing) and external factors (competitors and technological aspects).

A review on business model frameworks can be found in Krumeich et al. (2012). In the following some frameworks are introduced.

- Business reference model

   Business reference model is a reference model, concentrating on the architectural aspects of the core business of an enterprise, service organization or government agency.

- Component business model

Although Webvan failed in its goal of disintermediating the North American supermarket industry, several supermarket chains (like Safeway Inc.) have launched their own delivery services to target the niche market to which Webvan catered.

Technique developed by IBM to model and analyze an enterprise. It is a logical representation or map of business components or "building blocks" and can be depicted on a single page. It can be used to analyze the alignment of enterprise strategy with the organization's capabilities and investments, identify redundant or overlapping business capabilities, etc.

- Industrialization of services business model

  Business model used in strategic management and services marketing that treats service provision as an industrial process, subject to industrial optimization procedures

- Business Model Canvas

  Developed by A. Osterwalder, Yves Pigneur, Alan Smith, and 470 practitioners from 45 countries, the business model canvas is one of the most used frameworks for describing the elements of business models.

- OGSM

  The OGSM is developed by Marc van Eck and Ellen van Zanten of Business Openers into the 'Business plan on 1 page'. Translated in several languages all over the world. #1 Management book in The Netherlands in 2015. The foundation of Business plan on 1 page is the OGSM. Objectives, Goals, Strageties and Measures (dashboard and actions).

Related Concepts

The process of business model design is part of business strategy. Business model design and innovation refer to the way a firm (or a network of firms) defines its business logic at the strategic level.

In contrast, firms implement their business model at the operational level, through their business operations. This refers to their process-level activities, capabilities, functions and infrastructure (for example, their business processes and business process modeling), their organisational structures (e.g. organigrams, workflows, human resources) and systems (e.g. information technology architecture, production lines).

Consequently, an operationally viable and feasible business model requires lateral alignment with the underlining business operations.

The brand is a consequence of the business model and has a symbiotic relationship with it, because the business model determines the brand promise, and the brand equity becomes a feature of the model. Managing this is a task of integrated marketing.

The standard terminology and examples of business models do not apply to most nonprofit organizations, since their sources of income are generally not the same as the beneficiaries. The term 'funding model' is generally used instead.

The model is defined by the organization's vision, mission, and values, as well as sets of boundaries for the organization—what products or services it will deliver, what customers or markets it will target, and what supply and delivery channels it will use. While the business model includes high-level strategies and tactical direction for how the organization will implement the model, it also includes the annual goals that set the specific steps the organization intends to undertake in the next year and the measures for their expected accomplishment. Each of these is likely to be part of internal documentation that is available to the internal auditor.

Omnichannel

Omnichannel is a cross-channel business model that companies use to increase customer experience. The approach has verticals in healthcare, government, financial services, retail and telecommunications industries, including channels such as physical locations, FAQ webpages, social media, live web chats, mobile applications and telephone communication. Companies that use omnichannel contend that a customer values the ability to be in constant contact with a company through multiple avenues at the same time.

History

"Omnis" is Latin for "every/all" and is considered the integration of all physical channels (offline) and digital channels (online) to offer a seamless and unified customer experience. According to *Frost & Sullivan*, omnichannel is defined as "seamless and effortless, high-quality customer experiences that occur within and between contact channels".

Until the early 1990s, retail was either a physical brick and mortar store or catalog sales where an order was placed by mail or via telephone. Sale by mail order dates back to when British entrepreneur Pryce Pryce-Jones set up the first modern mail order in 1861, selling Welsh flannel. Catalog sales for an assortment of general goods started in the late 1800s when Sears & Roebuck issued its first catalog in 1896. In the early 1900s, L.L. Bean started its catalog business in United States.

AOL, CompuServe and Prodigy experimented with selling through their proprietary online services in the early 1990s. These companies started sales channel expansion, while general merchants had evolved to department stores and Big-box store electronic ordering. In August 1994, NetMarket processed the first Internet sale where the credit card was encrypted. Shortly thereafter, Amazon.com was founded and the eCommerce sales channel was established. Mobile commerce arrived in 1997, and multichannel retailing really took off.

Omnichannel's origins date back to Best Buy's use of customer centricity to compete with Walmart's electronic department in 2003. The company created an approach that centered around the customer both in-store and online, while providing post-sales support. Omnichannel was coined as a form of "assembled commerce" and spread into the healthcare and financial services industries.

Finance

Omnichannel banking developed in response to the popularity of digital banking transactions through ATMs, the web, and mobile applications. The most popular parts of omnichannel banking include 'zero drop rate' channel integration, individualizing channels for customers and marketing other channel options. Banks receive in-depth research about customers to build relationships and increase profitability.

Government

In 2009, the omnichannel platform started to be used in governments through Twitter interaction. Governments are developing web and mobile-enabled interfaces to improve and personalize the citizen experience. The United States government digital strategy includes information and customer-centric shared platforms that provide security and privacy. Omnichannel is used to communicate with citizens through the platform of their choice at their convenience and use feedback to analyze the citizen experience to better serve.

Healthcare

Due to fragmentation between health providers, hospitals, pharmaceutical companies and patients, omnichannel is developing to improve the customer experience in the healthcare industry. Omnichannel healthcare centers around integrating data, technology, content and communication, while coordinating patient's results through digital channels. In September 2015, the University of Pittsburgh Medical Center received media attention for its customer service technology, which was integrated in 2009. The UPMC Health Plan uses an omnichannel system to improve customer engagement and contact resolution.

Retail

Omnichannel retailing uses a variety of channels in a customer's shopping experience including research before a purchase. Such channels include retail stores, online stores, mobile stores, mobile app stores, telephone sales and any other method of transacting with a customer. Transacting includes browsing, buying, returning as well as pre-sale and after-sale service. Omnichannel pertains to the seamless integration of online and in-store sales channels. Extending across channels and devices, shoppers can visit stores, how and when they want.

Outlook

Although omnichannel is said to be dictated by systems and processes, it is the customer that dictates how a transaction occurs. Systems and processes facilitate the customer journey to transact and be served. Omnichannel is moving toward increased personalization based on analytics to make the customer experience more seamless. According to an *MIT* report, omnichannel "is the central force shaping the future of e-commerce and brick-and-mortar stores alike."

Business-to-business

The "electronic components district" of Guangzhou, where numerous shops sell electronic components to other companies that would use them to manufacture consumer goods

Business-to-business (B2B) refers to a situation where one business makes a commercial transaction with another. This typically occurs when:

- A business is sourcing materials for their production process (e.g. a food manufacturer purchasing salt).

- A business needs the services of another for operational reasons (e.g. a food manufacturer employing an accountancy firm to audit their finances).

- A business re-sells goods and services produced by others (e.g. a retailer buying the end product from the food manufacturer).

B2B is often contrasted against business-to-consumer (B2C). In B2B commerce it is often the case that the parties to the relationship have comparable negotiating power, and even when they don't, each party typically involves professional staff and legal counsel in the negotiation of terms, whereas B2C is shaped to a far greater degree by economic implications of information asymmetry.

Comparison with B2C

In most cases, the overall volume of B2B (business-to-business) transactions is much higher than the volume of B2C transactions. The primary reason for this is that in a typical supply chain there will be many B2B transactions involving sub-components or raw materials, and only one B2C transaction, specifically sale of the finished product to the end customer. For example, an automobile manufacturer makes several B2B transactions such as buying tires, glass for windscreens, and rubber hoses for its vehicles. The final transaction, a finished vehicle sold to the consumer, is a single (B2C) transaction.

However, in certain cases, for example a toothbrush manufacturer may make lesser B2B transactions of raw materials than the number of B2C transactions of toothbrush units that are sold.

Consumer-to-business

Consumer-to-business (C2B) is a business model in which consumers (individuals) create value and businesses consume that value. For example, when a consumer writes reviews or when a consumer gives a useful idea for new product development then that consumer is creating value for the business if the business adopts the input. Excepted concepts are crowd sourcing and co-creation.

C2B model, also called a reverse auction or demand collection model, enables buyers to name or demand their own price, which is often binding, for a specific good or service. The website collects the demand bids then offers the bids to participating sellers.

Another form of C2B is the electronic commerce business model in which consumers can offer products and services to companies, and the companies pay the consumers. This business model is a complete reversal of the traditional business model in which companies offer goods and services to consumers (business-to-consumer = B2C). We can see the C2B model at work in blogs or internet forums in which the author offers a link back to an online business thereby facilitating the purchase of a product (like a book on Amazon.com), for which the author might receive affiliate revenues from a successful sale. Elance was the first C2B model e-commerce site.

C2B is a kind of economic relationship that is qualified as an inverted business type. The advent of the C2B scheme is due to:

- The internet connecting large groups of people to a bidirectional network; the large traditional media outlets are one-directional relationships whereas the internet is bidirectional.

- Decreasing costs of technology; individuals now have access to technologies that were once only available to large companies (digital printing and acquisition technology, high performance computers, and powerful software).

Customer to Customer

Customer to customer (C2C) markets are innovative ways to allow customers to interact with each other. While traditional markets require business to customer relationships, in which a customer goes to the business in order to purchase a product or service. In customer to customer markets the business facilitates an environment where customers can sell these goods or services to each other. Other types of markets include business to business (B2B) and business to customer (B2C).

Consumer to consumer (or citizen-to-citizen) electronic commerce involves the electronically facilitated transactions between consumers through some third party. A common example is the online auction, in which a consumer posts an item for sale and other consumers bid to purchase it; the third party generally charges a flat fee or commission. The sites are only intermediaries, just there to match consumers. They do not have to check quality of the products being offered.

Consumer to consumer (C2C) marketing is the creation of a product or service with the specific promotional strategy being for consumers to share that product or service with others as brand advocates based on the value of the product. The investment into concepting and developing a top of the line product or service that consumers are actively looking for is equitable to a retail pre-launch product awareness marketing.

Origins

There are many different classifications of marketing. From Government to Business (G2B), Business to Business (B2B), Business to Consumer (B2C), to Customer to Customer (C2C). While many companies usually operate in one or more of these areas, Customer to Customer businesses operate only within that specific area. Customer to Customer marketing has become more popular recently with the advent of the internet. Companies such as Craigslist, eBay, and other classified and auction based sites have allowed for greater interaction between consumers, facilitating the Customer to Customer model. Furthermore, as it becomes more economical for individuals to network on the internet via social websites and individual content creation, this marketing model has been greatly leveraged by businesses and individuals alike.

There are two implementations of customer to customer markets that are credited with its origin. These are classifieds and auctions.

Newspapers and other similar publications were in frequent circulation and therefore were able to be used to facilitate a common need. Some people wanted things, other people had things and wanted to sell them. This was the birth of classifieds. The use of classifieds is referred to as classified advertisement. Normally used in text based print, classified advertisement is a now a strong vertical market that allows customers to communicate their needs with each other. In 2003 US classifieds market totaled $30.00 billion for both newspapers and online classified ad services.

The oldest auction house is Stockholm Auction House (Stockholms Auktionsverk), which was established in Sweden in 1674. Auctions however, have been recorded as far back as 500 B.C. Deriving from the Latin word augēre, which means to "'increase' (or 'augment')". Auctions have since a widely used method of liquidating assets, and has evolved into many different variations. The most successful current form of auctions is based on the internet, such as eBay.

Business Model

Most C2C websites, such as eBay, have both streamlined and globalized traditional person-to-person trading, which was usually conducted through such forms as garage sales, collectibles shows, flea markets and more, with their web interface. This facilitates easy exploration for buyers and enables the sellers to immediately list an item for sale within minutes of registering.

When an item is listed on a C2C site, a nonrefundable insertion fee is charged based on the seller's opening bid on the item. Once the auction is completed, a final value fee is charged. This fee generally ranges from 1.25 percent to 5 percent of the final sale price.

After the C2C site sets up the system in which bids could be placed, items can be put up for sale, transactions can be completed, seller fees are charged, and feedback can be left, while the C2C site stays in the background. For example, at the end of an auction, the C2C site notifies the buyer via e-mail that he or she has won. The C2C site also e-mails the seller to report who won and at what price the auction finished. At that point it's up to the seller and buyer finish the transaction independently of the C2C site.

C2C sites make money by charging fees to sellers. Although it's free to shop and place bids, sellers place fees to list items for sale, add on promotional features, and successfully complete transactions.

Many C2C sites have expanded and developed existing product categories by introducing category-specific bulletin boards and chat rooms, integrating category-specific content, advertising its service in targeted publications and participating in targeted trade shows. eBay specifically has also broadened the range of products that it offers to facilitate trading on the site, including payment services, shipping services, authentication, appraisal, vehicle inspection and escrow services.

Specialty marketplaces have also been added to serve the specialized needs of buyers and sellers. For example, eBay Motors serves the automotive marketplace, including vehicles, parts and accessories; and Half.com is focused on providing a fixed-price trading environment, initially for books music, videos and video games.

Many online auction sites use a system called PayPal for sellers to receive online payments securely and quickly. A traditional credit card is not required to use this site because PayPal can be linked directly to you bank account.

Product or Service

Consumer to Consumer transactions often involve products sold via either a classified or auction-like system. As such, the products and services bought and sold are usually varied in type and have a short development and sale cycle. Products sold may often be used or second-hand, since consumer to consumer sales are often facilitated through auction or classified sites.

Development

Since products are usually second-hand, surplus, or used there is seldom a long development cycle associated with the products that are marketed via this method. However, in the case of individuals who are looking to sell a product or service they have developed to be sold on the small-scale, there is a product development life cycle. However, even when a product goes through a development life cycle when marketed in this manner, seldom does traditional marketing research occur. Oftentimes individuals are looking to make a quick profit, and simply place their product in the market place in hopes that it will be sold.

Communications

Advertising

Advertising is essential towards the success of any business. In the case of customer to customer marketing, advertising often relates to online auctions and listings. As opposed to the pricey costs to advertise in medias such as newspapers and magazines, products are already being promoted and publicized once users decide to officially put them on the internet. Potential buyers will become aware of products or services by conducting searches on the websites. Aside from possible fees and commissions imposed by the auction or listing site, advertising in this market does not require a substantial amount of money.

Advantages

Customer to Customer marketing has become very popular in the recent years. Customers can directly contact sellers and eliminate the middle man. Moreover, anyone can now sell and advertise a product in the convenience of one's home – enabling one to easily start a business. Therefore, a wide variety of products can often be found on auction sites such as eBay, including second-hand goods. Since majority of these sales occur over the internet, sellers can reach both national and international customers and greatly increase their market. Feedback on the purchased product is often requested to aid both the seller and potential customers. The actual buying and searching process is simplified and search costs, distribution costs, and inventory costs are all reduced. Moreover, the transactions occur at a swift rate with the use of online payment systems such as PayPal.

Disadvantages

Although online auctions allow one to display his or her products, there is often a fee associated with such exhibitions. Other times, websites may charge a commission when products are sold. With the growing use of online auctions, the number of internet-related auction frauds have also increased. For instance, a seller may create two accounts on an auction site. When an interested buyer bids for an item, the seller will use another account to bid on the same item and thus, increasing the price. Consequently, many users have purchased products at unnecessarily inflated prices.

Identity theft has become a rising issue. Scam artists often create sites with popular domain names such as "ebay" in order to attract unknowing eBay customers. These sites will ask for personal information including credit card numbers. Numerous cases have been documented in which users find unknown charges on their credit card statements and withdrawals in their bank statements after purchasing something online. Unfortunately, websites often have a liability statement claiming that they are not responsible for any losses or damages. Furthermore, illegal or restricted products and services have been found on auction sites. Anything from illegal drugs, pirated works, prayers, and even sex have appeared on such sites. Although most of these items are blacklisted, some still find their way onto the internet.

Examples

Internet Auctions

Despite the success of eBay, numerous other online auction sites have either shut down or consolidated with other similar sites. Creating an innovative and efficient business model is vital towards success. Online auctions can be categorized into five main models: C2C, B2C, B2B, B2G, and G2P. C2C refers to customer to customer, B2C signifies business to customer, B2B refers to business to business, B2G signifies business to government, and G2P refers to government to public. In recent years, online auctions have even appealed to major businesses. For instance, Sears has reported selling items at higher prices on these auctions when compared to discounting them in stores.

The success of an online auction site largely depends on six variables: interactivity, product offering, level of trust, rate of growth and adoption, networking, level of commitment, and payment options. Interactions among users are crucial and thus, websites must be accessible and easily navigable. E-mails, community boards, and feedback all aid in increasing the interactivity. With the growing need for convenience, the variety of products offered can greatly attribute to the client basis. Especially with the growing number of online frauds, trust is essential in auction sites. Users must be guaranteed that their personal information will remain secured and that they will receive their purchased product in a perfect condition and in a timely manner. With the fast-paced advancements in technology, auction sites must respond to these changes by staying updated. Moreover, sites also need to constantly search for business opportunities in order to expand their market. A large network of users is also crucial. Having an array of different sellers, buyers, suppliers, and delivery agents will increase the number of users, which would also raise the level of interactivity. In addition, forming alliances with different partners will also aid in the site's success. The level of commitment in buyers and sellers also plays a role in the auction's success. Similar to the level of trust, buyers must be ensured that they receive their purchased item, and sellers must actually receive payment. Although most prefer speedy online transactions, it is beneficial to offer different payment options that will accommodate different buyers.

Internet Classifieds

Internet classifieds are another example of customer to customer marketing. An example of an internet classified company, is Craigslist. Craigslist utilizes the internet to attract a wide customer and buyer base which employs the website to list and sell items.

Since the customer to customer marketing strategy is strongly focused on serving the customer, the business model of Craigslist is simple: serve the customer first. Utilizing this model, Craigslist has developed into a prime example of a customer to customer driven 'machine', which focuses on the customer selling to the customer.

Revenues which support the company are derived through subsidiary channels, while maintaining the model and convenience of the site. In fact, Craigslist makes no money off the customer to customer interactions that occur on the classifieds of the website. All of their revenue is derived from portion of the website targeted at businesses. Thus, in other words, their revenue is derived solely from their business to customer model utilized by businesses to post jobs and hire new workers.

As such, it becomes apparent that companies who focuses on this particular model and, specifically classifieds, whether online or off, are often not focused on profit; but rather, on delivery of the service or product to ensure customer to customer interaction.

Internet classifieds sites such as olx, quikr, loogga etc. are gaining prominence in emerging economies such as India, Brazil and Nigeria. Olx and quikr recently enabled their users to sell cows and buffaloes in rural India

Marketing

C2C marketing is of critical importance to retailers. When a shopper buys a product, if it can be shared with the shopper's friends, that drives significant traffic back to the customer site. Additionally, shoppers trust user generated recommendations much higher than recommendations pushed by the retailer. Retailers like CafePress have implemented C2C marketing on their website and companies like ShopSocially are building C2C marketing platforms for retailers. Recent trends by Facebook and Wavespot that leverage free WIFI at a local business are indicative of C2C marketing's importance in SMB space.

Most companies think of C2C marketing as the use of social media channels such as Facebook and Twitter. However, in many cases, the messaging tends to be business to consumer.

Business-to-government

Business-to-government (B2G) is a derivative of B2B marketing and often referred to as a market definition of "public sector marketing" which encompasses marketing products and services to various government levels - including federal, state and local - through integrated marketing communications techniques such as strategic public relations, branding, marcom, advertising, and web-based communications.

B2G networks provide a platform for businesses to bid on government opportunities which are presented as solicitations in the form of RFPs in a reverse auction fashion. Public sector organizations (PSOs) post tenders in the form of RFPs, RFIs, RFQs, Sources Sought, etc. and suppliers respond to them.

Government agencies typically have pre-negotiated standing contracts vetting the vendors/suppliers and their products and services for set prices. These can be state, local or federal contracts and some may be grandfathered in by other entities (i.e. California's MAS Multiple Award Schedule will recognize the federal government contract holder's prices on a General Services Administration Schedule).

There are multiple social platforms dedicated to this vertical market and they have risen in popularity with the onset of the ARRA/Stimulus Program and increased government funds available to commercial entities for both grants and contracts.

E-procurement

E-procurement (electronic procurement, sometimes also known as supplier exchange) is the business-to-business or business-to-consumer or business-to-government purchase and sale of supplies, work, and services through the Internet as well as other information and networking systems, such as electronic data interchange and enterprise resource planning.

The e-procurement value chain consists of indent management, e-Informing, e-Tendering, e-Auctioning, vendor management, catalogue management, Purchase Order Integration, Order Status, Ship Notice, e-invoicing, e-payment, and contract management. Indent management is the workflow involved in the preparation of tenders. This part of the value chain is optional, with individual procuring departments defining their indenting process. In works procurement, administrative approval and technical sanction are obtained in electronic format. In goods procurement, indent generation activity is done online. The end result of the stage is taken as inputs for issuing the NIT.

Elements of e-procurement include request for information, request for proposal, request for quotation, RFx (the previous three together), and eRFx (software for managing RFx projects).

In the Public Sector

Public sector organizations use e-procurement for contracts to achieve benefits such as increased efficiency and cost savings (faster and cheaper) in government procurement and improved transparency (to reduce corruption) in procurement services. E-procurement in the public sector has seen rapid growth in recent years. Act 590 of Louisiana's 2008 Regular Legislative Session requires political subdivisions to make provisions for the receipt of electronic bids.

E-procurement in the public sector is emerging internationally. Hence, initiatives have been implemented in Singapore, Estonia, UK, United States, Malaysia, Indonesia, Australia, European Union , Kazakhstan, and South Africa

E-procurement projects are often part of the country's larger e-Government efforts to better serve its citizens and businesses in the digital economy. For example, Singapore's GeBIZ was implemented as one of the programmes under its e-Government masterplan. The Procurement G6 leads the use of e-procurement instruments in Public procurement.

Vendors

This field is populated by two types of vendors: big enterprise resource planning (ERP) providers which offer e-procurement as one of their services, and the more affordable services focused specifically of e-procurement.

E-procurement Systems

Implementing an e Procurement system benefits all levels of an organisation. E Procurement systems offer improved spend visibility and control and help finance officers match purchases with purchase orders, receipts and job tickets. An e-procurement system also manages tenders through a web site. This can be accessed anywhere globally and has greatly improved the accessibility of tenders. An example is the System for Acquisition Management (SAM), which on July 30, 2013 combined information from the former Central Contractor Registration and Online Representations and Certifications Application (ORCA), in the United States.

Public eProcurement

The term Public eProcurement ("electronic procurement" in the public sector) refers, in Singapore, Europe and Canada, to the use of electronic means in conducting a public procurement procedure for the purchase of goods, works or services.

Phases

The term of the Electronic Public Procurement can be defined as the usage of e-Government platform over the electronic resources (Internet and Web-based applications) to conduct transactions for purchasing the products and services from suppliers to authority's buyers.

The following sub-phases of the electronic public procurement process could be identified:

- eSourcing: preparatory activities conducted by the contracting authority/entity to collect and reuse information for the preparation of a call; potential bidders may be contacted, if admitted by the legal rules, by electronic means to provide quotations or manifest interest.

- eNoticing: advertisement of calls for tenders through the publication of appropriate contract notices in electronic format in the relevant Official Journal (national/EU); electronic access to tender documents and specifications as well as additional related documents are provided in a non-discriminatory way.

- eAccess: electronic access to tender documents and specifications as well support to economic operators for the preparation of an offer, e.g. clarifications, questions and answers.

- eSubmission: submission of offers in electronic format to the contracting authority/entity, which is able to receive, accept and process it in compliance with the legal requirements.

- eTendering: is the union of the eAccess and eSubmission phases.

- eAwarding: opening and evaluation of the electronic tenders received, and award of the contract to the best offer in terms of the lowest price or economically most advantageous bid.

- eContract: conclusion, enactment and monitoring of a contract / agreement through electronic means between the contracting authority/entity and the winning tenderer.

- eOrders: preparation and issuing of an electronic order by the contracting authority/entity and its acceptance by the contractor.

- eOrder Status: preparation and delivery of status information against the eOrder.

- eInvoicing: preparation and delivery of an invoice in electronic format.

- ePayment: electronic payment of the ordered goods, services or works.

Einvoicing

eInvoicing is currently defined in multiple ways. A simple search finds 3 simple variations: "an invoice issued, received and processed electronically", "an invoice sent by electronic means to the recipient", and "an invoice received by the customer electronically". Driving a single strategy requires a single definition; a common language. The best definition should be customer centric. "an invoice received by the customer electronically"

The same common language divides the tiers of eInvocing based on cash management impacts.

- Tier 3 reduces delivery time (e.g. email delivery of pdf versions of invoices)

- Tier 2 reduces delivery time and digitizes the data for easier management by customers (e.g. electronic files (xml, edi, flat, etc.) which match the sellers sales invoice)

- Tier 1 reduces delivery time, digitizes data and reduces reconciliation time (e.g. electronic files (xml, edi, flat,etc.) which match the customers purchase order, or web invoicing solutions).

Enabling Systems

To successfully conduct electronic procurement across borders, eProcurement systems rely on some "key-enablers"

- eSignature: data in electronic form which are attached to or logically associated with other electronic data and which serve as a method of authentication with regard to this data.

- eIdentity: dynamic collection of all attributes, in electronic format, related to a specific entity (citizen, enterprise, or object) which serve to ascertain a specific identity.

- eAttestations (Virtual Company Dossier): set of certificates and attestations, in electronic format, to be provided by a supplier to prove compliance with the selection and exclusion criteria of a procurement procedure.

- eCatalogues: electronic supplier catalogue prospect uses used to prepare and submit offers or parts of them.

- eArchiving: use of electronic means for long-term preservation of documents in digitalised format, ensuring that they can be easily retrieved without conversions.

References

- George,G and Bock AJ. 2012. Models of opportunity: How entrepreneurs design firms to achieve the unexpected. Cambridge University Press, ISBN 978-0-521-17084-0

- Vitasek, Kate. Vested Outsourcing: Five Rules that will Transform Outsourcing" (New York: Palgrave Macmillan, 2012) ISBN 978-1-137-29719-8

- Wasserman, Tom (December 30, 2015). "Creating a seamless omni-channel customer experience". Mobile Business Insights. Retrieved May 31, 2016.

- Fallon, Nicole (August 6, 2014). "The New Customer Service Is Here, There & Everywhere". Business News Daily. Retrieved May 31, 2016.

- Solomon, Micah (April 8, 2015). "Omnichannel Customer Experience: Expert Systems, 360 Degree Views And AI". Forbes. Retrieved May 31, 2016.

- "Omnichannel Customer Engagement Drives Great Customer Experiences at Every Touchpoint". Genesys. Retrieved May 31, 2016.

- Butte, Brian (December 4, 2015). "Cloud: The engine of the omni-channel customer experience". Network World. Retrieved June 4, 2016.

- "'Digital' & 'Omnichannel' Remains Elusive in Banking". The Financial Brand. February 2, 2015. Retrieved June 5, 2016.

- Marous, Jim (March 24, 2014). "Omnichannel Banking: More Than a Buzzword". The Financial Brand. Retrieved June 5, 2016.

- Estopace, Eden (August 20, 2014). "Governments also going omnichannel". Enterprise Innovation. Retrieved June 5, 2016.

- Solomon, Micah (October 16, 2014). "Omnichannel Beyond Retail: The Customer Experience In Healthcare, B2B, Professional Services". Forbes. Retrieved June 5, 2016.

- Tierney, Jim (September 1, 2015). "Customer Engagement Rises with University of Pittsburgh Medical Center Health Plan". Loyalty360. Retrieved June 5, 2016.

- Everett, Cath (November 2015). "First steps taken on 'omni-channel' customer experience". Computer Weekly. Retrieved June 4, 2016.

- Green, James (January 27, 2014). "Why And How Brands Must Go Omni-Channel in 2014". Marketing Land. Retrieved June 4, 2016.

- Unpacking Sourcing Business Models: 21st Century Solutions for Sourcing Services, The University of Tennessee, 2014

- "CCR Moving to SAM". U.S. Department of Health and Human Services, Health Resources and

Services Administration. Retrieved 27 June 2013.

- "Project Update: Leases—Joint Project of the FASB and the IASB". Financial Accounting Standards Board. August 1, 2012. Retrieved 2012-08-02.

- "An optimist sees the opportunity in every difficulty: is IFRS 9 an opportunity or a difficulty?". Ernst & Young. December 2010. Retrieved 2011-06-03.

- "Exposure Draft:Leases" (PDF). International Accounting Standards Board. August 2010. p. 31. Retrieved 2011-06-03.

Various E-commerce Softwares

Shopping cart software, jigshop, inventory management software and track and trace are the softwares used in e-commerce. The systems used for tracking orders, sales and deliveries are known as inventory management software whereas the process of determining the location of an item or property is track and trace. The topics discussed in the section are of great importance to broaden the existing knowledge on various e-commerce softwares.

Shopping Cart Software

In online marketing, a shopping cart is a piece of e-commerce software on a web server that allows visitors to an Internet site to select items for eventual purchase, analogous to the American English term "shopping cart." In British English, it is generally known as a shopping basket, almost exclusively shortened on websites to "basket."

The software allows online shopping customers to accumulate a list of items for purchase, described metaphorically as "placing items in the shopping cart" or "add to cart." Upon checkout, the software typically calculates a total for the order, including shipping and handling (i.e., postage and packing) charges and the associated taxes, as applicable.

History

The development of web shop systems took place right after the Internet became a mass medium. This was a result of the launch of the browser Mosaic in 1993 and Netscape in 1994. It created an environment in which web shops were possible. The Internet therefore acted as the key infrastructure developments that contributed to the rapid diffusion of the e-commerce, a subset of e-business that describes all computer-aided business transactions. In 1998 a total of 11 e-business models were observed, one of which was the e-shop business model for a B2C (business-to-consumer) business—also called the "online shop" The two terms "online shop" and "electronic" or "e-shop" are used interchangeably. The term "online shopping" was invented much earlier in 1984; for example TV shopping often used the term before the popularity of the online method. Today the term primarily refers to the B2C transactional business model. In order to enable "online shopping" a software system is needed. Since "online shopping", in the context of the B2C business model, became broadly available to the end consumer, internet-based "online shops" evolved.

For online shopping systems in this context the narrower term "web shop" is used. No term has become solidly established for a B2C e-commerce software system. Whereas in the German-speaking region terms such as "web shop software" or "online shop software" are used, the term "shopping cart software" has become established in the United States.

Technical Definition

These applications typically provide a means of capturing a client's payment information, but in the case of a credit card they rely on the software module of the secure gateway provider, in conjunction with the secure payment gateway, in order to conduct secure credit card transactions online.

Some setup must be done in the HTML code of the website, and the shopping cart software must be installed on the server which hosts the site, or on the secure server which accepts sensitive ordering information. E-shopping carts are usually implemented using HTTP cookies or query strings. In most server based implementations however, data related to the shopping cart is kept in the session object and is accessed and manipulated on the fly, as the user selects different items from the cart. Later at the process of finalizing the transaction, the information is accessed and an order is generated against the selected item thus clearing the shopping cart.

Although the most simple shopping carts strictly allow for an item to be added to a basket to start a checkout process (e.g., the free PayPal shopping cart), most shopping cart software provides additional features that an Internet merchant uses to fully manage an online store. Data (products, categories, discounts, orders, customers, etc.) is normally stored in a database and accessed in real time by the software.

Shopping Cart Software is also known as e-commerce software, e-store software, online store software or storefront software and online shop.

Components

- Storefront: the area of the Web store that is accessed by visitors to the online shop. Category, product, and other pages (e.g., search, bestsellers, etc.) are dynamically generated by the software based on the information saved in the store database. The look of the storefront can normally be changed by the store owner so that it merges with the rest of the web site (i.e., with the pages not controlled by the shopping cart software in use on the store).

- Administration: the area of the Web store that is accessed by the merchant to manage the online shop. The amount of store management features changes depending on the sophistication of the shopping cart software chosen by the merchant, but in general a store manager is able to add and edit products, categories, discounts, shipping and payment settings, etc. Order management features are also included in many shopping cart programs. The administration area can be:

- o Web-based (accessed through a web browser)
- o Desktop-based (a desktop application that runs on the user's computer and then transfers changes to the storefront component).

Types

Shopping cart software can be generally categorized into three types of E-commerce software:

- Open source software: The software is released under an open source licence and is very often free of charge. The merchant has to host the software with a Web hosting service. It allows users to access and modify the source code of the entire online store.

- Licensed software: The software is downloaded and then installed on a Web-server. This is most often associated with a one-time fee, the main advantages of this option are that the merchant owns a license and therefore can host it on any web server that meets the server requirements.

- Hosted service: The software is never downloaded, but rather is provided by a host-ed service provider and is generally paid for on a monthly or annual basis; also known as the application service provider (ASP) software model. Some of these services also charge a percentage of sales in addition to the monthly fee. This model often has predefined templates that a user can choose from to customize their look and feel. Predefined templates limit how much users can modify or customize the software with the advantage of having the vendor continuously keep the software up to date for security patches as well as adding new features.

PCI Compliance

The PCI security standards are a blanket of regulations set in place to safeguard payment account data security. The council that develops and monitors these regulations is composed of the leading providers in the payment industry: American Express, Discover Financial Services, JCB International, MasterCard Worldwide, and Visa Inc. Essentially, they define the best practices for storing, transmitting, and handling of sensitive information over the internet.

Visa Inc.can hold shopping cart software providers responsible for liability that may occur as a result of non-compliance to Visa's regulations. For this reason, Visa Inc. may require that online merchants use shopping cart software providers from their list of PCI DSS-validated service providers.

Jigoshop

Jigoshop is an open-source content management system for eCommerce web sites based on WordPress.

Jigoshop was initially developed as a free eCommerce software solution for small and medium enterprises (SMEs) with WordPress websites.

History

Jigoshop began its life as a product of UK based company Jigowatt Ltd. The first version was released on 31 May 2011 and it went on to grow in strength throughout 2011 and 2012.

Proxar IT Consulting purchased Jigoshop in March 2014. From April 2014, under new management, Jigoshop was under active development.

Inventory Management Software

Inventory management software is a computer-based system for tracking inventory levels, orders, sales and deliveries. It can also be used in the manufacturing industry to create a work order, bill of materials and other production-related documents. Companies use inventory management software to avoid product overstock and outages. It is a tool for organizing inventory data that before was generally stored in hard-copy form or in spreadsheets.

Features

Inventory management software is made up of several key components, all working together to create a cohesive inventory for many organizations' systems. These features include:

Order Management

Should inventory reach a specific threshold, a company's inventory management system can be programmed to tell managers to reorder that product. This helps companies avoid running out of products or tying up too much capital in inventory.

Asset Tracking

When a product is in a warehouse or store, it can be tracked via its barcode and/or other tracking criteria, such as serial number, lot number or revision number. Systems. for Business, Encyclopedia of Business, 2nd ed. Nowadays, inventory management software often utilizes barcode, radio-frequency identification (RFID), and/or wireless tracking technology.

Service Management

Companies that are primarily service-oriented rather than product-oriented can use inventory management software to track the cost of the materials they use to provide services, such as cleaning supplies. This way, they can attach prices to their services that reflect the total cost of performing them.

Product Identification

Barcodes are often the means whereby data on products and orders is inputted into inventory management software. A barcode reader is used to read barcodes and look up information on the products they represent. Radio-frequency identification (RFID) tags and wireless methods of product identification are also growing in popularity.

Modern inventory software programs may use QR codes or NFC tags to identify inventory items and smartphones as scanners. This method provides an option for small businesses to track inventory using barcode scanning without a need to purchase expensive scanning hardware.

Inventory Optimization

A fully automated demand forecasting and inventory optimization system to attain key inventory optimization metrics such as:

- Reorder point: the number of units that should trigger a replenishment order

- Order quantity: the number of units that should be reordered, based on the reorder point, stock on hand and stock on order

- Lead demand: the number of units that will be sold during the lead time

- Stock cover: the number of days left before a stockout if no reorder is made

- Accuracy: the expected accuracy of the forecasts

History

The Universal Product Code (UPC) was adopted by the grocery industry in April 1973 as the standard barcode for all grocers, though it was not introduced at retailing locations until 1974. This helped drive down costs for inventory management because retailers in the United States and Canada didn't have to purchase multiple barcode readers to scan competing barcodes. There was now one primary barcode for grocers and other retailers to buy one type of reader for.

In the early 1980s, personal computers began to be popular. This further pushed down the cost of barcodes and readers. It also allowed the first versions of inventory management software to be put into place. One of the biggest hurdles in selling readers and barcodes to retailers was the fact that they didn't have a place to store the information they scanned. As computers became more common and affordable, this hurdle was overcome. Once barcodes and inventory management programs started spreading through grocery stores, inventory management by hand became less practical. Writing inventory data by hand on paper was replaced by scanning products and inputting information into a computer by hand.

Starting in the early 2000s, inventory management software progressed to the point where businesspeople no longer needed to input data by hand but could instantly update their database with barcode readers.

Also, the existence of cloud based business software and their increasing adoption by businesses mark a new era for inventory management software. Now they usually allow integrations with other business backend processes, like accounting and online sales.

Purpose

Companies often use inventory management software to reduce their carrying costs. The software is used to track products and parts as they are transported from a vendor to a warehouse, between warehouses, and finally to a retail location or directly to a customer.

Inventory management software is used for a variety of purposes, including:

- Maintaining a balance between too much and too little inventory.
- Tracking inventory as it is transported between locations.
- Receiving items into a warehouse or other location.
- Picking, packing and shipping items from a warehouse.
- Keeping track of product sales and inventory levels.
- Cutting down on product obsolescence and spoilage.
- Avoiding missing out on sales due to out-of-stock situations.

Manufacturing Uses

Manufacturers primarily use inventory management software to create work orders and bills of materials. This facilitates the manufacturing process by helping manufacturers efficiently assemble the tools and parts they need to perform specific tasks. For more complex manufacturing jobs, manufacturers can create multilevel work orders and bills of materials, which have a timeline of processes that need to happen in the proper order to build a final product. Other work orders that can be created using inventory management software include reverse work orders and auto work orders. Manufacturers also use inventory management software for tracking assets, receiving new inventory and additional tasks businesses in other industries use it for.

Advantages of ERP Inventory Management Software

There are several advantages to using inventory management software in a business setting.

Cost Savings

A company's inventory represents one of its largest investments, along with its workforce and locations. Inventory management software helps companies cut expenses by minimizing the amount of unnecessary parts and products in storage. It also helps companies keep lost sales to a minimum by having enough stock on hand to meet demand.

Increased Efficiency

Inventory management software often allows for automation of many inventory-related tasks. For example, software can automatically collect data, conduct calculations, and create records. This not only results in time savings, cost savings, but also increases business efficiency.

Warehouse Organization

Inventory management software can help distributors, wholesalers, manufacturers and retailers optimize their warehouses. If certain products are often sold together or are more popular than others, those products can be grouped together or placed near the delivery area to speed up the process of picking. By 2018, 66% of warehouses "are poised to undergo a seismic shift, moving from still prevalent pen and paper processes to automated and mechanized inventory solutions. With these new automated processes, cycle counts will be performed more often and with less effort, increasing inventory visibility, and leading to more accurate fulfillment, fewer out of stock situations and fewer lost sales. More confidence in inventory accuracy will lead to a new focus on optimizing mix, expanding a selection and accelerating inventory turns."

Updated Data

Up-to-date, real-time data on inventory conditions and levels is another advantage inventory management software gives companies. Company executives can usually access the software through a mobile device, laptop or PC to check current inventory numbers. This automatic updating of inventory records allows businesses to make informed decisions.

Data Security

With the aid of restricted user rights, company managers can allow many employees to assist in inventory management. They can grant employees enough information access to receive products, make orders, transfer products and do other tasks without compromising company security. This can speed up the inventory management process and save managers' time.

Insight into Trends

Tracking where products are stocked, which suppliers they come from, and the length of time they are stored is made possible with inventory management software. By analysing such data, companies can control inventory levels and maximize the use of warehouse space. Furthermore, firms are more prepared for the demands and supplies of the market, especially during special circumstances such as a peak season on a particular month. Through the reports generated by the inventory management software, firms are also able to gather important data that may be put in a model for it to be analyzed.

Disadvantages of ERP Inventory Management Software

The main disadvantages of inventory management software are its cost and complexity.

Expense

Cost can be a major disadvantage of inventory management software. Many large companies use inventory management software, but small businesses can find it difficult to afford it. Barcode readers and other hardware can compound this problem by adding even more cost to companies. The advantage of allowing multiple employees to perform inventory management tasks is tempered by the cost of additional barcode readers. Use of smartphones as QR code readers has been a way that smaller companies avoid the high expense of custom hardware for inventory management.

Complexity

Inventory management software is not necessarily simple or easy to learn. A company's management team must dedicate a certain amount of time to learning a new system, including both software and hardware, in order to put it to use. Most inventory management software includes training manuals and other information available to users. Despite its apparent complexity, inventory management software offers a degree of stability to companies. For example, if an IT employee in charge of the system leaves the company, a replacement can be comparatively inexpensive to train compared to if the company used multiple programs to store inventory data.

Benefits of Cloud Inventory Management Software

The main benefits of a cloud inventory management software include:

Real Time Tracking of Inventory

For startups and SMBs, tracking inventory in real time is very important. Not only can business owners track and collect data but also generate reports. At the same time, entrepreneurs can access cloud-based inventory data from a wide range of internet enabled devices, including: smartphones, tablets, laptops, as well as traditional desktop PCs. In addition, users do not have to be inside business premises to use web based inventory program and can access the inventory software while on the road.

Cut Down Hardware Expenses

Because the software resides in the cloud, business owners do not have to purchase and maintain expensive hardware. Instead, SMBs and startups can direct capital and profits towards expanding the business to reach a wider audience. Cloud-based solutions also eliminate the need to hire a large IT workforce. The service provider will take care of maintaining the inventory software.

Fast Deployment

Deploying web based inventory software is quite easy. All business owners have to do is sign up for a monthly or yearly subscription and start using the inventory management software via the internet. Such flexibility allows businesses to scale up relatively quickly without spending a large amount of money.

Easy Integration

Cloud inventory management software allows business owners to integrate with their existing systems with ease. For example, business owners can integrate the inventory software with their eCommerce store or cloud-based accounting software. The rise in popularity of 3rd party marketplaces, such as Amazon, eBay and Shopify, prompted cloud-based inventory management companies to include the integration of such sites with the rest of a business owner's retail business, allowing one to view and control stock across all channels.

Enhanced Efficiency

Cloud inventory systems increase efficiency in a number of ways. One is real-time inventory monitoring. A single change can replicate itself company-wide instantaneously. As a result, businesses can have greater confidence in the accuracy of the information in the system, and management can more easily track the flow of supplies and products – and generate reports. In addition, cloud-based solutions offer greater accessibility.

Improved Coordination

Cloud inventory programs also allow departments within a company to work together more efficiently. Department A can pull information about Department B's inventory directly from the software without needing to contact Department B's staff for the information. This inter-departmental communication also makes it easier to know when to restock and which customer orders have been shipped, etc. Operations can run more smoothly and efficiently, enhancing your customer's experience. Accurate inventory information can also have a huge impact on your company's bottom line. It allows you to see where the bottlenecks and workflow issues are – and to calculate break-even points as well as profit margins.

Disadvantages of Cloud Inventory Management Software

Security & Privacy

Using the cloud means that your data is managed by a Third Party provider and there can be a risk of your data being accessed by unauthorized users.

Dependency

Since maintenance is managed by the vendor, you are essentially fully dependant on your provider. Before signing up for an account or purchasing the software, it is essential that you research on the best providers available in the market to ensure that the vendor is reliable and the software has all the features that meets your business needs.

Decreased Flexibility

Depending on which Cloud Service Provider you decide to work with, system and software upgrades will be performed based on their schedule, hence businesses may experience some limitations in flexibility in the process.

Integration

Not all on-premises systems or service providers can be synced with the cloud software used.

Track and Trace

In distribution and logistics of many types of products, track and trace or tracking and tracing, concerns a process of determining the current and past locations (and other information) of a unique item or property.

This concept can be supported by means of reckoning and reporting of the position of vehicles and containers with the property of concern, stored, for example, in a real-time database. This approach leaves the task to compose a coherent depiction of the subsequent status reports.

Another approach is to report the arrival or departure of the object and recording the identification of the object, the location where observed, the time, and the status. This approach leaves the task to verify the reports regarding consistency and completeness. An example of this method might be the package tracking provided by shippers, such as Deutsche Post, United Parcel Service, AirRoad, or FedEx.

Technology

An example of a generic RFID chip.

Some produce traceability makers use matrix barcodes to record data on specific produce.

The international standards organization EPCglobal under GS1 has ratified the EPC network standards (esp. the EPC information services EPCIS standard) which codify the syntax and semantics for supply chain events and the secure method for selectively sharing supply chain events with trading partners. These standards for Tracking and Tracing have been used in successful deployments in many industries and there are now a wide range of products that are certified as being compatible with these standards.

In response to a growing number of recall incidents (food, pharmaceutical, toys, etc.), a wave of software, hardware, consulting and systems vendors have emerged over the last few years to offer a range of traceability solutions and tools for industry. Radio-frequency identification and barcodes are two common technology methods used to deliver traceability.

RFID is synonymous with track-and-trace solutions, and has a critical role to play in supply chains. RFID is a code-carrying technology, and can be used in place of a barcode to enable non-line of sight-reading. Deployment of RFID was earlier inhibited by cost limitations but the usage is now increasing.

Barcoding is a common and cost-effective method used to implement traceability at both the item and case-level. Variable data in a barcode or a numeric or alphanumeric code format can be applied to the packaging or label. The secure data can be used as a pointer to traceability information and can also correlate with production data such as time to market and product quality.

Packaging converters have a choice of three different classes of technology to print barcodes:

- Inkjet (dot on demand or continuous) systems are capable of printing high resolution (300 dpi or higher for dot on demand) images at press speed (up to 1000fpm). These solutions can be deployed either on-press or off-line.

- Laser marking can be employed to ablate a coating or to cause a color change in certain materials. The advantage of laser is fine detail and high speed for character printing, and no consumables. Not all substrates accept a laser mark, and certain colors (e.g. red) are not suitable for barcode reading.

- Thermal transfer and direct thermal. For lower speed off-press applications, thermal transfer and direct thermal printers are ideal for printing variable data on labels.

Consumers can access web sites to trace the origins of their purchased products or to find the status of shipments. Consumers can type a code found on an item into a search box at the tracing website and view information. This can also be done via a smartphone taking a picture of a 2D barcode and thereby opening up a website that verifies the product (i.e. product authentication).

References

- "Integrations and Apps for Online Inventory Management Software | TradeGecko". www.tradegecko.com. Retrieved 2015- 11-24.

- Lu, Clara (March 27, 2014). "Recent Study Shows that 66% of Warehouses Plan to Expand Technology Investments by 2018". TradeGecko Blog.

- Lockard, Robert (29 November 2010). "3 Advantages of Using Inventory Management Software". Inventory System Software Blog. Retrieved 23 November 2012.

- MF Treutner, H Ostermann. Evolution of Standard Web Shop Software Systems: A Review and Analysis of Literature and Market Surveys. Retrieved 25 October 2011.

- Polsson, Ken. "Chronology of Personal Computers – 1981". Polsson's WebWorld. Retrieved August 17, 2010.

- Piasecki, Dave. "Optimizing Economic Order Quantity – Carrying Costs". Inventoryops.com. Retrieved August 17, 2010.

Mobile Commerce: A Comprehensive Study

Mobile commerce is an emerging field of study. Mobile commerce is worth billions, with Asia representing almost half of the market. Some of the services of mobile commerce discussed in this chapter are mobile ticketing, mobile banking, mobile payment and mobile marketing. The topics discussed in the chapter are of great importance to broaden the existing knowledge on mobile commerce.

Mobile Commerce

The phrase mobile commerce was originally coined in 1997 by Kevin Duffey at the launch of the Global Mobile Commerce Forum, to mean "the delivery of electronic commerce capabilities directly into the consumer's hand, anywhere, via wireless technology." Many choose to think of Mobile Commerce as meaning "a retail outlet in your customer's pocket."

Mobile commerce is worth US$230 billion, with Asia representing almost half of the market, and has been forecast to reach US$700 billion in 2017. According to BI Intelligence in January 2013, 29% of mobile users have now made a purchase with their phones. Walmart estimated that 40% of all visits to their internet shopping site in December 2012 was from a mobile device. Bank of America predicts $67.1 billion in purchases will be made from mobile devices by European and U.S. shoppers in 2015. Mobile retailers in UK alone are expected to increase revenues up to 31% in FY 2013–14.

History

The Global Mobile Commerce Forum, which came to include over 100 organisations, had its fully minuted launch in London on 10 November 1997. Kevin Duffey was elected as the Executive Chairman at the first meeting in November 1997. The meeting was opened by Dr Mike Short, former chairman of the GSM Association, with the very first forecasts for mobile commerce from Kevin Duffey (Group Telecoms Director of Logica) and Tom Alexander (later CEO of Virgin Mobile and then of Orange). Over 100 companies joined the Forum within a year, many forming mobile commerce teams of their own, e.g. MasterCard and Motorola. Of these one hundred companies, the first two were Logica and Cellnet (which later became O2). Member organisations such as Nokia, Apple, Alcatel, and Vodafone began a series of trials and collaborations.

Mobile commerce services were first delivered in 1997, when the first two mobile-phone enabled Coca Cola vending machines were installed in the Helsinki area in Finland. The machines accepted payment via SMS text messages. This work evolved to several new mobile applications such as the first mobile phone-based banking service was launched in 1997 by Merita Bank of Finland, also using SMS. Finnair mobile check-in was also a major milestone, first introduced in 2001.

The m-Commerce(tm) server developed in late 1997 by Kevin Duffey and Andrew Tobin at Logica won the 1998 Financial Times award for "most innovative mobile product," in a solution implemented with De La Rue, Motorola and Logica. The Financial Times commended the solution for "turning mobile commerce into a reality." The trademark for m-Commerce was filed on 7 April 2008.

In 1998, the first sales of digital content as downloads to mobile phones were made possible when the first commercial downloadable ringtones were launched in Finland by Radiolinja (now part of Elisa Oyj).

Two major national commercial platforms for mobile commerce were launched in 1999: Smart Money in the Philippines, and NTT DoCoMo's i-Mode Internet service in Japan. i-Mode offered a revenue-sharing plan where NTT DoCoMo kept 9 percent of the fee users paid for content, and returned 91 percent to the content owner.

Mobile-commerce-related services spread rapidly in early 2000. Norway launched mobile parking payments. Austria offered train ticketing via mobile device. Japan offered mobile purchases of airline tickets.

In April 2002, building on the work of the Global Mobile Commerce Forum (GMCF), the European Telecommunications Standards Institute (ETSI) appointed Joachim Hoffmann of Motorola to develop official standards for mobile commerce. In appointing Mr Hoffman, ETSI quoted industry analysts as predicting "that m-commerce is poised for such an exponential growth over the next few years that could reach US$200 billion by 2004".

As of 2008, UCL Computer Science and Peter J. Bentley demonstrated the potential for medical applications on mobile devices.

PDAs and cellular phones have become so popular that many businesses are beginning to use mobile commerce as a more efficient way to communicate with their customers.

In order to exploit the potential mobile commerce market, mobile phone manufacturers such as Nokia, Ericsson, Motorola, and Qualcomm are working with carriers such as AT&T Wireless and Sprint to develop WAP-enabled smartphones. Smartphones offer fax, e-mail, and phone capabilities.

"Profitability for device vendors and carriers hinges on high-end mobile devices and the accompanying killer applications," said Burchett. Perennial early adopters, such as the youth market, which are the least price sensitive, as well as more open to premium mobile content and applications, must also be a key target for device vendors.

Since the launch of the iPhone, mobile commerce has moved away from SMS systems and into actual applications. SMS has significant security vulnerabilities and congestion problems, even though it is widely available and accessible. In addition, improvements in the capabilities of modern mobile devices make it prudent to place more of the resource burden on the mobile device.

More recently, brick and mortar business owners, and big-box retailers in particular, have made an effort to take advantage of mobile commerce by utilizing a number of mobile capabilities such as location-based services, barcode scanning, and push notifications to improve the customer experience of shopping in physical stores. By creating what is referred to as a 'bricks & clicks' environment, physical retailers can allow customers to access the common benefits of shopping online (such as product reviews, information, and coupons) while still shopping in the physical store. This is seen as a bridge between the gap created by e-commerce and in-store shopping, and is being utilized by physical retailers as a way to compete with the lower prices typically seen through online retailers. By mid summer 2013, "omnichannel" retailers (those with significant e-commerce and in-store sales) were seeing between 25% and 30% of traffic to their online properties originating from mobile devices. Some other pure play/online-only retail sites (especially those in the travel category) as well as flash sales sites and deal sites were seeing between 40% and 50% of traffic (and sometimes significantly more) originate from mobile devices.

The Google Wallet Mobile App launched in September 2011 and the m-Commerce joint venture formed in June 2011 between Vodafone, O2, Orange and T-Mobile are recent developments of note. Reflecting the importance of m-Commerce, in April 2012 the Competition Commissioner of the European Commission ordered an in-depth investigation of the m-Commerce joint venture between Vodafone, O2, Orange and T-Mobile. A recent survey states that 2012, 41% of smartphone customers have purchased retail products with their mobile devices.

Products and Services Available

Mobile Money Transfer

In Kenya money transfer is mainly done through the use of mobile phones. This was an initiative of a multimillion shillings company in Kenya named Safaricom. Currently, the companies involved are Safaricom and Airtel. Mobile money transfer services in Kenya are now provided by the two companies under the names M-PESA and Airtel Money respectively.

A similar system called MobilePay has been operated by Danske Bank in Denmark since 2013. It has gained considerable popularity with about 1.6 million users by mid-2015. Another similar system called Vipps was introduced in Norway in 2015.

mobile automated teller machine (ATM) is a special type of ATM. Most ATMs are meant to be stationary, and they're often found attached to the side of financial institutions, in stores, and in malls. A mobile ATM machine, on the other hand, is meant to be moved from location to location. This type of ATM is often found at special events for which ATM service is only needed temporarily. For example, they may be found at carnivals, fairs, and parades. They may also be used at seminars and workshops when there is no regular ATM nearby.

Mobile ATMs are usually self-contained units that don't need a building or en-closure. Usually, a mobile ATM can be placed in just about any location and can transmit transaction information wirelessly, so there's no need to have a phone line handy. Mobile ATMs may, however, require access to an electrical source, though there are some capable of running on alternative sources of power. Often, these units are constructed of weather-resistant materials, so they can be used in practi-cally any type of weather conditions. Additionally, these machines typically have in-ternal heating and air conditioning units that help keep them functional despite the temperature of the environment.ion of mobile money services for the unbanked, operators are now looking for efficient ways to roll out and manage distribution networks that can support cash-in and cash-out. Unlike traditional ATM, sicap Mo-bile ATM have been specially engineered to connect to mobile money platforms and provide bank grade ATM quality. In Hungary, Vodafone allows cash or bank card payments of monthly phone bills. The Hungarian market is one where direct debits are not standard practice, so the facility eases the burden of queuing for the post-paid half of Vodafone's subscriber base in Hungary.

Mobile Ticketing

Tickets can be sent to mobile phones using a variety of technologies. Users are then able to use their tickets immediately, by presenting their mobile phone at the ticket check as a digital boarding pass. Most number of users are now moving towards this technology. Best example would be IRCTC where ticket comes as SMS to users.

Mobile Vouchers, Coupons and Loyalty Cards

Mobile ticketing technology can also be used for the distribution of vouchers, coupons, and loyalty cards. These items are represented by a virtual token that is sent to the mobile phone. A customer presenting a mobile phone with one of these tokens at the point of sale receives the same benefits as if they had the traditional token. Stores may send coupons to customers using location-based services to determine when the customer is nearby.

Content Purchase and Delivery

Currently, mobile content purchase and delivery mainly consists of the sale of ring-tones, wallpapers, and games for mobile phones. The convergence of mobile phones, portable audio players, and video players into a single device is increasing the purchase and delivery of full-length music tracks and video. The download speeds available with 4G networks make it possible to buy a movie on a mobile device in a couple of seconds.

Location-based Services

The location of the mobile phone user is an important piece of information used during mobile commerce or m-commerce transactions. Knowing the location of the user allows for location-based services such as:

- Local discount offers

- Local weather

- Tracking and monitoring of people

Information Services

A wide variety of information services can be delivered to mobile phone users in much the same way as it is delivered to PCs. These services include:

- News

- Stock quotes

- Sports scores

- Financial records

- Traffic reporting

- Emergency Alerts

Customized traffic information, based on a user's actual travel patterns, can be sent to a mobile device. This customized data is more useful than a generic traffic-report broadcast, but was impractical before the invention of modern mobile devices due to the bandwidth requirements.

Mobile Banking

Banks and other financial institutions use mobile commerce to allow their customers to access account information and make transactions, such as purchasing stocks, remitting money. This service is often referred to as *mobile banking*, or m-banking.

Mobile Brokerage

Stock market services offered via mobile devices have also become more popular and are known as Mobile Brokerage. They allow the subscriber to react to market developments in a timely fashion and irrespective of their physical location.

Auctions

Over the past three years mobile reverse auction solutions have grown in popularity. Unlike traditional auctions, the reverse auction (or low-bid auction) bills the consumer's phone each time they place a bid. Many mobile SMS commerce solutions rely on a one-time purchase or one-time subscription; however, reverse auctions offer a high return for the mobile vendor as they require the consumer to make multiple transactions over a long period of time.

Mobile Browsing

Using a mobile browser—a World Wide Web browser on a mobile device—customers can shop online without having to be at their personal computer. Many mobile marketing apps with geo-location capability are now delivering user-specific marketing messages to the right person at the right time.

Mobile Purchase

Catalog merchants can accept orders from customers electronically, via the customer's mobile device. In some cases, the merchant may even deliver the catalog electronically, rather than mailing a paper catalog to the customer. Consumers making mobile purchases can also receive value-add upselling services and offers. Some merchants provide mobile web sites that are customized for the smaller screen and limited user interface of a mobile device.

In-application Mobile Phone Payments

Payments can be made directly inside of an application running on a popular smartphone operating system, such as Google Android. Analyst firm Gartner expects in-application purchases to drive 41 percent of app store (also referred to as mobile software distribution platforms) revenue in 2016. In-app purchases can be used to buy virtual goods, new and other mobile content and is ultimately billed by mobile carriers rather than the app stores themselves. Ericsson's IPX mobile commerce system is used by 120 mobile carriers to offer payment options such as try-before-you-buy, rentals and subscriptions.

Mobile Marketing and Advertising

In the context of mobile commerce, mobile marketing refers to marketing sent to mobile devices. Companies have reported that they see better response from mobile marketing campaigns than from traditional campaigns. The primary reason for this is the instant nature of customer decision-making that mobile apps and websites enable. The consumer can receive a marketing message or discount coupon and, within a few seconds, make a decision to buy and go on to complete the sale - without disrupting their current real-world activity.

For example, a busy mom tending to her household chores with a baby in her arm could receive a marketing message on her mobile about baby products from a local store. She can and within a few clicks, place an order for her supplies without having to plan ahead for it. No more need to reach for her purse and hunt for credit cards, no need to log in to her laptop and try to recall the web address of the store she visited last week, and surely no need to find a babysitter to cover for her while she runs to the local store.

Research demonstrates that consumers of mobile and wireline markets represent two distinct groups who are driven by different values and behaviors, and who exhibit dissimilar psychographic and demographic profiles. What aspects truly distinguish between a traditional online shopper from home and a mobile on-the-go shopper? Research shows that how individuals relate to four situational dimensions- place, time, social context and control determine to what extent they are ubiquitous or situated as consumers. These factors are important in triggering m-commerce from e-commerce. As a result, successful mobile commerce requires the development of marketing campaigns targeted to these particular dimensions and according user segments.

Influence on Youth Markets

Mobile media is a rapidly changing field. New technologies, such as WiMax, act to accelerate innovation in mobile commerce. Early pioneers in mobile advertising include Vodafone, Orange, and SK Telecom.

Mobile devices are heavily used in South Korea to conduct mobile commerce. Mobile companies in South Korea believed that mobile technology would become synonymous with youth life style, based on their experience with previous generations of South Koreans. "Profitability for device vendors and carriers hinges on high-end mobile devices and the accompanying killer applications," said Gibran Burchett.

Payment Methods

Consumers can use many forms of payment in mobile commerce, including:

- Contactless payment for in-person transactions through a mobile phone (such as Apple Pay or Android Pay). In a system like EMV, these are interoperable with contactless credit and debit cards.

- Premium-rate telephone numbers, which apply charges to the consumer's long-distance bill

- Mobile-Operator Billing allows charges to be added to the consumer's mobile telephone bill, including deductions to pre-paid calling plans

- Credit cards and debit cards

  o Some providers allow credit cards to be stored in a phone's SIM card or secure element

  o Some providers are starting to use host card emulation, or HCE (e.g. Google Wallet and Softcard)

  o Some providers store credit card or debit card information in the cloud; usually in tokenized. With tokenization, payment verification, authentication, and authorization are still required, but payment card numbers don't need to be stored, entered, or transmitted from the mobile device

- Micropayment services

- Stored-value cards, often used with mobile-device application stores or music stores (e.g. iTunes)

App Design for M-commerce

Interaction Design and UX design has been at the core of the m-commerce experience from its conception, producing apps and mobile web pages that create highly usable interactions for users. However, much debate has occurred as to the focus that should be given to the apps. In recent research, Parker and Wang demonstrated that within Fashion M-Commerce apps the degree that the app helps the user shop (increasing convenience) were the most prominent functions. They also showed that shopping for others was a motivator for engaging in M-Commerce apps with great preference for close integration with social media.

Services of Mobile Commerce

Mobile Ticketing

Mobile ticketing is the process whereby customers can order, pay for, obtain and/or validate tickets using mobile phones or other mobile handsets. Mobile tickets reduce the production and distribution costs connected with traditional paper-based ticketing channels and increase customer convenience by providing new and simple ways to purchase tickets.

The term can also refer to a method by which law enforcement agencies use in-car computers to create traffic citations in the field, then print a hard copy for the offender. The advantages of mobile ticketing include reduced paperwork time, reduced chance of tickets being made void by human error and immediate accessibility of citation information by other departments.

Applications

- Airline check-in
- Airline ticketing
- Tourist Attraction Ticketing
- Zoo Ticketing
- Museum Ticketing
- Cinema ticketing
- Railway & Bus ticketing
- Concert/Event ticketing
- Consumer voucher distribution
- Mass transit
- Trade shows
- Bus ticket

Advantage of Mobile Ticketing

- Improved consumer convenience
- Increased revenue by increasing accessibility of tickets
- Reduced infrastructure costs (scanners retail at 30 times the cost of 1d scanners)
- Reduced ticket printing/mailing cost
- Ability to enforce no resale conditions and engage in price discrimination

Disadvantages

- Many company phones block premium SMS messages (not an issue where payment is linked to a credit card)
- Foreign subscription phones do not work in connection with premium SMS messages
- Some people do not own a mobile phone, so for this and the above reasons, other payment methods must be available

- If the phone battery runs out, the mobile ticket is made unusable

- Forgery (risk varies by mobile solution provider)

Usage

Mobile Purchase

The International Air Transport Association (IATA) 2007 announced a global standard that paves the way for global mobile phone check-in using two-dimensional (2D) bar codes. The industry has set a deadline of the end of 2010 to implement 100% bar coded boarding passes (BCBP). Upon full implementation, BCBP is said to be able to save the industry over US $500 million annually.

Mobile tickets can be purchased in a variety of ways including online, via text messaging or over the phone from a voice call, WAP page, or a secure mobile application. For repeated purchases such as daily train tickets, mobile applications or text messaging can be used. The drawbacks to text message purchasing is that either the vendor loses 40% of their revenue to the mobile operator, or any credit card purchase has to be achieved through a web page as the SMS has no security suitable for credit card entry, and very few ticket choices can be easily remembered and entered by SMS.

SMS Purchase

There are two distinct forms of SMS purchases: so-called 'premium SMS' purchases charged to the mobile operator bill; and SMS purchases charged to a payment card. Mobile ticket purchases are primarily user-initiated messages whereby a keyword is sent to a short code service number (e.g. GV for a single adult ticket in Gothenburg, Sweden or GN as a night-tariff ticket). A return message is sent containing the mobile ticket as either an MMS message, a URL leading to a 2D barcode, or as plain text with the ticket information.

With premium SMS the price of the ticket can be added to the users mobile phone bill or debited from their pre-paid service using SMS billing. The main business limitation is that when premium SMS is used for billing, by default around 20-40% of the transaction value is retained by the mobile operator and sms aggregator. Normally, this would not be viable for low margin tickets, however, in many cases much more favourable commercial terms have been negotiated e.g. between the public transport organisations and mobile operators. Payments charged to payment cards require an initial registration to associate the user's mobile phone number to their credit card, but have a far more favorable fee structure for service providers.

Online Purchase

Online purchase is still an option for mobile tickets, allowing the user to set up an account and choosing payment options etc.

Delivery

Delivery of tickets to mobile phones can be done in a variety of ways:

- Text messaging (SMS) - visual inspection or OCR

- Text messaging with WAP Push - visual inspection or OCR

- Picture messaging (SMS, EMS, WAP Push and MMS) - usually uses a barcode

- Dedicated Mobile application - which can store and render barcodes delivered via SMS, GPRS, Bluetooth, IRDA or RFID. Barcodes rendered on the device by a dedicated application have the advantage of being full screen without clutter, meaning faster and more successful scanning. A dedicated mobile application can also help the user to organise and sort their tickets better than when an SMS or MMS inbox is full of similar tickets, which is especially useful for transport tickets.

- Device RFID - This is the method proposed under the Near Field Communication (NFC) specification but not yet in general use, except of Japanese Osaifu-Keitai.

Southend United Football Club is currently the only team in the UK to have a mobile ticketing facility offered to fans.

Very few phones outside Japan have RFID/NFC tags and so this method of delivery is largely unsupported. Picture messaging is supported by almost all phones and is generally the delivery method of choice. It usually requires the sender to know the phone model in advance so that the picture is rendered at the correct resolution. Text-only messaging is supported by all mobile phones and is the simplest method of delivery.

Scanning

Visually validated mobile tickets do not require a scan device. Most forms of mobile tickets require some form of device to read the ticket from the user's device. Picture-based messages require a laser scanner (for 1-dimensional/linear barcodes) or camera based imager (for 2-dimensional barcodes) to photograph the message and decode it into a ticket ID. Text-based codes use OCR software for mTicket. Near Field Communication devices scan using an RFID reader.

Each of the above methods has its specific benefits and drawbacks. Optically reading the display of a cell phone is heavily influenced by the quality of the display (resolution, size of pixels, reflections). RFID is only supported by a very few phones yet.

Redemption

Visually validated mobile tickets are validated without connection to a back office system. Other forms of mobile ticket systems contact a server that is able to verify the ticket and record that it has been used.

New systems that make use of encryption of the data inside the barcode enable off-line scanning and validation, which is especially important if users are purchasing tickets immediately prior to use, and the portable venue or on-vehicle scanning devices cannot always have a connection to the live ticket database. (Many transport ticketing systems, such as the London Oyster card travel system and the M-PhaTic system of the Swedish state railways SJ are designed so that scanners can operate as disconnected islands when connectivity to central systems is lost.)

Mobile Banking

Mobile banking is a service provided by a bank or other financial institution that allows its customers to conduct a range of financial transactions remotely using a mobile device such as a mobile phone or tablet, and using software, usually called an app, provided by the financial institution for the purpose. Mobile banking is usually available on a 24-hour basis. Some financial institutions have restrictions on which accounts may be accessed through mobile banking, as well as a limit on the amount that can be transacted.

The types of financial transactions which a customer may transact through mobile banking include obtaining account balances and list of latest transactions, electronic bill payments, and funds transfers between a customer's or another's accounts. Some also enable copies of statements to be downloaded and sometimes printed at the customer's premises; and some banks charge a fee for mailing hardcopies of bank statements.

From the bank's point of view, mobile banking reduces the cost of handling transactions by reducing the need for customers to visit a bank branch for non-cash withdrawal and deposit transactions. Transactions involving cash aren't handled using mobile banking, and a customer needs to visit an ATM or bank branch for cash withdrawals or deposits. Many apps now have a mobile cheque deposit option; using the device's camera to digitally transmit cheques to their financial institution.

Mobile banking differs from mobile payments, which involves the use of a mobile device to pay for goods or services either at the point of sale or remotely, analogously to the use of a debit or credit card to effect an EFTPOS payment.

History

The earliest mobile banking services used SMS, a service known as SMS banking. With the introduction of smart phones with WAP support enabling the use of the mobile web in 1999, the first European banks started to offer mobile banking on this platform to their customers.

Mobile banking before 2010 was most often performed via SMS or the mobile web. Apple's initial success with iPhone and the rapid growth of phones based on Google's

Android (operating system) have led to increasing use of special mobile apps, downloaded to the mobile device. With that said, advancements in web technologies such as HTML5, CSS3 and JavaScript have seen more banks launching mobile web based services to complement native applications. A recent study (May 2012) by Mapa Research suggests that over a third of banks have mobile device detection upon visiting the banks' main website. A number of things can happen on mobile detection such as redirecting to an app store, redirection to a mobile banking specific website or providing a menu of mobile banking options for the user to choose from.

A Mobile Banking Conceptual

In one academic model, mobile banking is defined as:

Mobile Banking refers to provision and availment of banking- and financial services with the help of mobile telecommunication devices.The scope of offered services may include facilities to conduct bank and stock market transactions, to administer accounts and to access customised information."

According to this model mobile banking can be said to consist of three inter-related concepts:

- Mobile accounting
- Mobile brokerage
- Mobile financial information services

Most services in the categories designated *accounting* and *brokerage* are transaction-based. The non-transaction-based services of an informational nature are however essential for conducting transactions - for instance, balance inquiries might be needed before committing a money remittance. The accounting and brokerage services are therefore offered invariably in combination with information services. Information services, on the other hand, may be offered as an independent module.

Mobile banking may also be used to help in business situations as well as financial

Mobile Banking Services

Typical mobile banking services may include:

Account Information

1. Mini-statements and checking of account history
2. Alerts on account activity or passing of set thresholds
3. Monitoring of term deposits

4. Access to loan statements

5. Access to card statements

6. Mutual funds / equity statements

7. Insurance policy management

Transaction

1. Funds transfers between the customer's linked accounts

2. Paying third parties, including bill payments and third party fund transfers.

3. Check Remote Deposit

Investments

1. Portfolio management services

2. Real-time stock quotes

3. Personalized alerts and notifications on security prices

Support

1. Status of requests for credit, including mortgage approval, and insurance coverage

2. Check (cheque) book and card requests

3. Exchange of data messages and email, including complaint submission and tracking

4. ATM Location

Content Services

1. General information such as weather updates, news

2. Loyalty-related offers

3. Location-based services

A report by the US Federal Reserve (March 2012) found that 21 percent of mobile phone owners had used mobile banking in the past 12 months. Based on a survey conducted by Forrester, mobile banking will be attractive mainly to the younger, more "tech-savvy" customer segment. A third of mobile phone users say that they may consider performing some kind of financial transaction through their mobile phone. But most of the users are interested in performing basic transactions such as querying for account balance and making bill payment.

Future Functionalities in Mobile Banking

Based on the 'International Review of Business Research Papers' from World business Institute, Australia, following are the key functional trends possible in world of Mobile Banking.

With the advent of technology and increasing use of smartphone and tablet based devices, the use of Mobile Banking functionality would enable customer connect across entire customer life cycle much comprehensively than before. With this scenario, current mobile banking objectives of say building relationships, reducing cost, achieving new revenue stream will transform to enable new objectives targeting higher level goals such as building brand of the banking organization. Emerging technology and functionalities would enable to create new ways of lead generation, prospecting as well as developing deep customer relationship and mobile banking world would achieve superior customer experience with bi-directional communications. Among digital channels, mobile banking is a clear IT investment priority in 2013 as retail banks attempt to capitalise on the features unique to mobile, such as location-based services.

Illustration of objective based functionality enrichment In Mobile Banking

- Communication enrichment: - Video Interaction with agents, advisors.

- Pervasive Transactions capabilities: - Comprehensive "Mobile wallet"

- Customer Education: - "Test drive" for demos of banking services

- Connect with new customer segment: - Connect with Gen Y – Gen Z using games and social network ambushed to surrogate bank's offerings

- Content monetization: - Micro level revenue themes such as music, e-book download

- Vertical positioning: - Positioning offerings over mobile banking specific industries

- Horizontal positioning: - Positioning offerings over mobile banking across all the industries

- Personalization of corporate banking services: - Personalization experience for multiple roles and hierarchies in corporate banking as against the vanilla based segment based enhancements in the current context.

- Build Brand: - Built the bank's brand while enhancing the "Mobile real estate".

Challenges for a Mobile Banking Solution

Key challenges in developing a sophisticated mobile banking application are :

Handset Accessability

There are a large number of different mobile phone devices and it is a big challenge for banks to offer a mobile banking solution on any type of device. Some of these devices support Java ME and others support SIM Application Toolkit, a WAP browser, or only SMS.

Initial interoperability issues however have been localized, with countries like India using portals like "R-World" to enable the limitations of low end java based phones, while focus on areas such as South Africa have defaulted to the USSD as a basis of communication achievable with any phone.

The desire for interoperability is largely dependent on the banks themselves, where installed applications(Java based or native) provide better security, are easier to use and allow development of more complex capabilities similar to those of internet banking while SMS can provide the basics but becomes difficult to operate with more complex transactions.

There is a myth that there is a challenge of interoperability between mobile banking applications due to perceived lack of common technology standards for mobile banking. In practice it is too early in the service lifecycle for interoperability to be addressed within an individual country, as very few countries have more than one mobile banking service provider. In practice, banking interfaces are well defined and money movements between banks follow the ISo-8583 standard. As mobile banking matures, money movements between service providers will naturally adopt the same standards as in the banking world.

On January 2009, Mobile Marketing Association (MMA) Banking Sub-Committee, chaired by CellTrust and VeriSign Inc., published the Mobile Banking Overview for financial institutions in which it discussed the advantages and disadvantages of Mobile Channel Platforms such as Short Message Services (SMS), Mobile Web, Mobile Client Applications, SMS with Mobile Web and Secure SMS.

Security

As with most internet-connected devices, as well as mobile-telephony devices, cybercrime rates are escalating year-on-year. The types of cybercrimes which may affect mobile-banking might range from unauthorized use while the owner is using the toilet, to remote-hacking, or even jamming or interference via the internet or telephone network datastreams. In the banking world, currency rates may change by the millisecond.

Security of financial transactions, being executed from some remote location and transmission of financial information over the air, are the most complicated challenges that need to be addressed jointly by mobile application developers, wireless network service providers and the banks' IT departments.

The following aspects need to be addressed to offer a secure infrastructure for financial transaction over wireless network :

1. Physical part of the hand-held device. If the bank is offering smart-card based security, the physical security of the device is more important.

2. Security of any thick-client application running on the device. In case the device is stolen, the hacker should require at least an ID/Password to access the application.

3. Authentication of the device with service provider before initiating a transaction. This would ensure that unauthorized devices are not connected to perform financial transactions.

4. User ID / Password authentication of bank's customer.

5. Encryption of the data being transmitted over the air.

6. Encryption of the data that will be stored in device for later / off-line analysis by the customer.

One-time password (OTPs) are the latest tool used by financial and banking service providers in the fight against cyber fraud. Instead of relying on traditional memorized passwords, OTPs are requested by consumers each time they want to perform transactions using the online or mobile banking interface. When the request is received the password is sent to the consumer's phone via SMS. The password is expired once it has been used or once its scheduled life-cycle has expired.

Because of the concerns made explicit above, it is extremely important that SMS gateway providers can provide a decent quality of service for banks and financial institutions in regards to SMS services. Therefore, the provision of service level agreements (SLAs) is a requirement for this industry; it is necessary to give the bank customer delivery guarantees of all messages, as well as measurements on the speed of delivery, throughput, etc. SLAs give the service parameters in which a messaging solution is guaranteed to perform.

Scalability and Reliability

Another challenge for the CIOs and CTOs of the banks is to scale-up the mobile banking infrastructure to handle exponential growth of the customer base. With mobile banking, the customer may be sitting in any part of the world (true anytime, anywhere banking) and hence banks need to ensure that the systems are up and running in a true

24 x 7 fashion. As customers will find mobile banking more and more useful, their expectations from the solution will increase. Banks unable to meet the performance and reliability expectations may lose customer confidence. There are systems such as Mobile Transaction Platform which allow quick and secure mobile enabling of various banking services. Recently in India there has been a phenomenal growth in the use of Mobile Banking applications, with leading banks adopting Mobile Transaction Platform and the Central Bank publishing guidelines for mobile banking operations.

Application Distribution

Due to the nature of the connectivity between bank and its customers, it would be impractical to expect customers to regularly visit banks or connect to a web site for regular upgrade of their mobile banking application. It will be expected that the mobile application itself check the upgrades and updates and download necessary patches (so called "Over The Air" updates). However, there could be many issues to implement this approach such as upgrade / synchronization of other dependent components.

User Adoption

It should be noted that studies have shown that a huge concerning factor of having mobil banking more widely used, is a banking customer's unwillingness to adapt. Many consumers, whether they are misinformed or not, do not want to begin using mobile banking for several reasons. These can include the learning curve associated with new technology, having fears about possible security compromises, just simply not wanting to start using technology, etc.

Personalization

It would be expected from the mobile application to support personalization such as :

1. Preferred Language

2. Date / Time format

3. Amount format

4. Default transactions

5. Standard Beneficiary list

6. Alerts

Mobile Banking in the World

This is a list of countries by mobile banking usage as measured by the percentage of people who had non-SMS mobile banking transactions in the previous three months.

The data is sourced from Bain, Research Now and Bain along with GMI NPS surveys in 2012.

Rank	Country/Territory	Usage in 2012
1	South Korea	47%
2	China	42%
3	Hong Kong	41%
4	Singapore	38%
5	India	37%
6	Spain	34%
7	United States	32%
8	Mexico	30%
9	Australia	27%
10	France	26%
11	United Kingdom	26%
12	Thailand	24%
13	Canada	22%
14	Germany	14%
15	Pakistan	9%

African nations such as Kenya would rank highly if SMS mobile banking were included in the above list. Kenya has 38% of the population as subscribers to M-Pesa as of 2011.

Mobile banking is used in many parts of the world with little or no infrastructure, especially remote and rural areas. This aspect of mobile commerce is also popular in countries where most of their population is unbanked. In most of these places, banks can only be found in big cities, and customers have to travel hundreds of miles to the nearest bank.

In Iran, banks such as Parsian, Tejarat, Pasargad Bank, Mellat, Saderat, Sepah, Edbi, and Bankmelli offer the service. Banco Industrial provides the service in Guatemala. Citizens of Mexico can access mobile banking with Omnilife, Bancomer and MPower Venture. Kenya's Safaricom (part of the Vodafone Group) has the M-Pesa Service, which is mainly used to transfer limited amounts of money, but increasingly used to pay utility bills as well. In 2009, Zain launched their own mobile money transfer business, known as ZAP, in Kenya and other African countries. Several other players in Kenya such as Tangerine, MobiKash and Funtrench Limited also have network-independent mobile money transfer. In Somalia, the many telecom companies provide mobile banking, the most prominent being Hormuud Telecom and its ZAAD service.

Telenor Pakistan has also launched a mobile banking solution, in coordination with Ta-ameer Bank, under the label Easy Paisa, which was begun in Q4 2009. Eko India Finan-cial Services, the business correspondent of State Bank of India (SBI) and ICICI Bank, provides bank accounts, deposit, withdrawal and remittance services, micro-insurance, and micro-finance facilities to its customers (nearly 80% of whom are migrants or the unbanked section of the population) through mobile banking.

In a year of 2010, mobile banking users soared over 100 percent in Kenya, China, Brazil and United States with 200 percent, 150 percent, 110 percent and 100 percent respec-tively.

Dutch Bangla Bank launched the very first mobile banking service in Bangladesh on 31 March 2011. This service is launched with 'Agent' and 'Network' support from mobile operators, Banglalink and Citycell. Sybase 365, a subsidiary of Sybase, Inc. has provided software solution with their local partner Neurosoft Technologies Ltd. There are around 160 million people in Bangladesh, of which, only 13 per cent have bank accounts. With this solution, Dutch-Bangla Bank can now reach out to the rural and unbanked population, of which, 45 per cent are mobile phone users. Un-der the service, any mobile handset with subscription to any of the six existing mo-bile operators of Bangladesh would be able to utilize the service. Under the mobile banking services, bank-nominated 'Agents' perform banking activities on behalf of the banks, like opening mobile banking account, providing cash services (receipts and payments) and dealing with small credits. Cash withdrawal from a mobile ac-count can also be done from an ATM validating each transaction by 'mobile phone & PIN' instead of 'card & PIN'. Other services that are being delivered through mobile banking system are person-to-person (e.g. fund transfer), person-to-busi-ness (e.g. merchant payment, utility bill payment), business-to-person (e.g. salary/ commission disbursement), government-to-person (disbursement of government allowance) transactions.

In May 2012, Laxmi Bank Limited launched the very first mobile banking in Nepal with its product Mobile Khata. Mobile Khata currently runs on a third-party platform called Hello Paisa that is interoperable with all the telecoms in Nepal viz. Nepal Telecom, NCell, Smart Tel and UTL, and is also interoperable with various banks in the country. The initial joining members to the platform after Laxmi Bank Limited were Siddartha Bank, Bank of Kathmandu, Commerz and Trust Bank Nepal and International Leasing and Finance Company.

Barclays offers a service called Barclays Pingit, and Hello Money offering services in Africa, allowing transfer of money from the United Kingdom to many parts of the world with a mobile phone. Pingit is owned by a consortium of banks. In April 2014, the UK Payments Council launched the Paym mobile payment system, allowing mobile pay-ments between customers of several banks and building societies using the recipient's mobile phone number.

Mobile Payment

Mobile payment (also referred to as mobile money, mobile money transfer, and mobile wallet) generally refer to payment services operated under financial regulation and performed from or via a mobile device. Instead of paying with cash, cheque, or credit cards, a consumer can use a mobile phone to pay for a wide range of services and digital or hard goods. Although the concept of using non-coin-based currency systems has a long history, it is only recently that the technology to support such systems has become widely available.

Mobile payment is being adopted all over the world in different ways. In 2008, the combined market for all types of mobile payments was projected to reach more than $600B globally by 2013, which would be double the figure as of February, 2011. The mobile payment market for goods and services, excluding contactless Near field communication or NFC transactions and money transfers, is expected to exceed $300B globally by 2013. Investment on mobile money services is expected to grow by 22.2% during the next two years across the globe. It will result in revenue share of mobile money reaching up to 9% by 2018. Asia and Africa will observe significant growth for mobile money with technological innovation and focus on interoperability emerging as prominent trends by 2018.

In developing countries mobile payment solutions have been deployed as a means of extending financial services to the community known as the "unbanked" or "underbanked," which is estimated to be as much as 50% of the world's adult population, according to Financial Access' 2009 Report "Half the World is Unbanked". These payment networks are often used for micropayments. The use of mobile payments in developing countries has attracted public and private funding by organizations such as the Bill & Melinda Gates Foundation, United States Agency for International Development and Mercy Corps.

Models

There are five primary models for mobile payments:

- Mobile wallets

- Card-based payments

- Carrier billing (Premium SMS or direct carrier billing)

- Contactless payments NFC (Near Field Communication)

- Direct transfers between payer and payee bank accounts in near real-time (bank-led model, intra/inter-bank transfers/payments that are both bank and mobile operator agnostic)

Additionally there is a new emerging model from Haiti: direct carrier/bank co-operation.

Financial institutions and credit card companies as well as Internet companies such as Google and a number of mobile communication companies, such as mobile network operators and major telecommunications infrastructure such as w-HA from Orange and handset multinationals such as Ericsson and BlackBerry have implemented mobile payment solutions.

Mobile Wallets

Online companies like PayPal, Amazon Payments, and Google Wallet also have mobile options.

Generally, this is the process:

First payment:

- User registers, inputs their phone number, and the provider sends them an SMS with a PIN

- User enters the received PIN, authenticating the number

- User inputs their credit card info or another payment method if necessary (not necessary if the account has already been added) and validates payment

Subsequent payments:

- The user re enters their PIN to authenticate and validates payment

Requesting a PIN is known to lower the success rate (conversion) for payments. These systems can be integrated with directly or can be combined with operator and credit card payments through a unified mobile web payment platform.

Credit Card

A simple mobile web payment system can also include a credit card payment flow allowing a consumer to enter their card details to make purchases. This process is familiar but any entry of details on a mobile phone is known to reduce the success rate (conversion) of payments.

In addition, if the payment vendor can automatically and securely identify customers then card details can be recalled for future purchases turning credit card payments into simple single click-to-buy giving higher conversion rates for additional purchases.

Carrier Billing

The consumer uses the mobile billing option during checkout at an e-commerce site—such as an online gaming site—to make a payment. After two-factor authentication involving a PIN and One-Time-Password (often abbreviated as *OTP*), the consumer's mobile account is charged for the purchase. It is a true alternative payment method that does not require the use of credit/debit cards or pre-registration at an online payment solution such as PayPal, thus bypassing banks and credit card companies altogether. This type of mobile payment method, which is extremely prevalent and popular in Asia, provides the following benefits:

1. *Security* - Two-factor authentication and a risk management engine prevents fraud.

2. *Convenience* - No pre-registration and no new mobile software is required.

3. *Easy* - It's just another option during the checkout process.

4. *Fast* - Most transactions are completed in less than 10 seconds.

5. *Proven* - 70% of all digital content purchased online in some parts of Asia uses the Direct Mobile Billing method

SMS/USSD-based Transactional Payments

Premium SMS / Premium MMS

In the predominant model for SMS payments, the consumer sends a payment request via an SMS text message or an USSD to a short code and a premium charge is applied to their phone bill or their online wallet. The merchant involved is informed of the payment success and can then release the paid for goods.

Since a trusted physical delivery address has typically not been given, these goods are most frequently digital with the merchant replying using a Multimedia Messaging Service to deliver the purchased music, ringtones, wallpapers etc.

A Multimedia Messaging Service can also deliver barcodes which can then be scanned for confirmation of payment by a merchant. This is used as an electronic ticket for access to cinemas and events or to collect hard goods.

Transactional payments by SMS have been popular in Asia and Europe and are now accompanied by other mobile payment methods, such as mobile web payments (WAP), mobile payment client (Java ME, Android...) and Direct Mobile Billing.

Inhibiting factors of Premium SMS include:

1. *Poor reliability* - transactional premium SMS payments can easily fail as messages get lost.

2. *Slow speed* - sending messages can be slow and it can take hours for a merchant to get receipt of payment. Consumers do not want to be kept waiting more than a few seconds.

3. *Security* - The SMS/USSD encryption ends in the radio interface, then the message is a plaintext.

4. *High cost* - There are many high costs associated with this method of payment. The cost of setting up short codes and paying for the delivery of media via a Multimedia Messaging Service and the resulting customer support costs to account for the number of messages that get lost or are delayed.

5. *Low payout rates* - operators also see high costs in running and supporting transactional payments which results in payout rates to the merchant being as low as 30%. Usually around 50%

6. *Low follow-on sales* - once the payment message has been sent and the goods received there is little else the consumer can do. It is difficult for them to remember where something was purchased or how to buy it again. This also makes it difficult to tell a friend.

Some mobile payment services accept "premium SMS payments." Here is the typical end user payment process:

1. User sends SMS with keyword and unique number to a premium short code.

2. User receives a PIN (User billed via the short code on receipt of the PIN)

3. User uses PIN to access content or services.

Remote Payment by SMS and Credit Card Tokenization

Even as the volume of Premium SMS transactions have flattened, many cloud-based payment systems continue to use SMS for presentment, authorization, and authentication, while the payment itself is processed through existing payment networks such as credit and debit card networks. These solutions combine the ubiquity of the SMS channel, with the security and reliability of existing payment infrastructure. Since SMS lacks end-to-end encryption, such solutions employ a higher-level security strategies known as 'tokenization' and 'target removal' whereby payment occurs without transmitting any sensitive account details, username, password, or PIN.

To date, point-of-sales mobile payment solutions have not relied on SMS-based authentication as a payment mechanism, but remote payments such as bill payments, seat upgrades on flights, and membership or subscription renewals are commonplace.

In comparison to premium short code programs which often exist in isolation, relationship marketing and payment systems are often integrated with CRM, ERP, marketing-automation platforms, and reservation systems. Many of the problems inherent with premium SMS have been addressed by solution providers. Remembering keywords is not required since sessions are initiated by the enterprise to establish a transaction specific context.

Reply messages are linked to the proper session and authenticated either synchronously through a very short expiry period (every reply is assumed to be to the last message sent) or by tracking session according to varying reply addresses and/or reply options.

Mobile Web Payments (WAP)

Mobile payment system in Norway.

The consumer uses web pages displayed or additional applications downloaded and installed on the mobile phone to make a payment. It uses WAP (Wireless Application Protocol) as underlying technology and thus inherits all the advantages and disadvantages of WAP. Benefits include:

1. *Follow-on sales* where the mobile web payment can lead back to a store or to other goods the consumer may like. These pages have a URL and can be bookmarked making it easy to re-visit or share.

2. *High customer satisfaction* from quick and predictable payments

3. *Ease of use* from a familiar set of online payment pages

However, unless the mobile account is directly charged through a mobile network operator, the use of a credit/debit card or pre-registration at online payment solution such as PayPal is still required just as in a desktop environment.

Mobile web payment methods are now being mandated by a number of mobile network operators.

Direct Operator Billing

Direct operator billing, also known as mobile content billing, WAP billing, and carrier billing, requires integration with the mobile network operator. It provides certain benefits:

1. Mobile network operators already have a billing relationship with consumers, the payment will be added to their bill.

2. Provides instantaneous payment

3. Protects payment details and consumer identity

4. Better conversion rates

5. Reduced customer support costs *for merchants*

6. Alternative monetization option in countries where credit card usage is low

One of the drawbacks is that the payout rate will often be much lower than with other mobile payments options. Examples from a popular provider:

- 92% with PayPal

- 85 to 86% with Credit Card

- 45 to 91.7% with operator billing in the US, UK and some smaller European countries, but usually around 60%

More recently, Direct operator billing is being deployed in an in-app environment, where mobile application developers are taking advantage of the one-click payment option that Direct operator billing provides for monetising mobile applications. This is a logical alternative to credit card and Premium SMS billing.

In 2012, Ericsson and Western Union partnered to expand the direct operator billing market, making it possible for mobile operators to include Western Union Mobile Money Transfers as part of their mobile financial service offerings. Given the international reach of both companies, the partnership is meant to accelerate the interconnection between the m-commerce market and the existing financial world.

Contactless Near Field Communication

Near Field Communication (NFC) is used mostly in paying for purchases made in physical stores or transportation services. A consumer using a special mobile phone equipped with a smartcard waves his/her phone near a reader module. Most transactions do not require authentication, but some require authentication using PIN, before transaction is completed. The payment could be deducted from a pre-paid account or charged to a mobile or bank account directly.

Mobile payment method via NFC faces significant challenges for wide and fast adoption, due to lack of supporting infrastructure, complex ecosystem of stakeholders, and standards. Some phone manufacturers and banks, however, are enthusiastic. Ericsson and Aconite are examples of businesses that make it possible for banks to create consumer mobile payment applications that take advantage of NFC technology.

NFC vendors in Japan are closely related to mass-transit networks, like the Mobile

Suica used on the JR East rail network. Osaifu-Keitai system, used for Mobile Suica and many others including Edy and nanaco, has become the *de facto* standard method for mobile payments in Japan. Its core technology, Mobile FeliCa IC, is partially owned by Sony, NTT DoCoMo and JR East. Mobile FeliCa utilize Sony's FeliCa technology, which itself is the de facto standard for contactless smart cards in the country.

Other NFC vendors mostly in Europe use contactless payment over mobile phones to pay for on- and off-street parking in specially demarcated areas. Parking wardens may enforce the parkings by license plate, transponder tags or barcode stickers. First conceptualized in the 1990s, the technology has seen commercial use in this century in both Scandinavia and Estonia. End users benefit from the convenience of being able to pay for parking from the comfort of their car with their mobile phone, and parking operators are not obliged to invest in either existing or new street-based parking infrastructures. Parking wardens maintain order in these systems by license plate, transponder tags or barcode stickers or they read a digital display in the same way as they read a pay and display receipt.

Other vendors use a combination of both NFC and a barcode on the mobile device for mobile payment, for example, Cimbal or DigiMo, making this technique attractive at the point of sale because many mobile devices in the market do not yet support NFC.

Others

QR Code Payments

QR Codes 2D barcode are square bar codes. QR codes have been in use since 1994. Originally used to track products in warehouses, QR codes were designed to replace traditional (1D bar codes). Traditional bar codes just represent numbers, which can be looked up in a database and translated into something meaningful. QR, or "Quick Response" bar codes were designed to contain the meaningful info right in the bar code.

QR Codes can be of two main categories:

- The QR Code is presented on the mobile device of the person paying and scanned by a POS or another mobile device of the payee

- The QR Code is presented by the payee, in a static or one time generated fashion and it's scanned by the person executing the payment

Mobile self-checkout allows for one to scan a QR code or barcode of a product inside a brick-and-mortar establishment in order to purchase the product on the spot. This theoretically eliminates reduces the incidence of long checkout lines, even at self-checkout kiosks.

Cloud-based Mobile Payments

Google, PayPal, GlobalPay and GoPago use a cloud-based approach to in-store mobile payment. The cloud based approach places the mobile payment provider in the middle of the transaction, which involves two separate steps. First, a cloud-linked payment method is selected and payment is authorized via NFC or an alternative method. During this step, the payment provider automatically covers the cost of the purchase with issuer linked funds. Second, in a separate transaction, the payment provider charges the purchaser's selected, cloud-linked account in a card-not-present environment to recoup its losses on the first transaction.

Audio Signal-based Payments

The audio channel of the mobile phone is another wireless interface that is used to make payments. Several companies have created technology to use the acoustic features of cell phones to support mobile payments and other applications that are not chip-based. The technologies Near sound data transfer (NSDT), Data Over Voice and NFC 2.0 produce audio signatures that the microphone of the cell phone can pick up to enable electronic transactions.

Direct Carrier/Bank Co-operation

In the T-Cash model, the mobile phone and the phone carrier is the front-end interface to the consumers. The consumer can purchase goods, transfer money to a peer, cash out, and cash in. A 'mini wallet' account can be opened as simply as entering *700# on the mobile phone, presumably by depositing money at a participating local merchant and the mobile phone number. Presumably, other transactions are similarly accomplished by entering special codes and the phone number of the other party on the consumer's mobile phone.

Bank Transfer Systems

Swish is the name of a system established in Sweden. It was established by major banks in 2012 and has been very successful with half the population as users in 2016. The main usage is payment between private people, but is also used by sports clubs for snack sales etc. In 2017 it will be extended to internet shopping. The smartphone app is the front-end. The phone number is used as user number when doing transactions. The connection between the phone number and the actual bank account number is registered in the internet bank. Users with a simple phone or without the app can receive money if the phone number is registered in the internet bank. Like many other mobile payment system, it has the problem that users have to do an effort to register and get the app, before being able to use the system. It managed to reach a critical mass and more reluctant people are now also using it.

Mobile Payment Service Provider Model

There are four potential mobile payment models:

1. *Operator-Centric Model*: The mobile operator acts independently to deploy

mobile payment service. The operator could provide an independent mobile wallet from the user mobile account(airtime). A large deployment of the Operator-Centric Model is severely challenged by the lack of connection to existing payment networks. Mobile network operator should handle the interfacing with the banking network to provide advanced mobile payment service in banked and under banked environment. Pilots using this model have been launched in emerging countries but they did not cover most of the mobile payment service use cases. Payments were limited to remittance and airtime top up.

2. *Bank-Centric Model*: A bank deploys mobile payment applications or devices to customers and ensures merchants have the required point-of-sale (POS) acceptance capability. Mobile network operator are used as a simple carrier, they bring their experience to provide Quality of service (QOS) assurance.

3. *Collaboration Model*: This model involves collaboration among banks, mobile operators and a trusted third party.

4. *Peer-to-Peer Model*: The mobile payment service provider acts independently from financial institutions and mobile network operators to provide mobile payment. For example, the MHITS SMS payment service uses a peer-to-peer model.

Mobile Browser

Web Browser for S60 is an example of a mobile browser.

A mobile browser is a web browser designed for use on a mobile device such as a mobile phone or PDA. Mobile browsers are optimized so as to display Web content most effectively for small screens on portable devices. Mobile browser software must be small and efficient to accommodate the low memory capacity and low-bandwidth of wireless handheld devices. Typically they were stripped-down web browsers, but some more modern mobile browsers can handle more recent technologies like CSS 2.1, JavaScript, and Ajax.

Websites designed for access from these browsers are referred to as *wireless portals* or collectively as the Mobile Web. They may automatically create "mobile" versions of each page, for example this one.

Underlying Technology

The mobile browser usually connects via cellular network, or increasingly via Wireless LAN, using standard HTTP over TCP/IP and displays web pages written in HTML, XHTML Mobile Profile (WAP 2.0), or WML (which evolved from HDML). WML and HDML are stripped-down formats suitable for transmission across limited bandwidth, and wireless data connection called WAP. In Japan, DoCoMo defined the i-mode service based on i-mode HTML, which is an extension of Compact HTML (C-HTML), a simple subset of HTML.

WAP 2.0 specifies XHTML Mobile Profile plus WAP CSS, subsets of the W3C's standard XHTML and CSS with minor mobile extensions.

Newer mobile browsers are full-featured Web browsers capable of HTML, CSS, ECMAScript, as well as mobile technologies such as WML, i-mode HTML, or cHTML.

To accommodate small screens, they use Post-WIMP interfaces.

History

The first mobile browser for a PDA was PocketWeb for the Apple Newton created at TecO in 1994, followed by the first commercial product NetHopper released in August 1996.

The so-called "microbrowser" technologies such as WAP, NTTDocomo's i-mode platform and Openwave's HDML platform fueled the first wave of interest in wireless data services.

The first deployment of a mobile browser on a mobile phone was probably in 1997 when Unwired Planet (later to become Openwave) put their "UP.Browser" on AT&T handsets to give users access to HDML content.

A British company, STNC Ltd., developed a mobile browser (HitchHiker) in 1997 that was intended to present the entire device UI. The demonstration platform for this mobile browser (Webwalker) had 1 MIPS total processing power. This was a single core platform, running the GSM stack on the same processor as the application stack. In 1999 STNC was acquired by Microsoft and HitchHiker became Microsoft Mobile Explorer 2.0, not related to the primitive Microsoft Mobile Explorer 1.0. HitchHiker is believed to be the first mobile browser with a unified rendering model, handling HTML and WAP along with ECMAScript, WMLScript, POP3 and IMAP mail in a single client. Although it was not used, it was possible to combine HTML and WAP in the same pages although this would render the pages invalid for any other device. Mobile Explorer 2.0 was available on the Benefon Q, Sony CMD-Z5, CMD-J5, CMD-MZ5, CMD-J6, CMD-Z7, CMD-J7 and CMD-J70. With the addition of a messaging kernel and a driver model, this was powerful enough to be the operating system for certain embedded devices. One such device was the Amstrad e-m@iler and e-m@iler 2. This code formed the basis for MME3.

Multiple companies offered browsers for the Palm OS platform. The first HTML browser for Palm OS 1.0 was HandWeb by Smartcode software, released in 1997. HandWeb included its own TCP/IP stack, and Smartcode was acquired by Palm in 1999. Mobile browsers for the Palm OS platform multiplied after the release of Palm OS 2.0, which included a TCP/IP stack. A freeware (although later shareware) browser for the Palm OS was Palmscape, written in 1998 by Kazuho Oku in Japan, who went on to found Ilinx. Still in limited use as late as 2003. Qualcomm also developed the Eudora Web browser, and launched it with the Palm OS based QCP smartphone. ProxiWeb was a proxy-based Web browsing solution, developed by Ian Goldberg and others at the University of California Berkeley and later acquired by PumaTech.

Released in 2001, Mobile Explorer 3.0 added iMode compatibility (cHTML) plus numerous proprietary schemes. By imaginatively combining these proprietary schemes with WAP protocols, MME3.0 implemented OTA database synchronisation, push email, push information clients (not unlike a 'Today Screen') and PIM functionality. The cancelled Sony Ericsson CMD-Z700 was to feature heavy integration with MME3.0. Although Mobile Explorer was ahead of its time in the mobile phone space, development was stopped in 2002.

Also in 2002, Palm, Inc. offered Web Pro on Tungsten PDAs based upon a Novarra browser. PalmSource offered a competing Web browser based on Access Netfront.

Opera Software pioneered with its Small Screen Rendering (SSR) and Medium Screen Rendering (MSR) technology. The Opera web browser is able to reformat regular web pages for optimal fit on small screens and medium-sized (PDA) screens. It was also the first widely available mobile browser to support Ajax and the first mobile browser to pass ACID2 test.

Distinct from a mobile browser is a web-based emulator, which uses a "Virtual Handset" to display WAP pages on a computer screen, implemented either in Java or as an HTML transcoder.

Popular Mobile Browsers

The following are some of the more popular mobile browsers. Some mobile browsers are really miniaturized Web browsers, so some mobile device providers also provide browsers for desktop and laptop computers.

Usage share of mobile (smartphone and tablet) browsers for June 2015						
Source	Android Browser	Chrome	Internet Explorer	Safari	Opera Mini	Other
StatCounter	15.81%	30.67%	1.76%	24.64%	10.37%	3.79%

Usage share of mobile (smartphone and tablet) browsers for June 2014						
Source	Android Browser	Chrome	Internet Explorer	Safari	Opera Mini	Other
NetApplications	22.77%	16.67%	2.01%	47.06%	7.82%	4.69%

Default Browsers for Mobile and Tablet

Mobile HTML Transcoders

Mobile transcoders reformat and compress web content for mobile devices and must be used in conjunction with built-in or user-installed mobile browsers. The following are several leading mobile transcoding services.

- Openwave Web Adapter - used by Vodacom
- Vision Mobile Server
- Skweezer - used by Orange, Etisalat, JumpTap, Medio, Miva, and others
- Teashark
- Opera Mini

1. *"Myriad -Mobile browsers". Myriad Group. 2010. Retrieved 2010-12-15.*
2. *"Series 40 Platform". Forum Nokia. 2010-06-04. Retrieved 2010-07-29.*
3. iOS Source Licenses
4. *"Mobile features". Mozilla. Retrieved 2012-06-26.*

Mobile Marketing

Mobile marketing is marketing on or with a mobile device, such as a smart phone. Mobile marketing can provide customers with time and location sensitive, personalized information that promotes goods, services and ideas. In a more theoretical manner, academic Andreas Kaplan defines mobile marketing as "any marketing activity conducted through a ubiquitous network to which consumers are constantly connected using a personal mobile device".

SMS Marketing

Marketing through cellphones' SMS (Short Message Service) became increasingly popular in the early 2000s in Europe and some parts of Asia when businesses started to collect mobile phone numbers and send off wanted (or unwanted) content. On average, SMS messages are read within four minutes, making them highly convertible.

Over the past few years SMS marketing has become a legitimate advertising channel in some parts of the world. This is because unlike email over the public internet, the carriers who police their own networks have set guidelines and best practices for the mobile media industry (including mobile advertising). The IAB (Interactive Advertising Bureau) and the Mobile Marketing Association (MMA), as well, have established guidelines and are evangelizing the use of the mobile channel for marketers. While this has been fruitful in developed regions such as North America, Western Europe and some other countries, mobile SPAM messages (SMS sent to mobile subscribers without a legitimate and explicit opt-in by the subscriber) remain an issue in many other parts of the world, partly due to the carriers selling their member databases to third parties. In India, however, government's efforts of creating National Do Not Call Registry have helped cellphone users to stop SMS advertisements by sending a simple SMS or calling 1909.

Mobile marketing via SMS has expanded rapidly in Europe and Asia as a new channel to reach the consumer. SMS initially received negative media coverage in many parts of Europe for being a new form of spam as some advertisers purchased lists and sent unsolicited content to consumer's phones; however, as guidelines are put in place by the mobile operators, SMS has become the most popular branch of the Mobile Marketing industry with several 100 million advertising SMS sent out every month in Europe alone.

In Europe the first cross-carrier SMS shortcode campaign was run by Txtbomb in 2001 for an Island Records release, In North America it was the Labatt Brewing Company in 2002. Over the past few years mobile short codes have been increasingly popular as a new channel to communicate to the mobile consumer. Brands have begun to treat the mobile short code as a mobile domain name allowing the consumer to text message the brand at an event, in store and off any traditional media.

SMS marketing services typically run off a short code, but sending text messages to an email address is another methodology (though this method is not supported by the carriers). Short codes are 5 or 6 digit numbers that have been assigned by all the mobile operators in a given country for the use of brand campaign and other consumer services. Due to the high price of short codes of $500–$1000 a month, many small businesses opt to share a short code in order to reduce monthly costs. The mobile operators vet every short code application before provisioning and monitor the service to make sure it does not diverge from its original service description. Another alternative to sending messages by short code or email is to do so through one's own dedicated phone number.

Besides short codes, inbound SMS can be received on long numbers (international number format, e.g. +44 7624 805000 or US number format, e.g. 757 772 8555), which can be used in place of short codes or premium-rated short messages for SMS reception in several applications, such as product promotions and campaigns. Long numbers are internationally available, as well as enabling businesses to have their own number, rather than short codes which are usually shared across a number of brands. Additionally, long numbers are non-premium inbound numbers.

One key criterion for provisioning is that the consumer opts into the service. The mobile operators demand a double opt in from the consumer and the ability for the consumer to opt out of the service at any time by sending the word STOP via SMS. These guidelines are established in the CTIA Playbook and the MMA Consumer Best Practices Guidelines which are followed by all mobile marketers in the United States. In Canada, opt in will be mandatory once the Fighting Internet and Wireless Spam Act comes in force in mid-2012.

MMS

MMS mobile marketing can contain a timed slideshow of images, text, audio and video. This mobile content is delivered via MMS (Multimedia Message Service). Nearly all new phones produced with a color screen are capable of sending and receiving standard MMS message. Brands are able to both send (mobile terminated) and receive (mobile originated) rich content through MMS A2P (application-to-person) mobile networks to mobile subscribers. In some networks, brands are also able to sponsor messages that are sent P2P (person-to-person).

Good examples of mobile-originated MMS marketing campaigns are Motorola's ongoing campaigns at House of Blues venues, where the brand allows the consumer to send their mobile photos to the LED board in real-time as well as blog their images online.

Push Notifications

Push notifications were first introduced to smartphones by Apple with the Push Notification Service in 2009. For Android devices, Google developed Android Cloud to Messaging or C2DM in 2010. Google replaced this service with Google Cloud Messaging in 2013. Commonly referred to as GCM, Google Cloud Messaging served as C2DM's successor, making improvements to authentication and delivery, new API endpoints and messaging parameters, and the removal of limitations on API send-rates and message sizes. It is a message that pops up on a mobile device. It is the delivery of information from a software application to a computing device without any request from the client or the user. They look like SMS notifications but they are reached only the users who installed the app. The specifications vary for iOS and android users. SMS and push notifications can be part of a well-developed inbound mobile marketing strategy.

According to mobile marketing company Leanplum, Android sees open rates twice as high as those on iOS. Android sees open rates of 3.48 percent for push notification, versus iOS which has open rates of 1.77 percent.

App-based Marketing

With the increasingly widespread use of smartphones, app usage has also greatly increased. Therefore, mobile marketers have increasingly taken advantage of smartphone apps as a marketing resource. Marketers will aim to increase the visibility of an app in a store, which will in turn help in getting more downloads. By optimizing the placement of the app usage, marketers can ensure a significant number of increases in download. This allows for direct engagement, payment, and targeted advertising.

There is a lot of competition in this field as well. However, just like other services, it is not easy anymore to rule the mobile application market.

The current wave of progression and growth highly depends upon the wise use of technology and Mobile App Development is one such technology that is benefiting various companies in order to maximize their profits. In the past couple of years the usage of mobile phones has increased at an astonishing rate. Most of the companies have slowly but surely acknowledged the potential that Mobile App possess in order to increase the interaction between a company and its target customers. While planning to invest in Mobile App for your business you must consider all the aspects of it. Always choose a reliable and experienced company to develop customized apps for your business as this would help to increase the chances of success of that App and minimize the chances of any technical glitches that might crop up. You must keep in mind that an App can prove to be a very beneficial element to promote your business on a vast level only if it is developed by efficient service provider.

In-game Mobile Marketing

There are essentially three major trends in mobile gaming right now: interactive real-time 3D games, massive multi-player games and social networking games. This means a trend towards more complex and more sophisticated, richer game play. On the other side, there are the so-called casual games, i.e. games that are very simple and very easy to play. Most mobile games today are such casual games and this will probably stay so for quite a while to come.

Brands are now delivering promotional messages within mobile games or sponsoring entire games to drive consumer engagement. This is known as mobile advergaming or ad-funded mobile game.

In in-game mobile marketing, advertisers pay to have their name or products featured in the mobile games. For instance, racing games can feature real cars made by Ford or Chevy. Advertisers have been both creative and aggressive in their attempts to integrate ads organically in the mobile games.

Although investment in mobile marketing strategies like advergaming is slightly more expensive than what is intended for a mobile app, a good strategy can make the brand derive a substantial revenue. Games that use advergaming make the users remember better the brand involved. This memorization increases virality of the content so that the users tend to recommend them to their friends and acquaintances, and share them via social networks.

QR Codes

QR codes allow a customer to visit a web page address by scanning a 2D image with their phone's camera, instead of manually entering a URL. The resultant URLs typically include tracking features which would be unwieldy if typed by the customer. Originally approved as an ISS standard in 1997, Denso-Wave first developed the standard for tracking automobile parts in Japan.

QR codes have been growing in popularity in Asia and Europe, but have been slow to be adopted in North America. Some high-profile QR campaigns in the United States have included billboards by Calvin Klein in Times Square, QR codes for every SKU in Home Depot and Best Buy stores, and a scavenger hunt promoting Starbucks and Lady Gaga.

Apple Passbook (application), implemented as a native app for iOS6, has employed QR codes as one of the ways that the iPhone (or iPod Touch) users can take a real world action. i.e. scan the Barcode on their Passbook Pass. In addition to QR codes, the Passbook (application) also supports PDF417 and Aztec 2D Barcodes

Bluetooth

Bluetooth technology is a global wireless standard enabling, convenient, secure connectivity for an expanding range of devices and services. Created by Ericsson in 1994, Bluetooth wireless technology was originally conceived as a wireless alternative to RS-232 data cables.

The use of Bluetooth gained traction around 2003 and a few companies in Europe have started establishing successful businesses. Most of these businesses offer "hotspot" systems which consist of some kind of content-management system with a Bluetooth distribution function. This technology has the advantages that it is permission-based, has higher transfer speeds and is a radio-based technology and thus can neither be metered nor billed. The likely earliest device built for mobile marketing via Bluetooth was the context tag of the AmbieSense project (2001-2004). More recently Tata Motors conducted one of the biggest Bluetooth marketing campaigns in India for its brand the Sumo Grande and more of such activities have happened for brands like Walt Disney promoting their movie *High School Musical*.

Proximity Systems

Mobile marketing via proximity systems, or proximity marketing, relies on GSM 03.41

which defines the Short Message Service - Cell Broadcast. SMS-CB allows messages (such as advertising or public information) to be broadcast to all mobile users in a specified geographical area. In the Philippines, GSM-based proximity broadcast systems are used by select Government Agencies for information dissemination on Government-run community-based programs to take advantage of its reach and popularity (Philippines has the world's highest traffic of SMS). It is also used for commercial service known as Proxima SMS. Bluewater, a super-regional shopping centre in the UK, has a GSM based system supplied by NTL to help its GSM coverage for calls, it also allows each customer with a mobile phone to be tracked though the centre which shops they go into and for how long. The system enables special offer texts to be sent to the phone. For example, a retailer could send a mobile text message to those customers in their database who have opted-in, who happen to be walking in a mall. That message could say "Save 50% in the next 5 minutes only when you purchase from our store." Snacks company, Mondelez International, makers of Cadbury and Oreo products has committed to exploring proximity-based messaging citing significant gains in point-of-purchase influence.

Location-based Services

Location-based services (LBS) are offered by some cell phone networks as a way to send custom advertising and other information to cell-phone subscribers based on their current location. The cell-phone service provider gets the location from a GPS chip built into the phone, or using radiolocation and trilateration based on the signal-strength of the closest cell-phone towers (for phones without GPS features). In the United Kingdom, which launched location-based services in 2003, networks do not use trilateration; LBS uses a single base station, with a "radius" of inaccuracy, to determine a phone's location.

Some location-based services work without GPS tracking technique, instead transmitting content between devices peer-to-peer.

Ringless Voice Mail

The advancement of mobile technologies has allowed the ability to leave a voice mail message on a mobile phone without ringing the line. The technology was pioneered by VoAPP, which used the technology in conjunction with live operators as a debt collection service. The FCC has ruled that the technology is compliant with all regulations. CPL expanded on the existing technology to allow for a completely automated process including the replacement of live operators with pre recorded messages. By optimizing the technology, marketers can utilize the process to increase engagement of their product or service.

User-controlled Media

Mobile marketing differs from most other forms of marketing communication in that it is often user (consumer) initiated (mobile originated, or MO) message, and requires the express consent of the consumer to receive future communications. A call delivered from a server (business) to a user (consumer) is called a mobile terminated (MT) message. This infrastructure points to a trend set by mobile marketing of consumer controlled marketing communications.

Due to the demands for more user controlled media, mobile messaging infrastructure providers have responded by developing architectures that offer applications to operators with more freedom for the users, as opposed to the network-controlled media. Along with these advances to user-controlled Mobile Messaging 2.0, blog events throughout the world have been implemented in order to launch popularity in the latest advances in mobile technology. In June 2007, Airwide Solutions became the official sponsor for the Mobile Messaging 2.0 blog that provides the opinions of many through the discussion of mobility with freedom.

GPS plays an important role in location-based marketing.

Privacy Concerns in Mobile Marketing

Mobile advertising has become more and more popular. However, some mobile advertising is sent without a required permission from the consumer causing privacy violations. It should be understood that irrespective of how well advertising messages are designed and how many additional possibilities they provide, if consumers do not have confidence that their privacy will be protected, this will hinder their widespread deployment. But if the messages originate from a source where the user is enrolled in a relationship/loyalty program, privacy is not considered violated and even interruptions can generate goodwill.

The privacy issue became even more salient as it was before with the arrival of mobile data networks. A number of important new concerns emerged mainly stemming from the fact that mobile devices are intimately personal and are always with the user, and four major concerns can be identified: mobile spam, personal identification, location information and wireless security. Aggregate presence of mobile phone users could be tracked in a privacy-preserving fashion.

Classification of Mobile Marketing

Kaplan categorizes mobile marketing along the degree of consumer knowledge and the trigger of communication into four groups: strangers, groupies, victims, and patrons. Consumer knowledge can be high or low and according to its degree organizations can customize their messages to each individual user, similar to the idea of one-to-one marketing. Regarding the trigger of communication, Kaplan differentiates between push communication, initiated by the organization, and pull communication, initiated by the consumer. Within the first group (low knowledge/push), organizations broadcast a general message to a large number of mobile users. Given that the organization cannot know which customers have ultimately been reached by the message, this group is referred to as "strangers". Within the second group (low knowledge/pull), customers opt to receive information but do not identify themselves when doing so. The organizations therefore does not know which specific clients it is dealing with exactly, which is why this cohort is called "groupies". In the third group (high knowledge/push) referred to as "victims", organizations know their customers and can send them messages and information without first asking permission. The last group (high knowledge/pull), the "patrons" covers situations where customers actively give permission to be contacted and provide personal information about themselves, which allows for one-to-one communication without running the risk of annoying them.

Apple Pay

Apple Pay is a mobile payment and digital wallet service by Apple Inc. that lets users make payments using the iPhone 6, 6 Plus, iPhone SE, and later, Apple Watch-compatible devices (iPhone 5 and later models), iPad Air 2, iPad Pro and iPad Mini 3 and later and Mac. Apple Pay does not require Apple Pay-specific contactless payment terminals, and can work with existing contactless terminals.

It it based on the EMV Payment Tokenisation Specification.

Service

Apple Pay lets mobile devices make payments at contactless points of sale and in iOS apps and On the Web. It digitizes and replaces the credit or debit card chip and PIN or magnetic stripe transaction at point-of-sale terminals. It is similar to contactless payments already used in many countries, with the addition of two-factor authentication. The service lets Apple devices wirelessly communicate with point of sale systems using a near field communication (NFC) antenna, a "dedicated chip that stores encrypted payment information" (known as the Secure Element), and Apple's Touch ID and Wallet. The service is compatible with the iPhone 6, 6 Plus, 6S and 6S Plus, iPhone SE, iPad Air 2, iPad Pro and the Apple Watch. Users with iPhone 5, 5C, 5S, 6, 6 Plus, 6S, 6S Plus, and iPhone SE can use the service through an Apple Watch, though it lacks Touch ID security. Instead, Apple Pay is activated with a passcode and will remain active for as long as the user wears the Apple Watch.

The service keeps customer payment information private from the retailer, and creates a "dynamic security code [...] generated for each transaction". Apple added that they would not track usage, which would stay between the customers, the vendors, and the banks. Users can also remotely halt the service on a lost phone via the Find My iPhone service.

To pay at points of sale, users hold their authenticated Apple device to the point of sale system. iPhone users authenticate by holding their fingerprint to the phone's Touch

ID sensor, whereas Apple Watch users authenticate by double clicking a button on the device. To pay in supported iOS apps, users choose Apple Pay as their payment method and authenticate with Touch ID. Users can add payment cards to the service in any of three ways: through their iTunes accounts, by taking a photo of the card, or by entering the card information manually.

In the United Kingdom, payments using contactless cards are limited to £30 (previously £20 until August 2015) as they have only one-factor authentication. Although payments using Apple Pay have two-factor authentication and no transaction limit, they are in practice subject to the previous £20-30 transaction limit until retailers upgrade the software in their terminals to support the latest network contactless specifications.

Apple assumes some liability for fraudulent use of the service. Banks are expected to carry the burden of the service, and Apple is said to have negotiated smaller transaction fees. In turn, the banks hoped to capture purchases that were formerly handled without credit. *Financial Times* reported that Apple receives 0.15% cut of US purchases made with the service, but, following the UK launch, reported that Apple's cut is much lower in the UK. This is largely because Regulation (EU) 2015/751 capped interchange fees in the European Economic Area at 0.3% for personal credit cards and 0.2% for personal debit cards with effect from June 8, 2015.

History

The service was announced at Apple's iPhone 6 event on September 9, 2014. At its announcement, Apple CEO Tim Cook described the magnetic stripe card payment process as broken for its reliance on plastic cards' "outdated and vulnerable magnetic interface", "exposed numbers", and insecure "security codes". The iOS 8.1 software update accompanying the service's launch activated Apple Pay on compatible devices. The company announced an API for app developers to build Apple Pay checkout into their apps.

The service was in preparation for "a long time", as Apple acquired startups, hired executives and filed patents related to payments. Apple partnered with American Express, Mastercard and Visa. Their joint project began in January 2013, though they had discussed Apple's potential involvement for years. Their joint solution was a system where single-use digital tokens would replace the transfer of personal information. A Visa executive said that 750 people at the company worked on the anonymized "token" system for a year, and the other partners had similar teams in collaboration. MasterCard began work on the project in 2013 and hoped that their joint work would become a "standard for mobile payments". The announcement of the service came at a time when Master-Card and Visa policy created strong incentives for upgrading to mobile payment-compatible point of sale systems. Apple then approached several big banks in mid 2013 and did not divulge the names of the other banks. To maintain secrecy, JPMorgan set up a windowless "war room" where the majority of the sensitive work was done. of their

300 people on the project, about 100 knew that the partner was Apple. Others close to the project did not know it was named "Apple Pay" until the announcement. The company's participation remained a secret leading up to its announcement.

The service initially supported US-issued payments cards. An international roll-out is ongoing, beginning with support for UK-issued payment cards in July 2015. On December 17, 2015, Apple announced that it will launch Apple Pay with 15 major banks in China, and Chinese users can use Apple Pay since February 18, 2016.

In October 2015, Apple Pay vice president Jennifer Bailey confirmed that KFC, Chili's, and Starbucks would launch Apple Pay in 2016.

On March 8, 2016, ExxonMobil officially launched Apple Pay support within its Speedpass+ iOS app, letting customers pay for gas or car washes directly from their iPhone, eliminating the need to use the ExxonMobil's physical NFC Speedpass keychain token at the point of transaction.

On April 27, 2016, ANZ made Apple Pay available to their American Express and Visa cardholders in Australia.

On May 4, 2016, Kohl's became the first retailer allow the use of Apple Pay with Kohl's Charge Cards or other credit or debit cards enrolled with Apple Pay and simultaneously earn Yes2You Rewards loyalty points with a single tap using Apple Pay. J. C. Penney announced that they will be rolling out the same in the near future.

On May 10, 2016, Apple Pay was expanded the service in Canada to customers of RBC, CIBC, ATB Financial and Canadian Tire Bank. The expansion includes varying support for Visa, MasterCard, and Interac, covering most major debit and credit cards in Canada. Apple Pay was previously only available in Canada for non-bank-issued American Express cards. Apple Pay will be further expanded to TD Canada Trust, Scotiabank, and the Bank of Montreal in the "coming months" to complete the rollout across the Canada's Big Five financial institutions. Apple Pay support is also coming soon to Air Canada, Aldo, Domino's, Pizza Pizza, Zulily, and the TTC transit system in Toronto. Additionally, the payment service is integrated into the iPhone and iPad applications for the Apple Store, Delta, Etsy, Fancy, Groupon, Kickstarter, Priceline, Starbucks, Ticketmaster, Uber, and Zara starting in June 2016.

On May 19, 2016, Chime Banking initiated its support of Apple Pay.

Apple Pay launched in Singapore on April 19, 2016 with American Express issued cards. On May 25, 2016, this was extended to support Visa and MasterCard credit and debit cards issued by Singapore's five major banks, translating to about 83 percent of credit and debit cards in the country.

BMO, Scotiabank, and TD Canada Trust, which make up three of the five largest banks in Canada, rolled out Apple Pay support on June 1, 2016.

On June 1, 2016, KFC has announced that it now accepts Apple Pay at some of its U.S. restaurants, with nationwide adoption to be completed by the end of the summer.

On June 3, 2016, Grubhub, the nation's leading online and mobile food-ordering and delivery platform began accepting payment from its customers using Apple Pay on its two applications; Grubhub and Seamless. The company is keeping up with its rivals in adopting the payment service as Caviar, DoorDash, and Postmates.

Apple announced at its WWDC 2016 keynote on June 13, 2016, that Apple Pay will be entering three new markets; France, Hong Kong, and Switzerland over the following months in partnerships with Visa, MasterCard, and American Express. Visa and MasterCard cards will be supported in all three markets, while American Express will also be available in Hong Kong. The specific credit, debit, and prepaid cards that can be used in each country vary depending on the participating issuers

- France at launch will include Banque Populaire, Boon, Caisse Epargne, Carrefour Banque, Orange, and Ticket Restaurant. It will also be accepted at many retailers in France, including Apple, Bocage, Boulanger, Cojean, Dior, Fnac, Le Bon Marché, Louis Vuitton, Orange, Pret a Manger, Parkeon, Sephora, and at other locations where contactless payments are already accepted.

- Hong Kong at launch will include the Bank of East Asia (BEA), Bank of China (Hong Kong), DBS Bank (Hong Kong), Hang Seng Bank, HSBC, and Standard Chartered. Apple Pay will also be accepted at 7-Eleven, Apple, Colourmix, KFC, Lane Crawford, Mannings, McDonald's, Pacific Coffee, Pizza Hut, Sasa, Senryo, Starbucks, ThreeSixty, and at other locations where contactless payments are already accepted.

- Switzerland's launch of the service was on July 7, 2016 with MasterCard and Visa. Initial banks deploying Apple Pay in Switzerland include Bonus Card, Cornèr Bank (Cornèrcard), and Swiss Bankers. Apple Pay will also be accepted at retail locations of Aldi Suisse, Apple, Avec, Hublot, K Kiosk, Lidl, Louis Vuitton, Mobilezone, Press & Books, SPAR, TAG Heuer, and at other locations where contactless payments are already accepted.

A month after Apple Pay launched in Hong Kong, the service has expanded to The Bank of East Asia (BEA) and Hong Kong Telekom (HKT)'s Tap & Go contactless payments network. BEA customers can add eligible MasterCard and Visa credit cards to Apple Pay and receive 5,000 bonus points between the launch and August 22, 2016 while the first 30,000 customers that complete three or more Apple Pay transactions between the launch and October 31 will receive a 25% cash rebate of up to $180. Also, HKT Tap & Go customers that add prepaid cards to Apple Pay, and complete three or more Apple Pay transactions between the launch and August 31, will receive a cash rebate of up to $50.

Under a partnership with American Express, Hong Kong and Spain will also get Apple Pay support in 2016.

Bank of America is outfitting some of its ATMs with Apple Pay support and the ability to withdraw cash using it. The new Apple Pay enabled ATM is outfitted with the NFC reader and logo that Apple Pay users have become used to seeing since the service launched. The NFC reader is located directly to the left of the card reader, although unlike the card reader, the NFC reader does not light up. Bank of America has launched a new website detailing the simple process of withdrawing cash with a smartphone (Android Pay, Samsung Pay, or Apple Pay). Currently, Bank of America says that "Consumer Debit Cards, U.S. Trust Debit Cards, Small Business Debit Cards (owner card only)" are supported. Wells Fargo and JPMorgan Chase are both working to integrate Apple Pay support into their ATMs.

On August 18, 2016, Apple announced it has added Apple Pay support for customers of Yorkshire Bank and Clydesdale Bank in the United Kingdom.

On August 29, 2016, ANZ Expanded their support for Apple Pay to support MasterCard holders in Australia.

On September 7, 2016, Apple announced that iPhone 7 and Apple Watch Series 2 users in Japan can now add both local credit cards and FeliCa cards to their Apple Pay wallets. As of now, only Suica cards are supported by Apple Pay, which now can be used at subway stations, convenience stores, etc., just like regular Suica cards. Apple Pay also supports payment via all QUICPay and iD enabled terminals that are already popular in Japan.

Taiwan's Financial Supervisory Commission began accepting applications from the country's banks offering Apple Pay to their customers on September 28, 2016. This includes the banks; CTBC Bank, Cathay, United Commercial Bank, E.SUN Commercial Bank, and Taishin International Bank.

Release dates	
Date	**Support for payment cards issued in**
October 20, 2014	United States
July 14, 2015	United Kingdom
November 17, 2015	Canada
November 19, 2015	Australia
February 18, 2016	China
April 19, 2016	Singapore
July 7, 2016	Switzerland
July 19, 2016	France
July 20, 2016	Hong Kong
October 4, 2016	Russia

October 13, 2016	New Zealand
Late October, 2016	Japan

Reception

Reviews

Journalists noted the multiple previously unsuccessful efforts of other retailers to build mobile payments services, including those of PayPal, Wal-Mart, Target, Google Wallet, and Softcard. They noted that previous efforts did not solve customer inconvenience issues, and felt that Apple Pay potentially did. *The Verge*'s Adrianne Jeffries noted that mobile payment market fragmentation was partially due to Apple's refusal to enter the market. *BusinessWeek*'s Joshua Brustein added that Apple has a history of letting "first movers fail" with an early version of the service before releasing "a more polished version of the same idea". *The Verge*'s Dieter Bohn called Apple Pay the "week's most revolutionary product" and the announcement "a classic Apple moment of simplification and integration", and the partnership between payments services and Apple "a rare piece of collaboration and agreement". He predicted that the service's effect on the mobile payments industry would be similar to the iPhone's effect on the smartphone industry. Nathaniel Popper of *The New York Times* referred to the banks' level of coordination with Apple as "elaborate" and indicative of mutual "preparation and investment". Some analysts added that the service could reduce the standard credit card transaction fees over time, since fees traditionally cover credit card fraud. The banks were willing to work with Apple in the face of efforts like Bitcoin and the Merchant Customer Exchange, which seeks to work around the card networks.

Early reviews of the service regarded it as easy to use, but were not sure whether the service would become widely adopted. *The Verge*'s Nilay Patel wrote that the product demo was "remarkably smooth" and "a cohesive user experience". Patel said the process took five to ten seconds at a retail card reader, and added that it may be less smooth at stores such as Walgreens, where cashiers prompt customers for loyalty cards and charity donations. *The New York Times*'s Neil Irwin wrote that Apple exaggerated the inconvenience of credit cards. Among the plastic card's benefits, he included how others could make purchases on another's behalf and how dead cell phones could leave the owner stranded.

There are many controversial topics as to whether or not Apple Pay is safe. The answer may vary from different perspectives. However, Apple has taken major steps to make it very secure. Besides the NFC-based chip architecture, Apple has integrated Touch ID and a complex passcode architecture into the mobile wallet system. Apple Pay also keeps your identity a secret throughout the process. Each Apple Pay transaction online or in-app is authorised with a one-time unique dynamic security code, instead of using the safety code from the back of your card.

Adoption

Paying for coffee with Square's Apple Pay reader

Apple announced that more than 1 million credit cards had been registered on Apple Pay in the first 3 days of its availability, making it the largest mobile payment system in the US at the time. There were 220,000 participating vendors when it launched. Outside the United States and the United Kingdom, Apple Pay can be used with American and British payment cards at compatible NFC-based payment terminals.

In the United States, Apple faced opposition by the mobile payments industry, particularly the Merchant Customer Exchange (MCX) which is trialling a competing system known as CurrentC. Several participants of CurrentC, such as Best Buy and Walmart, had initially stated that they would not accept Apple Pay as a result of exclusivity deals. CVS Pharmacy and Rite-Aid subsequently disabled all NFC payment systems in favor of CurrentC, although due to the exclusivity period ending in August 2015, Rite Aid has begun accepting it August 15, 2015. Best Buy has begun to accept Apple Pay at all stores starting in October 2015. Target's CEO Brian Cornell said that they would be open to accepting Apple Pay eventually after chip and PIN is done, but they remain involved with MCX.

Transport for London, one of Apple Pay's official UK launch partners and one of the largest contactless merchants in the world, became the UK's most used Apple Pay merchant.

As of February 11, 2016, 20% of iPhone 6 users in the United States reported using the service at least once. Apple maintains an up-to-date list of merchants who accept Apple Pay on its website.

On June 2, 2016, according to *Fortune*, Apple said its mobile payment platform is gaining a million new users each week, yet the company did not reveal the total number of Apple Pay users. Apple also revealed that transaction volume through the service is five times what it was a year ago, and that payment volume within apps more than doubled in the second half of 2015.

With the launch of Apple Pay in China, the service hit three million provisions inside its first three days, while, more generally, it is adding one million new users per week worldwide.

On July 11, 2016 LCBO (Liquor Control Board of Ontario) confirmed that it accepts

Apple Pay at all of its over 850 stores in Ontario, Canada. LCBO had been gradually rolling out Apple Pay support since June at its stores, which had NFC-based terminals for contactless payments.

Starting on August 19, 2016, Apple Pay will be available in Chick-fil-A restaurants across the United States, allowing fast food buyers to make their purchases both in-store and at the drive thru using Apple Pay.

On September 7, 2016, Wayfair announced that they will support Apple Pay in Safari on iPhone, iPad, and Mac at launch.

References

- Titcomb, James (June 24, 2015). "Most Apple Pay UK transactions will be limited to £20, for now". The Telegraph. Retrieved July 13, 2015.

- Arnold, Martin (July 14, 2015). "UK banks put squeeze on Apple Pay fees". Financial Times. Retrieved July 15, 2015.

- "Regulation (EU) 2015/751 of the European Parliament and of the Council of 29 April 2015 on interchange fees for card-based payment transactions". European Commission. Retrieved July 25, 2015.

- Patel, Nilay (September 9, 2014). "Apple Pay hands-on: is this the future of payments?". The Verge. Archived from the original on September 13, 2014. Retrieved September 13, 2014.

- Irwin, Neil (September 10, 2014). "Apple Pay Tries to Solve a Problem That Really Isn't a Problem". The New York Times. Archived from the original on September 14, 2014. Retrieved September 14, 2014.

- Perez, Sarah (September 9, 2014). "Apple Announces Mobile Payment Solution Called Apple Pay". TechCrunch. AOL. Archived from the original on September 22, 2014. Retrieved September 22, 2014.

- Snider, Mike (September 9, 2014). "Apple hopes to jump-start mobile payments with Apple Pay". USA Today. Archived from the original on September 22, 2014. Retrieved September 22, 2014.

- Smith, Chris (October 21, 2014). "Apple Pay works in countries outside the U.S. with this simple trick". Boy Genius Report. Retrieved July 26, 2015.

- Gokey, Malarie (October 22, 2014). "Apple Pay Works Abroad! ... If You Have a U.S. Credit Card". Digital Trends. Retrieved July 26, 2015.

- Jeffries, Adrianne (September 9, 2014). "Apple Pay allows you to pay at the counter with your iPhone 6". The Verge. Archived from the original on September 13, 2014. Retrieved September 13, 2014.

- "Clever trick will safeguard Apple Watch from thieves". Cult Of Mac. September 10, 2014. Retrieved November 10, 2014.

- Popper, Nathaniel (September 11, 2014). "Banks Did It Apple's Way in Payments by Mobile". The New York Times. Archived from the original on September 15, 2014.

- Fiveash, Kelly (September 13, 2014). "Apple Pay is a tidy payday for Apple with 0.15% cut, sources say". The Register. Archived from the original on September 13, 2014. Retrieved September 13, 2014.

- Bohn, Dieter (September 10, 2014). "Apple Pay was this week's most revolutionary product". The Verge. Archived from the original on September 13, 2014. Retrieved September 13, 2014.

- "Ericsson and Aconite collaborate on mobile contactless payments". Mobile Payments Today. Retrieved 2013-01-25.

5

Applications of E-commerce

Online banking helps the customer of any bank manage financial transactions through the bank's website. Online advertising on the other hand are the advertisements used on the Internet to promote marketing messages to consumers. Some of the applications of E-commerce discussed in the text are online banking, online auction, online advertising, electronic publishing and net market.

Online Banking

Online banking, also known as internet banking, e-banking or virtual banking, is an electronic payment system that enables customers of a bank or other financial institution to conduct a range of financial transactions through the financial institution's website. The online banking system will typically connect to or be part of the core banking system operated by a bank and is in contrast to branch banking which was the traditional way customers accessed banking services.

To access a financial institution's online banking facility, a teacher with internet access would need to register with the institution for the service, and set up a password and other credentials for customer verification. The credentials for online banking is normally not the same as for telephone or mobile banking. Financial institutions now routinely allocate customers numbers, whether or not customers have indicated an intention to access their online banking facility. Customer numbers are normally not the same as account numbers, because a number of customer accounts can be linked to the one customer number. Technically, the customer number can be linked to any account with the financial institution that the customer controls, though the financial institution may limit the range of accounts that may be accessed to, say, cheque, savings, loan, credit card and similar accounts.

The customer visits the financial institution's secure website, and enters the online banking facility using the customer number and credentials previously set up. The types of financial transactions which a customer may transact through online banking are determined by the financial institution, but usually includes obtaining account balances, a list of the recent transactions, electronic bill payments and funds transfers between a customer's or another's accounts. Most banks also enable a customer to download copies of bank statements, which can be printed at the customer's premises (some banks charge a fee for mailing hard copies of bank statements). Some banks also enable customers to download transactions directly into the customer's accounting software.

The facility may also enable the customer to order a cheque book, statements, report loss of credit cards, stop payment on a cheque, advise change of address and other routine actions.

Today, many banks are internet-only institutions. These "virtual banks" have lower overhead costs than their brick-and-mortar counterparts. In the United States, many online banks are insured by the Federal Deposit Insurance Corporation (FDIC) and can offer the same level of protection for the customers' funds as traditional banks.

History

Precursors

The precursor for the modern home online banking services were the distance banking services over electronic media from the early 1980s. The term 'online' became popular in the late 1980s and referred to the use of a terminal, keyboard and TV (or monitor) to access the banking system using a phone line. 'Home banking' can also refer to the use of a numeric keypad to send tones down a phone line with instructions to the bank. Online services started in New York in 1981 when four of the city's major banks (Citibank, Chase Manhattan, Chemical and Manufacturers Hanover) offered home banking services. using the videotex system. Because of the commercial failure of videotex these banking services never became popular except in France where the use of videotex (Minitel) was subsidised by the telecom provider and the UK, where the Prestel system was used.

Internet and Customer Reluctance

When the clicks-and-bricks euphoria hit in the late 1990s, many banks began to view web-based banking as a strategic imperative. The attraction of banks to online banking are fairly obvious: diminished transaction costs, easier integration of services, interactive marketing capabilities, and other benefits that boost customer lists and profit margins. Additionally, online banking services allow institutions to bundle more services into single packages, thereby luring customers and minimizing overhead.

A mergers-and-acquisitions wave swept the financial industries in the mid- and late 1990s, greatly expanding banks' customer bases. Following this, banks looked to the Web as a way of maintaining their customers and building loyalty. A number of different factors are causing bankers to shift more of their business to the virtual realm.

While financial institutions took steps to implement e-banking services in the mid-1990s, many consumers were hesitant to conduct monetary transactions over the internet. It took widespread adoption of electronic commerce, based on trailblazing companies such as America Online, Amazon.com and eBay, to make the idea of paying for items online widespread. By 2000, 80% of U.S. banks offered e-banking. Customer use grew slowly. At Bank of America, for example, it took 10 years to acquire 2 million e-banking customers. However, a significant cultural change took place after the Y2K scare ended. In 2001, Bank of America became the first bank to top 3 million online banking customers, more than 20% of its customer base. In comparison, larger national institutions, such as Citigroup claimed 2.2 million online relationships globally, while J.P. Morgan Chase estimated it had more than 750,000 online banking customers. Wells Fargo had 2.5 million online banking customers, including small businesses. Online customers proved more loyal and profitable than regular customers. In October 2001, Bank of America customers executed a record 3.1 million electronic bill payments, totaling more than $1 billion. In 2009, a report by Gartner Group estimated that 47% of United States adults and 30% in the United Kingdom bank online.

The early 2000s saw the rise of the branch-less banks as internet only institutions. These internet-based banks incur lower overhead costs than their brick-and-mortar counterparts. Many online banks like Bank of Internet USA, Ally Bank and Bank5 Connect in the United States are FDIC-insured and offer the same level of protection for the funds of their customers as do traditional banks.

First Online Banking Services in the United States

Online banking was first introduced in the early 1980s in New York, United States. Four major banks — Citibank, Chase Manhattan, Chemical Bank and Manufacturers Hanover — offered home banking services. Chemical introduced its Pronto services for individuals and small businesses in 1983, which enabled individual and small-business clients to maintain electronic checkbook registers, see account balances, and transfer funds between checking and savings accounts. Pronto failed to attract enough customers to break even and was abandoned in 1989. Other banks had a similar experience.

First Online Banking in the United Kingdom

Almost simultaneously with the United States, online banking arrived in the United Kingdom. The UK's first home online banking services known as Homelink was set up by Bank of Scotland for customers of the Nottingham Building Society (NBS) in 1983. The system used was based on the UK's Prestel viewlink system and used a computer, such as the BBC Micro, or keyboard (Tandata Td1400) connected to the telephone system and television set. The system allowed on-line viewing of statements, bank transfers and bill payments. In order to make bank transfers and bill payments, a written instruction giving details of the intended recipient had to be sent to the NBS who set the details up on the Homelink system. Typical recipients were gas, electricity and telephone companies and accounts with other banks. Details of payments to be made were input into the NBS system by the account holder via Prestel. A cheque was then sent by NBS to the payee and an advice giving details of the payment was sent to the account holder. BACS was later used to transfer the payment directly.

Stanford Federal Credit Union was the first financial institution to offer online internet banking services to all of its members in October 1994.

Banks and the World Wide Web

Around 1994, banks saw the rising popularity of the internet as an opportunity to advertise their services. Initially, they used the internet as another brochure, without interaction with the customer. Early sites featured pictures of the bank's officers or buildings, and provided customers with maps of branches and ATM locations, phone numbers to call for further information and simple listings of products.

Interactive Banking on the Web

In 1995, Wells Fargo was the first U.S. bank to add account services to its website, with other banks quickly following suit. That same year, Presidential became the first U.S. bank to open bank accounts over the internet. According to research by Online Banking Report, at the end of 1999 less than 0.4% of households in the U.S. were using online banking. At the beginning of 2004, some 33 million U.S. households (31%) were using some form of online banking. Five years later, 47% of Americans used online banking, according to a survey by Gartner Group. Meanwhile, in the UK online banking grew from 63% to 70% of internet users between 2011 and 2012.

Features

Online banking facilities typically have many features and capabilities in common, but also have some that are application specific. The common features fall broadly into several categories:

- A bank customer can perform non-transactional tasks through online banking, including –
  - Viewing account balances
  - Viewing recent transactions
  - Downloading bank statements, for example in PDF format
  - Viewing images of paid cheques
  - Ordering cheque books
  - Download periodic account statements
  - Downloading applications for M-banking, E-banking etc.
- Bank customers can transact banking tasks through online banking, including –
  - Funds transfers between the customer's linked accounts
  - Paying third parties, including bill payments and third party fund transfers

     ○ Investment purchase or sale

     ○ Loan applications and transactions, such as repayments of enrollments

     ○ Credit card applications

     ○ Register utility billers and make bill payments

- Financial institution administration

- Management of multiple users having varying levels of authority

- Transaction approval process

Some financial institutions offer special internet banking services, for example:

- Personal financial management support, such as importing data into personal accounting software. Some online banking platforms support account aggregation to allow the customers to monitor all of their accounts in one place whether they are with their main bank or with other institutions.

Advantages

There are some advantages on using e-banking both for banks and customers:

- Permanent access to the bank

- Lower transaction costs / general cost reductions

- Access anywhere

- Less time consuming

- Very safe and secure method

Security

Five security token devices for online banking.

Security of a customer's financial information is very important, without which online banking could not operate. Similarly the reputational risks to the banks themselves are important. Financial institutions have set up various security processes to reduce the risk of unauthorized online access to a customer's records, but there is no consistency to the various approaches adopted.

The use of a secure website has been almost universally embraced.

Though single password authentication is still in use, it by itself is not considered secure enough for online banking in some countries. Basically there are two different security methods in use for online banking:

- The PIN/TAN system where the PIN represents a password, used for the login and TANs representing one-time passwords to authenticate transactions. TANs can be distributed in different ways, the most popular one is to send a list of TANs to the online banking user by postal letter. Another way of using TANs is to generate them by need using a security token. These token generated TANs depend on the time and a unique secret, stored in the security token (two-factor authentication or 2FA).

  More advanced TAN generators (chipTAN) also include the transaction data into the TAN generation process after displaying it on their own screen to allow the user to discover man-in-the-middle attacks carried out by Trojans trying to secretly manipulate the transaction data in the background of the PC.

  Another way to provide TANs to an online banking user is to send the TAN of the current bank transaction to the user's (GSM) mobile phone via SMS. The SMS text usually quotes the transaction amount and details, the TAN is only valid for a short period of time. Especially in Germany, Austria and the Netherlands many banks have adopted this "SMS TAN" service.

  Usually online banking with PIN/TAN is done via a web browser using SSL secured connections, so that there is no additional encryption needed.

- Signature based online banking where all transactions are signed and encrypted digitally. The Keys for the signature generation and encryption can be stored on smartcards or any memory medium, depending on the concrete implementation (see, e.g., the Spanish ID card *DNI electrónico*).

Attacks

Attacks on online banking used today are based on deceiving the user to steal login data and valid TANs. Two well known examples for those attacks are phishing and pharming. Cross-site scripting and keylogger/Trojan horses can also be used to steal login information.

A method to attack signature based online banking methods is to manipulate the used software in a way, that correct transactions are shown on the screen and faked transactions are signed in the background.

A 2008 U.S. Federal Deposit Insurance Corporation Technology Incident Report, compiled from suspicious activity reports banks file quarterly, lists 536 cases of computer intrusion, with an average loss per incident of $30,000. That adds up to a nearly $16-million loss in the second quarter of 2007. Computer intrusions increased by 150 percent between the first quarter of 2007 and the second. In 80 percent of the cases, the source of the intrusion is unknown but it occurred during online banking, the report states.

Another kind of attack is the so-called man-in-the-browser attack, a variation of the man-in-the-middle attack where a Trojan horse permits a remote attacker to secretly modify the destination account number and also the amount in the web browser.

As a reaction to advanced security processes allowing the user to cross-check the transaction data on a secure device there are also combined attacks using malware and social engineering to persuade the user himself to transfer money to the fraudsters on the ground of false claims (like the claim the bank would require a "test transfer" or the claim a company had falsely transferred money to the user's account and he should "send it back"). Users should therefore never perform bank transfers they have not initiated themselves.

Countermeasures

There exist several countermeasures which try to avoid attacks. Digital certificates are used against phishing and pharming, in signature based online banking variants (HBCI/FinTS) the use of "Secoder" card readers is a measurement to uncover software side manipulations of the transaction data. To protect their systems against Trojan horses, users should use virus scanners and be careful with downloaded software or e-mail attachments.

In 2001, the U.S. Federal Financial Institutions Examination Council issued guidance for multifactor authentication (MFA) and then required to be in place by the end of 2006.

In 2012, the European Union Agency for Network and Information Security advised all banks to consider the PC systems of their users being infected by malware by default and therefore use security processes where the user can cross-check the transaction data against manipulations like for example (provided the security of the mobile phone holds up) SMS TAN where the transaction data is sent along with the TAN number or standalone smartcard readers with an own screen including the transaction data into the TAN generation process while displaying it beforehand to the user to counter man-in-the-middle attacks.

Regulations

Since its inception in the United States, online banking has been federally governed by the *Electronic Funds Transfer Act of 1978*.

Forms of Online Banking

Electronic Money

Electronic money, or e-money, is the money balance recorded electronically on a stored-value card. These cards have microprocessors embedded which can be loaded with a monetary value. Another form of electronic money is network money, software that allows the transfer of value on computer networks, particularly the internet. Electronic money is a floating claim on a private bank or other financial institution that is not linked to any particular account. Examples of electronic money are bank deposits, electronic funds transfer, direct deposit, payment processors, and digital currencies.

Electronic money can either be centralized, where there is a central point of control over the money supply, or decentralized, where the control over the money supply can come from various sources. Electronic money that is decentralized is also known as digital currencies. The major difference between E-money and digital currencies is that E-money doesn't change the value of the fiat currency (USD, EUR) it represents, but digital currency is not equivalent to any fiat currency. In other words, all digital currency is Electronic money, but Electronic money is not necessarily digital currency. Many mobile sub-systems have been introduced in the past few years including Google Wallet and Apple Pay.

History

In 1983, a research paper by David Chaum introduced the idea of digital cash. In 1990, he founded DigiCash, an electronic cash company, in Amsterdam to commercialize the ideas in his research. It filed for bankruptcy in 1998. In 1999, Chaum left the company.

In 1997, Coca Cola offered buying from vending machines using mobile payments. After that PayPal emerged in 1998. Other system such as e-gold followed suit, but faced issues because it was used by criminals and was raided by US Feds in 2005. In 2008, bitcoin was introduced, which marked the start of Digital currencies.

Law

Since 2001, the European Union has implemented the E-Money Directive "on the taking up, pursuit and prudential supervision of the business of electronic money institutions" last amended in 2009. Doubts on the real nature of EU electronic money have arisen, since calls have been made in connection with the 2007 EU Payment Services

Directive in favor of merging payment institutions and electronic money institutions. Such a merger could mean that electronic money is of the same nature as bank money or scriptural money.

In the United States, electronic money is governed by Article 4A of the Uniform Commercial Code for wholesale transactions and the Electronic Fund Transfer Act for consumer transactions. Provider's responsibility and consumer's liability are regulated under Regulation E.

Uses of Electronic Money Worldwide

- Hong Kong's Octopus card system: Launched in 1997 as an electronic purse for public transportation, is the most successful and mature implementation of contactless smart cards used for mass transit payments. After only 5 years, 25 percent of Octopus card transactions are unrelated to transit, and accepted by more than 160 merchants.

- London Transport's Oyster card system: Oyster is a plastic smartcard which can hold pay as you go credit, Travelcards and Bus & Tram season tickets. You can use an Oyster card to travel on bus, Tube, tram, DLR, London Overground and most National Rail services in London.

- Japan's FeliCa: A contactless RFID smart card, used in a variety of ways such as in ticketing systems for public transportation, e-money, and residence door keys.

- Netherlands' Chipknip: As an electronic cash system used in the Netherlands, all ATM cards issued by the Dutch banks had value that could be loaded via Chipknip loading stations. For people without a bank, pre-paid Chipknip cards could be purchased at various locations in the Netherlands. As of January 1, 2015, you can no longer pay with Chipknip.

- Belgium's Proton: An electronic purse application for debit cards in Belgium. Introduced in February 1995, as a means to replace cash for small transactions. The system was retired in December 31, 2014.

Types of Systems

Centralized Systems

Many systems—such as PayPal, eCash, WebMoney, Payoneer, cashU, and Hub Culture's Ven will sell their electronic currency directly to the end user. Other systems only sell through third party digital currency exchangers. The M-Pesa system is used to transfer money through mobile phones in Africa, India, Afghanistan, and Eastern Europe. Some community currencies, like some local exchange trading systems (LETS) and the Community Exchange System, work with electronic transactions.

Mobile Sub-systems/Digital Wallets

A number of electronic money systems use contactless payment transfer in order to facilitate easy payment and give the payee more confidence in not letting go of their electronic wallet during the transaction.

- In 1994 Mondex and National Westminster Bank provided an 'electronic purse' to residents of Swindon

- In about 2005 Telefónica and BBVA Bank launched a payment system in Spain called Mobipay which used simple short message service facilities of feature phones intended for pay-as you go services including taxis and pre-pay phone recharges via a BBVA current bank account debit.

- In Jan 2010, Venmo launched as a mobile payment system through SMS, which transformed into a social app were friends can pay each other for minor expenses like a cup of coffee, rent and paying your share of the restaurant bill when you forget your wallet. It is popular with college students, but has some security issues. It can be linked to your bank account, credit/debit card or have a loaded value to limit the amount of loss in case of a security breach. Credit cards and non-major debit cards incur a 3% processing fee.

- On September 19, 2011, Google Wallet was released in the US only, which makes it easy to carry all your credit/debit cards on your phone.

- In 2012 O2 (Ireland) (owned by Telefónica)launched Easytrip to pay road tolls which were charged to the mobile phone account or prepay credit.

- O2 (United Kingdom) invented O2 Wallet at about the same time. The wallet can be charged with regular bank accounts or cards and discharged by participating retailers using a technique known as 'money messages' The service closed in 2014

- On September 9, 2014 Apple Pay was announced at the iPhone 6 event. In October 2014 it was released as an update to work on iPhone 6 and Apple Watch. It is very similar to Google Wallet, but for Apple devices only.

- GNU Taler is an anonymous, open source electronic payment system currently (September 2015) in development.

Decentralized Systems

Cryptocurrencies allow electronic money systems to be decentralized, systems include:

- Bitcoin, a peer-to-peer electronic monetary system based on cryptography.

- Litecoin, originally based on the bitcoin protocol, intended to improve upon its alleged inefficiencies.

- Ripple monetary system, a monetary system based on trust networks.

- Dogecoin, a Litecoin-derived system meant by its author to reach broader demographics.

- Nxt, conceived as flexible platform to build applications and financial services around.

Hard vs. Soft Electronic Currencies

A *hard electronic currency* is one that does not have services to dispute or reverse charges. In other words, it is akin to cash in that it only supports non-reversible transactions. Reversing transactions, even in case of a legitimate error, unauthorized use, or failure of a vendor to supply goods is difficult, if not impossible. The advantage of this arrangement is that the operating costs of the electronic currency system are greatly reduced by not having to resolve payment disputes. Additionally, it allows the electronic currency transactions to clear instantly, making the funds available immediately to the recipient. This means that using hard electronic currency is more akin to a cash transaction. Examples are Western Union, KlickEx and Bitcoin.

A *soft electronic currency* is one that allows for reversal of payments, for example in case of fraud or disputes. Reversible payment methods generally have a "clearing time" of 72 hours or more. Examples are PayPal and credit card. A hard currency can be *softened* by using a trusted third party or an escrow service.

Electronic Bill Payment

Electronic bill payment is a feature of online, mobile and telephone banking, similar in its effect to a giro, allowing a customer of a financial institution to transfer money from their transaction or credit card account to a creditor or vendor such as a public utility, department store or an individual to be credited against a specific account. These payments are typically executed electronically as a direct deposit through a national payment system, operated by the banks or in conjunction with the government. Payment is typically initiated by the payer but can also be set up as a direct debit.

In addition to the bill payment facility, most banks will also offer various features with their electronic bill payment systems. These include the ability to schedule payments in advance to be made on a specified date (convenient for installments such as mortgage and support payments), to save the biller information for reuse at a future time and various options for searching the recent payment history. In many cases the payment data can also be downloaded and posted directly into the customer's accounting or personal finance software.

History

Although this technology was available from the mid 1990s, uptake was initially slow until internet access by households increased. By 2000, adoption of electronic bill payment systems started to dramatically increase.

Impact

From the consumers point of view, electronic payment of bills is cheaper, faster, and more convenient than writing, posting and reconciling cheques. In addition, though limitations exist, a wider range of bank accounts or credit cards can be used for the electronic payment of bills.

Using electronic bill presentment and payment enables businesses to fast-track customer payments and get access to funds faster, which in turn results in cash flow improvement.

For banks the advantages of electronic bill payments are a reduction in processing costs minimizing paperwork and an increase in customer loyalty. In a 2003 study, the banks said that "customers who pay online show more loyalty and are more receptive to other offers".

Electronic Signature

An electronic signature, or e-signature, refers to data in electronic form, which is logically associated with other data in electronic form and which is used by the signatory to sign. This type of signature provides the same legal standing as a handwritten signature as long as it adheres to the requirements of the specific regulation it was created under (e.g., eIDAS in the European Union, NIST-DSS in the USA or ZertES in Switzerland).

Increasingly, digital signatures are used in e-commerce and in regulatory filings to implement electronic signature in a cryptographically protected way. Standardization agencies like NIST or ETSI provide standards for their implementation (e.g., NIST-DSS, XAdES or PAdES). The concept itself is not new, with common law jurisdictions having recognized telegraph signatures as far back as the mid-19th century and faxed signatures since the 1980s.

Description

An electronic signature is intended to provide a secure and accurate identification method for the signatory to provide a seamless transaction. Definitions of electronic signatures vary depending on the applicable jurisdiction. A common denominator in most countries is the level of an advanced electronic signature requiring that:

1. The signatory can be uniquely identified and linked to the signature

2. The signatory must have sole control of the private key that was used to create the electronic signature

3. The signature must be capable of identifying if its accompanying data has been tampered with after the message was signed

4. In the event that the accompanying data has been changed, the signature must be invalidated

Electronic signatures may be created with increasing levels of security, with each having its own set of requirements and means of creation on various levels that prove the validity of the signature. To provide an even stronger probative value than the above described advanced electronic signature, some countries like the European Union or Switzerland introduced the qualified electronic signature. It is difficult to challenge the authorship of a statement signed with a qualified electronic signature - the statement is non-reputable. Technically, a qualified electronic signature is implemented through an advanced electronic signature that utilizes a digital certificate, which has been encrypted through a security signature-creating device and which has been authenticated by a qualified trust service provider.

In Contract Law

Since well before the American Civil War began in 1861, morse code was used to send messages electrically by telegraphy. Some of these messages were agreements to terms that were intended as enforceable contracts. An early acceptance of the enforceability of telegraphic messages as electronic signatures came from the New Hampshire Supreme Court in 1869.

In the 1980s, many companies and even some individuals began using fax machines for high-priority or time-sensitive delivery of documents. Although the original signature on the original document was on paper, the image of the signature and its transmission was electronic.

Courts in various jurisdictions have decided that enforceable electronic signatures can include agreements made by email, entering a personal identification number (PIN) into a bank ATM, signing a credit or debit slip with a digital pen pad device (an application of graphics tablet technology) at a point of sale, installing software with a clickwrap software license agreement on the package, and signing electronic documents online.

The first agreement signed electronically by two sovereign nations was a Joint Communiqué recognizing the growing importance of the promotion of electronic commerce, signed by the United States and Ireland in 1998.

Enforceability

In 1996 the United Nations published the UNCITRAL Model Law on Electronic Commerce. Article 7 of the UNCITRAL Model Law on Electronic Commerce was highly influential in the development of electronic signature laws around the world, including in the US. In 2001, UNCITRAL concluded work on a dedicated text, the UNCITRAL Model Law on Electronic Signatures, which has been adopted in some 30 jurisdictions. The latest UNCITRAL text dealing with electronic signatures is article 9, paragraph 3 of the United Nations Convention on the Use of Electronic Communications in International Contracts, 2005, which establishes a mechanism for functional equivalence between electronic and handwritten signatures at the international level as well as for the cross-border recognition.

Canadian law (PIPEDA) attempts to clarify the situation by first defining a generic electronic signature as "a signature that consists of one or more letters, characters, numbers or other symbols in digital form incorporated in, attached to or associated with an electronic document", then defining a secure electronic signature as an electronic signature with specific properties. PIPEDA's secure electronic signature regulations refine the definition as being a digital signature applied and verified in a specific manner.

In the European Union EU REGULATION No 910/2014 on electronic identification and trust services for electronic transactions in the European internal market (eIDAS) sets the legal frame for electronic signatures . It repeals Directive 1999/93/EC. The current and applicable version of eIDAS was published by the European Parliament and the European Council on July 23, 2014. Following Article 25 (1) of the eIDAS regulation, an advanced electronic signature shall "not be denied legal effect and admissibility as evidence in legal proceedings". However it will reach a higher probative value when enhanced to the level of a qualified electronic signature. By requiring the use of a qualified electronic signature creation device and being based on a certificate that has been issued by a qualified trust service provider, the upgraded advanced signature then carries according to Article 25 (2) of the eIDAS Regulation the same legal value as a handwritten signature. However, this is only regulated in the European Union and similarly through ZertES in Switzerland. A qualified electronic signature is not defined in the United States.

The U.S. Code defines an electronic signature for the purpose of US law as "an electronic sound, symbol, or process, attached to or logically associated with a contract or other record and executed or adopted by a person with the intent to sign the record." It may be an electronic transmission of the document which contains the signature, as in the case of facsimile transmissions, or it may be encoded message, such as telegraphy using Morse code.

In the United States, the definition of what qualifies as an electronic signature is wide and is set out in the Uniform Electronic Transactions Act ("UETA") released by the National Conference of Commissioners on Uniform State Laws (NCCUSL) in 1999. It was influenced by ABA committee white papers and the uniform law promulgated by NCCUSL. Under UETA, the term means "an electronic sound, symbol, or process, attached to or logically associated with a record and executed or adopted by a person with the intent to sign the record." This definition and many other core concepts of UETA are echoed in the U.S. ESign Act of 2000. 47 US states, the District of Columbia, and the US Virgin Islands have enacted UETA. Only New York, Washington State, and Illinois have not enacted UETA, but each of those states has adopted its own electronic signatures statute.

Legal Definitions

Various laws have been passed internationally to facilitate commerce by the use of electronic records and signatures in interstate and foreign commerce. The intent is to ensure the validity and legal effect of contracts entered into electronically. For instance,

PIPEDA (Canadian federal law)

> (1) An electronic signature is "a signature that consists of one or more letters, characters, numbers or other symbols in digital form incorporated in, attached to or associated with an electronic document";

> (2) A secure electronic signature is as an electronic signature that

> (a) is unique to the person making the signature;

> (b) the technology or process used to make the signature is under the sole control of the person making the signature;

> (c) the technology or process can be used to identify the person using the technology or process; and

> (d) the electronic signature can be linked with an electronic document in such a way that it can be used to determine whether the electronic document has been changed since the electronic signature was incorporated in, attached to or associated with the electronic document.

ESIGN Act Sec 106 (US federal law)

> (2) ELECTRONIC- The term 'electronic' means relating to technology having electrical, digital, magnetic, wireless, optical, electromagnetic, or similar capabilities.

> (4) ELECTRONIC RECORD- The term 'electronic record' means a contract or other record created, generated, sent, communicated, received, or stored by electronic means.

> (5) ELECTRONIC SIGNATURE- The term 'electronic signature' means an electronic sound, symbol, or process, attached to or logically associated with a contract or other record and executed or adopted by a person with the intent to sign the record.

GPEA Sec 1710 (US federal law)

> (1) ELECTRONIC SIGNATURE.—the term "electronic signature" means a method of signing an electronic message that—
>
> (A) identifies and authenticates a particular person as the source of the electronic message; and
>
> (B) indicates such person's approval of the information contained in the electronic message.

UETA Sec 2 (US state law)

> (5) "Electronic" means relating to technology having electrical, digital, magnetic, wireless, optical, electromagnetic, or similar capabilities.
>
> (6) "Electronic agent" means a computer program or an electronic or other automated means used independently to initiate an action or respond to electronic records or performances in whole or in part, without review or action by an individual.
>
> (7) "Electronic record" means a record created, generated, sent, communicated, received, or stored by electronic means.
>
> (8) "Electronic signature" means an electronic sound, symbol, or process attached to or logically associated with a record and executed or adopted by a person with the intent to sign the record.

Federal Reserve 12 CFR 202 (US federal regulation)

> refers to the ESIGN Act

Commodity Futures Trading Commission 17 CFR Part 1 Sec. 1.3 (US federal regulations)

> (tt) Electronic signature means an electronic sound, symbol, or process attached to or logically associated with a record and executed or adopted by a person with the intent to sign the record.

Food and Drug Administration 21 CFR Sec. 11.3 (US federal regulations)

> (5) Digital signature means an electronic signature based upon cryptographic methods of originator authentication, computed by using a set of rules and a set of parameters such that the identity of the signer and the integrity of the data can be verified.
>
> (7) Electronic signature means a computer data compilation of any symbol or series of symbols executed, adopted, or authorized by an individual to be the legally binding equivalent of the individual's handwritten signature.

United States Patent and Trademark Office 37 CFR Sec. 1.4 (federal regulation)

(d)(2) *S-signature.* An S-signature is a signature inserted between forward slash marks, but not a handwritten signature ... (i)The S-signature must consist only of letters, or Arabic numerals, or both, with appropriate spaces and commas, periods, apostrophes, or hyphens for punctuation... (e.g., /Dr. James T. Jones, Jr./)...

(iii) The signer's name must be:

(A) Presented in printed or typed form preferably immediately below or adjacent the S-signature, and

(B) Reasonably specific enough so that the identity of the signer can be readily recognized.

Laws Regarding their Use

- Australia - Electronic Transactions Act 1999 (which incorporates amendments from Electronic Transactions Amendment Act 2011), Section 10 - Signatures specifically relates to electronic signatures.

- Canada - PIPEDA, its regulations, and the Canada Evidence Act.

- China - Law of the People's Republic of China on Electronic Signature (effective April 1, 2005)

- Costa Rica - Digital Signature Law 8454 (2005)

- Croatia 2002, updated 2008

- Czech Republic – Zákon o elektronickém podpisu 227/2000 Sb.

- European Union - eIDAS regulation on implementation within the EU is set out in the Digital Signatures and the Law.

- India - Information Technology Act

- Ireland - Electronic Commerce Act 2000

- Japan - Law Concerning Electronic Signatures and Certification Services, 2000

- Mexico - E-Commerce Act

- New Zealand - Electronic Transactions Act 2002

- Paraguay - Ley 4017: De validez jurídica de la Firma Electrónica, la Firma Digital, los Mensajes de Datos y el Expediente Electrónico (12/23/2010) (Spanish), Ley 4610: Que modifica y amplia la Ley 4017/10 (05/07/2012) (Spanish)

- Peru - Ley N° 27269. Ley de Firmas y Certificados Digitales (28MAY2000) (Spanish)

- Philippines - Electronic Commerce Act of 2000

- Poland - Ustawa o podpisie elektronicznym (Dziennik Ustaw z 2001 r. Nr 130 poz. 1450)

- Romania - Legea nr. 455 din 18 iulie 2001 privind semnătura electronică

- Russian Federation - Federal Law of Russian Federation about Electronic Signature (06.04.2011)

- Singapore - Singapore Electronic Transactions Act (1998, 2010)

- Slovakia - Zákon č.215/2002 o elektronickom podpise

- Slovenia - Slovene Electronic Commerce and Electronic Signature Act

- South Africa - The Electronic Communications and Transactions Act 25, 2002

- Spain - Ley 59/2003, de 19 de diciembre, de firma electrónica

- Switzerland - ZertES

- Republika Srpska (entity of the Bosnia and Herzegovina) 2005

- Turkey - Electronic Signature Law

- Ukraine - Electronic Signature Law, 2003

- UK - s.7 Electronic Communications Act 2000

- U.S. - Electronic Signatures in Global and National Commerce Act

- U.S. - Uniform Electronic Transactions Act - adopted by 48 states

- U.S. - Digital Signature And Electronic Authentication Law

- U.S. - Government Paperwork Elimination Act (GPEA)

- U.S. - The Uniform Commercial Code (UCC)

Technological Implementations (Underlying Technology)

Digital Signatures

Digital signatures are cryptographic implementations of electronic signatures used as a proof of authenticity, data integrity and non-repudiation of communications conducted over the Internet. When implemented in compliance to digital signature standards, digital signing should offer end-to-end privacy with the signing process being user-friendly and secure. Digital signatures are generated and verified through standardized frameworks such as the Digital Signature Algorithm (DSA). by NIST or in compliance to the XAdES, PAdES or CAdES standards, specified by the ETSI.

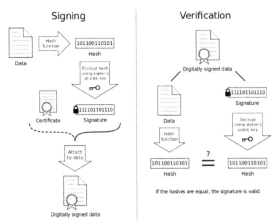

A diagram showing how a digital signature is applied and then verified.

There are typically three algorithms involved with the digital signature process:

- Key generation – This algorithm provides a private key along with its corresponding public key.

- Signing – This algorithm produces a signature upon receiving a private key and the message that is being signed.

- Verification – This algorithm checks for the authenticity of the message by verifying it along with the signature and public key.

The process of digital signing requires that the signature generated by both the fixed message and private key can then be authenticated by its accompanied public key. Using these cryptographic algorithms, the user's signature cannot be replicated without having access to their private key. A secure channel is not typically required. By applying asymmetric cryptography methods, the digital signature process prevents several common attacks where the attacker attempts to gain access through the following attack methods.

The most relevant standards on digital signatures with respect to size of domestic markets are the Digital Signature Standard (DSS) by the National Institute of Standards and Technology (NIST) and the eIDAS Regulation enacted by the European Parliament. OpenPGP is a non-proprietary protocol for email encryption through public key cryptography. It is supported by PGP and GnuPG, and some of the S/MIME IETF standards and has evolved into the most popular email encryption standard in the world.

Biometric Signatures

Electronic signature may also refer to electronic forms of processing or verifying identity through use of biometric "signatures" or biologically identifying qualities of an individual. Such signatures use the approach of attaching some biometric measurement, or hash of said measurement, to a document as evidence. For instance, fingerprints, hand geometry (finger lengths and palm size), iris patterns, or even retinal patterns. All of these are collected using electronic sensors of some kind. Since each of these physical characteristics has claims to uniqueness among humans, each is to some extent useful as a signature method.

Biometric measurements of this type are useless as passwords, as they can't be changed if compromised. However, they might be serviceable as electronic signatures of a kind - except that, to date they have been so easily spoofable that they can carry little assurance that the person who purportedly signed a document was actually the person who did. Unfortunately, each is easily spoofable by a replay of the electronic signal produced and submitted to the computer system responsible for 'affixing' a signature to a document. Wiretapping techniques often suffice for this. In the particular case of fingerprints, a Japanese professor and some graduate students managed to spoof all of the commercially available fingerprint readers available to them with some ordinary kitchen chemistry (gummy bear candy gel) and a little ingenuity. No actual fingers were needed to successfully spoof every reading device. In addition, some German journalists at a CeBit conference were able to fool several iris pattern scanners with improvised masks.

Electronic Ticket

An electronic ticket (commonly abbreviated as e-ticket) is a digital ticket. The term is most commonly associated with airline issued tickets. Electronic ticketing for urban or rail public transport is usually referred to as travel card or transit pass. It is also used in ticketing in the entertainment industry.

A sample itinerary for an open jaw electronic ticket from Montreal to Amsterdam, and returning from Munich

An electronic ticket system is a more efficient method of ticket entry, processing and marketing for companies in the railways, flight and other transport and entertainment industries.

Airline Ticket

Electronic ticketing in the airline industry was devised in about 1994. E-ticketing has largely replaced the older multi-layered paper ticketing systems, and since 1 June 2008, it has been mandatory for IATA members. Where paper tickets are still available, some airlines charge a fee for issuing paper tickets.

When a reservation is confirmed, the airline keeps a record of the booking in its computer reservations system. Customers can print out or are provided with a copy of their e-ticket itinerary receipt which contains the record locator or reservation number and the e-ticket number. It is possible to print multiple copies of an e-ticket itinerary receipt.

Besides providing itinerary details, an e-ticket itinerary receipt also contains:

- An official ticket number (including the airline's 3-digit ticketing code, a 4-digit form number, a 6-digit serial number, and sometimes a check digit).

- Carriage terms and conditions, (or at least a reference to them)

- Fare and tax details, including fare calculation details and some additional data such as tour codes. The exact cost might not be stated, but a "fare basis" code will always identify the fare used.

- A short summary of fare restrictions, usually specifying only whether change or refund are permitted but not the penalties to which they are subject.

- Form of payment.

- Issuing office.

- Baggage allowance.

Checking in with an E-ticket

To check in for a flight with an e-ticket, the passenger usually goes to the check-in counter in the usual manner. There they may be required to present some personal identification, a credit card or the e-ticket itinerary receipt. Theoretically it is not even necessary to present the e-ticket itinerary receipt document or quote the confirmation code or e-ticket number as the reservation is confirmed solely on the basis of the passenger's identity, which may be proven by a passport or the matching credit card. However, producing a print-out of the itinerary receipt is required to enter the terminal of some airports as well as to satisfy immigration regulations in most countries.

At the check-in counter, the passenger checks-in his/her luggage and receives a boarding pass. However, electronic ticketing allows various enhancements to checking-in.

Self-service and Remote Check-in

- online/telephone/self-service kiosk check-in (if the airline makes this option available)

- early check-in

- printing boarding passes at airport kiosks and at locations other than an airport

- delivery of boarding pass bar-codes via SMS or email to a mobile device

Several websites assist people holding e-tickets to check in online in advance of the twenty-four-hour airline restriction. These sites store a passenger's flight information and then when the airline opens up for online check-in the data is transferred to the airline and the boarding pass is emailed back to the customer. With this e-ticket technology, if a passenger receives his boarding pass remotely and is travelling without check-in luggage, he may bypass traditional counter check-in.

E-ticket Limitations

The ticketing systems of most airlines are only able to produce e-tickets for itineraries of no more than 16 segments, including surface segments. This is the same limit that applied to paper tickets.

Another critical limitation is that at the time e-tickets were initially designed, most airlines still practiced product bundling. By the time the industry began 100% e-ticket implementation, more and more airlines began to unbundle previously included services (like checked baggage) and add them back in as optional fees (ancillary revenue). However, the e-ticket standard did not anticipate and did not include a standardized mechanism for such optional fees.

IATA later implemented the Electronic Miscellaneous Document (EMD) standard for such information. This way, airlines could consistently expose and capture such fees at time of booking through travel reservation systems, rather than having to surprise passengers with them at check-in.

IATA Mandated Transition

As part of the IATA Simplifying the Business initiative, the association instituted a program to switch the industry to 100% electronic ticketing. The program concluded on June 1, 2008, with the association saying that the resulting industry savings were approximately US$3 billion.

In 2004, IATA Board of Governors set the end of 2007 as the deadline for airlines to make the transition to 100% electronic ticketing for tickets processed through the IATA billing and settlement plan; in June 2007, the deadline was extended to May 31, 2008.

As of June 1, 2008 paper tickets can no longer be issued on neutral stock by agencies reporting to their local BSP. Agents reporting to the ARC using company-provided stock or issuing tickets on behalf of an airline (GSAs and ticketing offices) are not subject to that restriction.

The industry was unable to comply with the IATA mandate and paper tickets remain in circulation as of February 2009.

Train Tickets

Amtrak started offering electronic tickets on all train routes on 30 July 2012. These tickets can be ordered over the internet and printed (as a PDF file), printed at a Quik-Trak kiosk, or at the ticket counter at the station. Electronic tickets can also be held in a smart phone and shown to the conductor using an app.

Several European train operators also offer self printable tickets. Often tickets can also be delivered as SMS or MMS. Railway operators in other countries also issue electronic tickets.

In India, an SMS sent by the Indian Railways, along with a valid proof of identity is considered equivalent to a ticket.

Sport & Concert Tickets

Many sport and concert venues offer electronic tickets to their events. Electronic tickets, or "eTickets" as they are sometimes referred, are often delivered as PDF's or another downloadable format that can be received via email or through a mobile app. Electronic tickets allow spectators to download their tickets, as opposed to waiting for physical tickets to arrive in the mail. A printed copy of these tickets or a digital copy on a mobile phone may be presented on coming to the venue. These tickets may also have a barcode, which may be scanned on entry into the venue to streamline crowd processing. Electronic tickets have become increasingly prevalent in the entertainment industry over the last decade.

Digital Economy

Digital economy refers to an economy that is based on digital computing technologies. The digital economy is also sometimes called the *Internet Economy*, the *New Economy*, or *Web Economy*. Increasingly, the "digital economy" is intertwined with the traditional economy making a clear delineation harder.

Definition

The term 'Digital Economy' was coined in Don Tapscott's 1995 best-seller *The Digital Economy: Promise and Peril in the Age of Networked Intelligence*. The Digital Economy was among the first books to show how the Internet would change the way we did business. It became an international best-seller within one month of its release, appearing on a number of best-seller lists, including the New York Times Business Book list and a seven-month run on the BusinessWeek best sellers list. BusinessWeek also named The Digital Economy the top selling business book for 1996.

According to Thomas Mesenbourg (2001), three main components of the 'Digital Economy' concept can be identified:

- supporting infrastructure (hardware, software, telecoms, networks, etc.),

- e-business (how business is conducted, any process that an organization conducts over computer-mediated networks),

- e-commerce (transfer of goods, for example when a book is sold online).

But, as Bill Imlah comments, new applications are blurring these boundaries and adding complexity – for example, social media, and Internet search.

In the last decade of the 20th century. Nicholas Negroponte (1995) used a metaphor of shifting from processing atoms to processing bits. He discussed the disadvantages of the former (e.g., mass, materials, transport) and advantages of the latter (e.g., weightlessness, virtual, instant global movement). In this new economy, digital networking and communication infrastructures provide a global platform over which people and organizations devise strategies, interact, communicate, collaborate and search for information. More recently, *Digital Economy* has been defined as the branch of economics studying zero marginal cost intangible goods over the Net.

Impact

It is widely accepted that the growth of the digital economy has widespread impact on the whole economy. Various attempts at categorising the size of the impact on traditional sectors have been made. The Boston Consulting Group discussed "four waves of change sweeping over consumer goods and retail", for instance. Deloitte ranked six industry sectors as having a "short fuse" and to experience a "big bang" as a result of the digital economy. Telstra, a leading Australian telecommunications provider, describes how competition will become more global and more intense as a result of the digital economy.

Response

Given its expected broad impact, traditional firms are actively assessing how to respond to the changes brought about by the digital economy. For corporations, timing of their response is of the essence. Banks are trying to innovate and use digital tools to improve their traditional business. Governments are investing in infrastructure. In 2013, the Australian National Broadband Network, for instance, aimed to provide a 1 GB/sec download speed fibre based broadband to 93% of the population over ten years.

Electronic Invoicing

Electronic invoicing (also called e-invoicing) is a form of electronic billing. E-invoicing methods are used by trading partners, such as customers and their suppliers, to present and monitor transactional documents between one another and ensure the terms of their trading agreements are being met. These documents include invoices, purchase orders, debit notes, credit notes, payment terms and instructions, and remittance slips.

E-invoicing includes a number of different technologies and entry options and is used as an umbrella term to describe any method by which an invoice is electronically presented to a customer for payment.

Purpose

The main responsibility of the accounts payable department is to ensure all outstanding invoices from its suppliers are approved, processed, and paid. Processing an invoice includes recording important data from the invoice and feeding it into the company's financial or bookkeeping systems. After the feed is accomplished, the invoices must go through the company's business process to be paid.

An e-invoice can be defined as structured invoice data issued in Electronic Data Interchange (EDI) or XML formats, possibly using Internet-based web forms. These documents can be exchanged in a number of ways including EDI, XML, or CSV files. They can be uploaded using emails, virtual printers, web applications, or FTP sites. The company may use imaging software to capture data from PDF or paper invoices and input it into their invoicing system. This streamlines the filing process while positively impacting sustainability efforts. Some companies have their own in-house e-invoicing process; however, many companies hire a third-party company to implement and support e-invoicing processes and to archive the data on their own servers.

History

Since the mid-1960s, companies began establishing data links with trading partners in order to transfer documents, such as invoices and purchase orders. Inspired by the idea of a paperless office and more reliable transfer of data, they developed the first EDI systems. These proprietary systems were fairly efficient, but rigid. Every set of trading partners seemed to have their own method of electronic data interchange. There was no standard that any trading partners could choose to adopt. Recognizing this, the Accredited Standards Committee X12, a standards institution under the umbrella of ANSI, moved to standardize EDI processes. The result is known today as the ANSI X12 EDI standard. This remained the main way to exchange transactional data between trading partners until the 1990s, when companies that offered more robust user interface web applications began to appear. These new web-based applications had functions that catered to both the supplier and customer. They allowed for online submission of individual invoices as well as EDI file uploads, including the CSV, PDF, and XML formats. These services allow suppliers to present invoices to their customers for matching and approval in a web application. Suppliers can also see a history of all the invoices they submitted to their customers without having direct access to the customers' systems. This is because all the transactional information is stored in the data centers of the third-party company that provides the invoicing web app. This transactional information can be regulated by the customer in order to control how much information the vendor is allowed to see.

As companies advance into the digital era, more and more are switching to electronic invoicing services to automate their accounts payable departments. The 2012 Global E-Invoicing Study illustrated the rate at which electronic invoicing is growing. According to the study, 73% of respondents used electronic invoicing to some degree in 2012, a 14% increase from 2011. Supplier resistance to e-invoicing has decreased from 46% in 2011 to 26% in 2012. According to a report done by the GXS in 2013, Europe is adopting government legislation encouraging businesses to adopt electronic invoicing practices. The United States treasury estimated that implementing e-invoicing across the entire federal government would reduce costs by 50% and save $450 million annually.

Usage

To enable e-invoicing, there must be an existing method of viewing the transactions, typically an ERP or accounting system. Routing and rules must be established in a project specification. This typically involves members of accounts payable, IT, and sometimes procurement. Once routing is established to the system, validation rules can be set up to reduce the amount of invoice exceptions. Further validation can be set up to automatically reject errors, three-way match invoices, purchase orders, and other documents. Validation can also notify suppliers of acceptance or rejections. Once the e-invoicing specification is finalized and testing is complete, the business's suppliers are connected electronically, and the e-invoicing system is ready.

Online Auction

An online auction is an auction which is held over the internet. Online auctions come in many different formats, but most popularly they are ascending English auctions, descending Dutch auctions, first-price sealed-bid, Vickrey auctions, or sometimes even a combination of multiple auctions, taking elements of one and forging them with another. The scope and reach of these auctions have been propelled by the Internet to a level beyond what the initial purveyors had anticipated. This is mainly because online auctions break down and remove the physical limitations of traditional auctions such as geography, presence, time, space, and a small target audience. This influx in reachability has also made it easier to commit unlawful actions within an auction. In 2002, online auctions were projected to account for 30% of all online e-commerce due to the rapid expansion of the popularity of the form of electronic commerce.

History

Online auctions were taking place even before the release of the first web browser for personal computers, NCSA Mosaic. Instead of users selling items through the Web they were instead trading through text-based newsgroups and email discussion lists. However, the first Web-based commercial activity regarding online auctions that made significant sales began in May 1995 with the company Onsale. In September that same year eBay also began trading.' Both of these companies used ascending bid. The Web offered new advantages such as the use of automated bids via electronic forms, a search engine to be able to quickly find items and the ability to allow users to view items by categories.

Online auctions have greatly increased the variety of goods and services that can be bought and sold using auction mechanisms along with expanding the possibilities for the ways auctions can be conducted and in general created new uses for auctions. In the current web environment there are hundreds, if not thousands, of websites dedicated to online auction practices.

Types of Online Auctions

There are six different basic types of online auctions:

English Auctions

In live terms, English auctions are where bids are announced by either an auctioneer or by the bidders and winners pay what they bid to receive the object. English auctions are claimed to be the most common form of third-party on-line auction format used and is deemed to appear the most simplistic of all the forms. The common operational method of the format is that it is an ascending bid auction in which bids are open for all to see. The winner is the highest bidder and the price is the highest bid. The popularity of the English auction is due to the fact that it uses a mechanism that people find familiar and intuitive and therefore reduces transaction costs. It also transcends the boundaries of a traditional English auction where physical presence is required by the bidders, making it increasingly popular even though there is a susceptibility to various forms of cheating.

Dutch Auctions

Dutch auctions are the reverse of English auctions whereby the price begins high and is systematically lowered until a buyer accepts the price. Dutch auction services are usually misleading and the term 'Dutch' tends to have become common usage for the use of a uniform-price rule in a single unit auction as opposed to how it is originally intended for that of a declining price auction. However, with actual on-line Dutch auctions where the price is descending, it was found that auctions have on average a 30% higher ending price than first-price auctions with speculation pointing to bidder impatience or the effect of endogenous entry on the Dutch auction.

First-price Sealed-bid

First-price sealed-bid auctions are when a single bid is made by all bidding parties and the single highest bidder wins, and pays what they bid. The main difference between this and English auctions is that bids are not openly viewable or announced as opposed to the competitive nature which is generated by public bids. From the game-theoretic point of view, the first-price sealed-bid auction is strategically equivalent to the Dutch auction; that is, in both auctions the players will be using the same bidding strategies.

Vickrey Auction

A Vickrey auction, sometimes known as a *second-price sealed-bid auction*, uses very much the same principle as a first-price sealed bid. However, the highest bidder and winner will only pay what the second highest bidder had bid. The Vickrey auction is suggested to prevent the incentive for buyers to bid strategically, due to the fact it requires them to speak the truth by giving their true value of the item.

Reverse Auction

Reverse auctions are where the roles of buyer and seller are reversed. Multiple sellers compete to obtain the buyer's business and prices typically decrease over time as new offers are made. They do not follow the typical auction format in that the buyer can see all the offers and may choose which they would prefer. Reverse auctions are used predominantly in a business context for procurement. Reverse auctions bring buyers and sellers together in a transparent marketplace. The practice has even been implemented for private jet travel on the online auction site Marmalade Skies. IP The term reverse auction is often confused with unique bid auctions, which are more akin to traditional auctions as there is only one seller and multiple buyers. However, they follow a similar price reduction concept except the lowest unique bid always wins, and each bid is confidential.

Bidding Fee Auction

A bidding fee auction (also known as a penny auction) requires customers to pay for bids, which they can increment an auction price one unit of currency at a time. On English auctions for example, the price goes up in 1 pence (0.01 GBP) increments. There has been criticism that compares this type of auction to gambling, as users can spend a considerable amount of money without receiving anything in return (other than the spent bids trying to acquire the item). The auction owner (typically the owner of the website) makes money in two ways, the purchasing of bids and the actual amount made from the final cost of the item.

Legalities

Shill Bidding

Placing fake bids that benefits the seller of the item is known as shill bidding. This is a method often used in Online auctions but can also happen in standard auctions. This is seen as an unlawful act as it unfairly raises the final price of the auction, so that the winning bidder pays more than they should have. If the shill bid is unsuccessful, the item owner needs to pay the auction fees. In 2011, a member of eBay became the first individual to be convicted of shill bidding on an auction. By taking part in the process, an individual is breaking the European Union fair trading rules which carries out a fine of up to £5,000 in the United Kingdom.

Fraud

The increasing popularity of using online auctions has led to an increase in fraudulent activity. This is usually performed on an auction website by creating a very appetising auction, such as a low starting amount. Once a buyer wins an auction and pays for it, the fradulent seller will either not pursue with the delivery, or send a less valuable version of the purchased item (replicated, used, refurbished, etc.). Protection to prevent such acts has become readily available, most notably Paypal's buyer protection policy. As Paypal handles the transaction, they have the ability to hold funds until a conclusion is drawn whereby the victim can be compensated.

Sale of Stolen Goods

Online auction websites are used by thieves or fences to sell stolen goods to unsuspecting buyers. According to police statistics there were over 8000 crimes involving stolen goods, fraud or deception reported on eBay in 2009. It has become common practice for organised criminals to steal in-demand items, often in bulk. These items are then sold online as it is a safer option due to the anonymity and worldwide market it provides. Auction fraud makes up a large percentage of complaints received by the FBI's Internet Crime Complaint Center (IC3). This was around 45% in 2006 and 63% in 2005.

Bidding Techniques

Auction Sniping

Auction sniping is a controversial bidding technique used in timed online auctions. It is the practice of placing a bid in the final stages of an auction with the aim of removing other bidder's ability to place another bid before the auction ends. These bids can either be placed by the bidder manually or automatically with the use of a tool. There are tools available that have been developed for this purpose. However, the use of these tools is the subject of much controversy.

There are two different approaches employed by sniping tools.

- Online: These are hosted on a remote server and are a service run by a third party.

- Local: This type is a script which can be downloaded onto the users computer which is then activated and run locally.

Online Advertising

Online advertising, also called online marketing or Internet advertising or web advertising, is a form of marketing and advertising which uses the Internet to deliver promotional marketing messages to consumers. Consumers view online advertising as an unwanted distraction with few benefits and have increasingly turned to ad blocking for a variety of reasons.

It includes email marketing, search engine marketing (SEM), social media marketing, many types of display advertising (including web banner advertising), and mobile advertising. Like other advertising media, online advertising frequently involves both a publisher, who integrates advertisements into its online content, and an advertiser, who provides the advertisements to be displayed on the publisher's content. Other potential participants include advertising agencies who help generate and place the ad copy, an ad server which technologically delivers the ad and tracks statistics, and advertising affiliates who do independent promotional work for the advertiser.

In 2011, Internet advertising revenues in the United States surpassed those of cable television and nearly exceeded those of broadcast television. In 2013, Internet advertising revenues in the United States totaled $42.8 billion, a 17% increase over the $36.57 billion in revenues in 2012. U.S. internet ad revenue hit a historic high of $20.1 billion for the first half of 2013, up 18% over the same period in 2012. Online advertising is widely used across virtually all industry sectors.

Many common online advertising practices are controversial and increasingly subject to regulation. Online ad revenues may not adequately replace other publishers' revenue streams. Declining ad revenue has led some publishers to hide their content behind paywalls.

History

In early days of the Internet, online advertising was mostly prohibited. For example, two of the predecessor networks to the Internet, ARPANET and NSFNet, had "acceptable use policies" that banned network "use for commercial activities by for-profit institutions". The NSFNet began phasing out its commercial use ban in 1991.

Email

The first widely publicized example of online advertising was conducted via electronic mail. On 3 May 1978, a marketer from DEC (Digital Equipment Corporation), Gary Thuerk, sent an email to most of the ARPANET's American west coast users, advertising an open house for a new model of a DEC computer. Despite the prevailing acceptable use policies, electronic mail marketing rapidly expanded and eventually became known as "spam."

The first known large-scale non-commercial spam message was sent on 18 January 1994 by an Andrews University system administrator, by cross-posting a religious message to all USENET newsgroups. Four months later, Laurence Canter and Martha Siegel, partners in a law firm, broadly promoted their legal services in a USENET posting titled "Green Card Lottery – Final One?" Canter and Siegel's Green Card USENET spam raised the profile of online advertising, stimulating widespread interest in advertising via both Usenet and traditional email. More recently, spam has evolved into a more industrial operation, where spammers use armies of virus-infected computers (botnets) to send spam remotely.

Display Ads

Online banner advertising began in the early 1990s as page owners sought additional revenue streams to support their content. Commercial online service Prodigy displayed banners at the bottom of the screen to promote Sears products. The first clickable web ad was sold by Global Network Navigator in 1993 to a Silicon Valley law firm. In 1994, web banner advertising became mainstream when HotWired, the online component of Wired Magazine, sold banner ads to AT&T and other companies. The first AT&T ad on HotWired had a 44% click-through rate, and instead of directing clickers to AT&T's website, the ad linked to an online tour of seven of the world's most acclaimed art museums.

Search Ads

GoTo.com (renamed Overture in 2001, and acquired by Yahoo! in 2003) created the first search advertising keyword auction in 1998. Google launched its "AdWords" search advertising program in 2000 and introduced quality-based ranking allocation in 2002, which sorts search advertisements by a combination of bid price and searchers' likeliness to click on the ads.

Recent Trends

More recently, companies have sought to merge their advertising messages into editorial content or valuable services. Examples include Red Bull's Red Bull Media House streaming Felix Baumgartner's jump from space online, Coca-Cola's online magazines, and Nike's free applications for performance tracking. Advertisers are also embracing social media and mobile advertising; mobile ad spending has grown 90% each year from 2010 to 2013.

Delivery Methods

Display Advertising

Display advertising conveys its advertising message visually using text, logos, animations, videos, photographs, or other graphics. Display advertisers frequently target users with particular traits to increase the ads' effect. Online advertisers (typically through their ad servers) often use cookies, which are unique identifiers of specific computers, to decide which ads to serve to a particular consumer. Cookies can track whether a user left a page without buying anything, so the advertiser can later retarget the user with ads from the site the user visited.

As advertisers collect data across multiple external websites about a user's online activity, they can create a detailed picture of the user's interests to deliver even more targeted advertising. This aggregation of data is called behavioral targeting. Advertisers can also target their audience by using contextual to deliver display ads related to the content of the web page where the ads appear. Retargeting, behavioral targeting, and contextual advertising all are designed to increase an advertiser's return on investment, or ROI, over untargeted ads.

Advertisers may also deliver ads based on a user's suspected geography through geotargeting. A user's IP address communicates some geographic information (at minimum, the user's country or general region). The geographic information from an IP can be supplemented and refined with other proxies or information to narrow the range of possible locations. For example, with mobile devices, advertisers can sometimes use a phone's GPS receiver or the location of nearby mobile towers. Cookies and other persistent data on a user's machine may provide help narrowing a user's location further.

Web Banner Advertising

Web banners or banner ads typically are graphical ads displayed within a web page. Many banner ads are delivered by a central ad server.

Banner ads can use rich media to incorporate video, audio, animations, buttons, forms, or other interactive elements using Java applets, HTML5, Adobe Flash, and other programs.

Frame Ad (Traditional Banner)

Frame ads were the first form of web banners. The colloquial usage of "banner ads" often refers to traditional frame ads. Website publishers incorporate frame ads by setting aside a particular space on the web page. The Interactive Advertising Bureau's Ad Unit Guidelines proposes standardized pixel dimensions for ad units.

Pop-ups/Pop-unders

A pop-up ad is displayed in a new web browser window that opens above a website visitor's initial browser window. A pop-under ad opens a new browser window under a website visitor's initial browser window. Pop-under ads and similar technologies are now advised against by online authorities such as Google, who state that they "do not condone this practice".

Floating Ad

A floating ad, or overlay ad, is a type of rich media advertisement that appears superimposed over the requested website's content. Floating ads may disappear or become less obtrusive after a preset time period.

Expanding Ad

An expanding ad is a rich media frame ad that changes dimensions upon a predefined condition, such as a preset amount of time a visitor spends on a webpage, the user's click on the ad, or the user's mouse movement over the ad. Expanding ads allow advertisers to fit more information into a restricted ad space.

Trick Banners

A trick banner is a banner ad where the ad copy imitates some screen element users commonly encounter, such as an operating system message or popular application message, to induce ad clicks. Trick banners typically do not mention the advertiser in the initial ad, and thus they are a form of bait-and-switch. Trick banners commonly attract a higher-than-average click-through rate, but tricked users may resent the advertiser for deceiving them.

News Feed Ads

"News Feed Ads", also called "Sponsored Stories", "Boosted Posts", typically exist on Social Media Platforms that offer a steady stream of information updates ("news feed") in regulated formats (i.e. in similar sized small boxes with a uniform style). Those advertisements are intertwined with non-promoted news that the users are reading through. Those advertisements can be of any content, such as promoting a website, a fan page, an app, or a product.

Some examples are: Facebook's "Sponsored Stories", LinkedIn's "Sponsored Updates", and Twitter's "Promoted Tweets".

This display ads format falls into its own category because unlike banner ads which are quite distinguishable, News Feed Ads' format blends well into non-paid news updates. This format of online advertisement yields much higher click-through rates than traditional display ads

Display Advertising Process Overview

The process by which online advertising is displayed can involve many parties. In the simplest case, the web site publisher selects and serves the ads. Publishers which operate their own advertising departments may use this method.

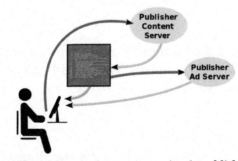

Online advertising serving process - simple publisher case

The ads may be outsourced to an advertising agency under contract with the publisher, and served from the advertising agency's servers.

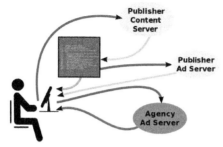

Online advertising serving process using an ad agency

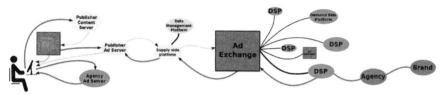

Online advertising serving process using online bidding

Alternatively, ad space may be offered for sale in a bidding market using an ad exchange and real-time bidding. This involves many parties interacting automatically in real time. In response to a request from the user's browser, the publisher content server sends the web page content to the user's browser over the Internet. The page does not yet contain ads, but contains links which cause the user's browser to connect to the publisher ad server to request that the spaces left for ads be filled in with ads. Information identifying the user, such as cookies and the page being viewed, is transmitted to the publisher ad server.

The publisher ad server then communicates with a supply-side platform server. The publisher is offering ad space for sale, so they are considered the supplier. The supply side platform also receives the user's identifying information, which it sends to a data management platform. At the data management platform, the user's identifying information is used to look up demographic information, previous purchases, and other information of interest to advertisers.

Broadly speaking, there are three types of data obtained through such a data management platform:

> *First party data* refers to the data retrieved from customer relationship management (CRM) platforms, in addition to website and paid media content or cross-platform data. This can include data from customer behaviors, actions or interests.

> *Second party data* refers to an amalgamation of statistics related to cookie pools on external publications and platforms. The data is provided directly from

the source (adservers, hosted solutions for social or an analytics platform). It is also possible to negotiate a deal with a particular publisher to secure specific data points or audiences.

Third party data is sourced from external providers and often aggregated from numerous websites. Businesses sell third-party data and are able to share this via an array of distribution avenues.

This customer information is combined and returned to the supply side platform, which can now package up the offer of ad space along with information about the user who will view it. The supply side platform sends that offer to an ad exchange.

The ad exchange puts the offer out for bid to demand-side platforms. Demand side platforms act on behalf of ad agencies, who sell ads which advertise brands. Demand side platforms thus have ads ready to display, and are searching for users to view them. Bidders get the information about the user ready to view the ad, and decide, based on that information, how much to offer to buy the ad space. According to the Internet Advertising Bureau, a demand side platform has 10 milliseconds to respond to an offer. The ad exchange picks the winning bid and informs both parties.

The ad exchange then passes the link to the ad back through the supply side platform and the publisher's ad server to the user's browser, which then requests the ad content from the agency's ad server. The ad agency can thus confirm that the ad was delivered to the browser.

This is simplified, according to the IAB. Exchanges may try to unload unsold ("remnant") space at low prices through other exchanges. Some agencies maintain semi-permanent pre-cached bids with ad exchanges, and those may be examined before going out to additional demand side platforms for bids. The process for mobile advertising is different and may involve mobile carriers and handset software manufacturers.

Interstitial

An interstitial ad displays before a user can access requested content, sometimes while the user is waiting for the content to load. Interstitial ads are a form of interruption marketing.

Text Ads

A text ad displays text-based hyperlinks. Text-based ads may display separately from a web page's primary content, or they can be embedded by hyperlinking individual words or phrases to advertiser's websites. Text ads may also be delivered through email marketing or text message marketing. Text-based ads often render faster than graphical ads and can be harder for ad-blocking software to block.

Search Engine Marketing (SEM)

Search engine marketing, or SEM, is designed to increase a website's visibility in search engine results pages (SERPs). Search engines provide sponsored results and organic (non-sponsored) results based on a web searcher's query. Search engines often employ visual cues to differentiate sponsored results from organic results. Search engine marketing includes all of an advertiser's actions to make a website's listing more prominent for topical keywords.

Search Engine Optimization (SEO)

Search engine optimization, or SEO, attempts to improve a website's organic search rankings in SERPs by increasing the website content's relevance to search terms. Search engines regularly update their algorithms to penalize poor quality sites that try to game their rankings, making optimization a moving target for advertisers. Many vendors offer SEO services.

Sponsored Search

Sponsored search (also called sponsored links, search ads, or paid search) allows advertisers to be included in the sponsored results of a search for selected keywords. Search ads are often sold via real-time auctions, where advertisers bid on keywords. In addition to setting a maximum price per keyword, bids may include time, language, geographical, and other constraints. Search engines originally sold listings in order of highest bids. Modern search engines rank sponsored listings based on a combination of bid price, expected click-through rate, keyword relevancy and site quality.

Social Media Marketing

Social media marketing is commercial promotion conducted through social media websites. Many companies promote their products by posting frequent updates and providing special offers through their social media profiles.

Mobile Advertising

Mobile advertising is ad copy delivered through wireless mobile devices such as smartphones, feature phones, or tablet computers. Mobile advertising may take the form of static or rich media display ads, SMS (Short Message Service) or MMS (Multimedia Messaging Service) ads, mobile search ads, advertising within mobile websites, or ads within mobile applications or games (such as interstitial ads, "advergaming," or application sponsorship). Industry groups such as the Mobile Marketing Association have attempted to standardize mobile ad unit specifications, similar to the IAB's efforts for general online advertising.

Mobile advertising is growing rapidly for several reasons. There are more mobile devices in the field, connectivity speeds have improved (which, among other things, allows for richer media ads to be served quickly), screen resolutions have advanced, mobile publishers are becoming more sophisticated about incorporating ads, and consumers are using mobile devices more extensively. The Interactive Advertising Bureau predicts continued growth in mobile advertising with the adoption of location-based targeting and other technological features not available or relevant on personal computers. In July 2014 Facebook reported advertising revenue for the June 2014 quarter of $2.68 billion, an increase of 67 percent over the second quarter of 2013. Of that, mobile advertising revenue accounted for around 62 percent, an increase of 41 percent on the previous year.

Email Advertising

Email advertising is ad copy comprising an entire email or a portion of an email message. Email marketing may be unsolicited, in which case the sender may give the recipient an option to opt out of future emails, or it may be sent with the recipient's prior consent (opt-in).

Chat Advertising

As opposed to static messaging, chat advertising refers to real time messages dropped to users on certain sites. This is done by the usage of live chat software or tracking applications installed within certain websites with the operating personnel behind the site often dropping adverts on the traffic surfing around the sites. In reality this is a subset of the email advertising but different because of its time window.

Online Classified Advertising

Online classified advertising is advertising posted online in a categorical listing of specific products or services. Examples include online job boards, online real estate listings, automotive listings, online yellow pages, and online auction-based listings. Craigslist and eBay are two prominent providers of online classified listings.

Adware

Adware is software that, once installed, automatically displays advertisements on a user's computer. The ads may appear in the software itself, integrated into web pages visited by the user, or in pop-ups/pop-unders. Adware installed without the user's permission is a type of malware.

Affiliate Marketing

Affiliate marketing (sometimes called lead generation) occurs when advertisers organize third parties to generate potential customers for them. Third-party affiliates receive payment based on sales generated through their promotion. Affiliate marketers generate traffic to offers from affiliate networks, and when the desired action is taken by the visitor, the affiliate earns a commission. These desired actions can be an email submission, a phone call, filling out an online form, or an online order being completed.

Content Marketing

Content marketing is any marketing that involves the creation and sharing of media and publishing content in order to acquire and retain customers. This information can be presented in a variety of formats, including blogs, news, video, white papers, e-books, infographics, case studies, how-to guides and more.

Considering that most marketing involves some form of published media, it is almost (though not entirely) redundant to call 'content marketing' anything other than simply 'marketing'. There are, of course, other forms of marketing (in-person marketing, telephone-based marketing, word of mouth marketing, etc.) where the label is more useful for identifying the type of marketing. However, even these are usually merely presenting content that they are marketing as information in a way that is different from traditional print, radio, TV, film, email, or web media.

Online Marketing Platform

Online marketing platform (OMP) is an integrated web-based platform that combines the benefits of a business directory, local search engine, search engine optimisation (SEO) tool, customer relationship management (CRM) package and content management system (CMS). Ebay and Amazon are used as online marketing and logistics management platforms. On Facebook, Twitter, YouTube, Pinterest, LinkedIn, and other Social Media, retail online marketing is also used. Online business marketing platforms such as Marketo, Aprimo, MarketBright and Pardot have been bought by major IT companies (Eloqua-Oracle, Neolane-Adobe and Unica-IBM).

Unlike television marketing in which Neilsen TV Ratings can be relied upon for viewing metrics, online advertisers do not have an independent party to verify viewing claims made by the big online platforms.

Compensation Methods

Advertisers and publishers use a wide range of payment calculation methods. In 2012, advertisers calculated 32% of online advertising transactions on a cost-per-impression basis, 66% on customer performance (e.g. cost per click or cost per acquisition), and 2% on hybrids of impression and performance methods.

CPM (Cost Per Mille)

Cost per mille, often abbreviated to CPM, means that advertisers pay for every thousand displays of their message to potential customers (mille is the Latin word for thousand). In the online context, ad displays are usually called "impressions." Definitions of an "impression" vary among publishers, and some impressions may not be charged because they don't represent a new exposure to an actual customer. Advertisers can use technologies such as web bugs to verify if an impression is actually delivered.

Publishers use a variety of techniques to increase page views, such as dividing content across multiple pages, repurposing someone else's content, using sensational titles, or publishing tabloid or sexual content.

CPM advertising is susceptible to "impression fraud," and advertisers who want visitors to their sites may not find per-impression payments a good proxy for the results they desire.

CPC (Cost Per Click)

CPC (Cost Per Click) or PPC (Pay per click) means advertisers pay each time a user clicks on the ad. CPC advertising works well when advertisers want visitors to their sites, but it's a less accurate measurement for advertisers looking to build brand awareness. CPC's market share has grown each year since its introduction, eclipsing CPM to dominate two-thirds of all online advertising compensation methods.

Like impressions, not all recorded clicks are valuable to advertisers. GoldSpot Media reported that up to 50% of clicks on static mobile banner ads are accidental and resulted in redirected visitors leaving the new site immediately.

CPE (Cost Per Engagement)

Cost per engagement aims to track not just that an ad unit loaded on the page (i.e., an impression was served), but also that the viewer actually saw and/or interacted with the ad.

CPV (Cost Per View)

Cost per view video advertising. Both Google and TubeMogul endorsed this standardized CPV metric to the IAB's (Interactive Advertising Bureau) Digital Video Committee, and it's garnering a notable amount of industry support. CPV is the primary benchmark used in YouTube Advertising Campaigns, as part of Google's AdWords platform.

CPI (Cost Per Install)

The CPI compensation method is specific to mobile applications and mobile advertising. In CPI ad campaigns brands are charged a fixed of bid rate only when the application was installed.

Attribution of Ad Value

In marketing, "attribution" is the measurement of effectiveness of particular ads in a consumer's ultimate decision to purchase. Multiple ad impressions may lead to a consumer "click" or other action. A single action may lead to revenue being paid to multiple ad space sellers.

Other Performance-based Compensation

CPA (Cost Per Action or Cost Per Acquisition) or PPP (Pay Per Performance) advertising means the advertiser pays for the number of users who perform a desired activity, such as completing a purchase or filling out a registration form. Performance-based compensation can also incorporate revenue sharing, where publishers earn a percentage of the advertiser's profits made as a result of the ad. Performance-based compensation shifts the risk of failed advertising onto publishers.

Fixed Cost

Fixed cost compensation means advertisers pay a fixed cost for delivery of ads online, usually over a specified time period, irrespective of the ad's visibility or users' response to it. One examples is CPD (cost per day) where advertisers pay a fixed cost for publishing an ad for a day irrespective of impressions served or clicks.

Benefits of Online Advertising

Cost

The low costs of electronic communication reduce the cost of displaying online advertisements compared to offline ads. Online advertising, and in particular social media, provides a low-cost means for advertisers to engage with large established communities. Advertising online offers better returns than in other media.

Measurability

Online advertisers can collect data on their ads' effectiveness, such as the size of the potential audience or actual audience response, how a visitor reached their advertisement, whether the advertisement resulted in a sale, and whether an ad actually loaded within a visitor's view. This helps online advertisers improve their ad campaigns over time.

Formatting

Advertisers have a wide variety of ways of presenting their promotional messages, including the ability to convey images, video, audio, and links. Unlike many offline ads, online ads also can be interactive. For example, some ads let users input queries or let users follow the advertiser on social media. Online ads can even incorporate games.

Targeting

Publishers can offer advertisers the ability to reach customizable and narrow market segments for targeted advertising. Online advertising may use geo-targeting to display relevant advertisements to the user's geography. Advertisers can customize each individual ad to a particular user based on the user's previous preferences. Advertisers can also track whether a visitor has already seen a particular ad in order to reduce unwanted repetitious exposures and provide adequate time gaps between exposures.

Coverage

Online advertising can reach nearly every global market, and online advertising influences offline sales.

Speed

Once ad design is complete, online ads can be deployed immediately. The delivery of online ads does not need to be linked to the publisher's publication schedule. Furthermore, online advertisers can modify or replace ad copy more rapidly than their offline counterparts.

Concerns

Security Concerns

According to a US Senate investigation, the current state of online advertising endangers the security and privacy of users.

Banner Blindness

Eye-tracking studies have shown that Internet users often ignore web page zones likely to contain display ads (sometimes called "banner blindness"), and this problem is worse online than in offline media. On the other hand, studies suggest that even those ads "ignored" by the users may influence the user subconsciously.

Fraud on the Advertiser

There are numerous ways that advertisers can be overcharged for their advertising. For example, click fraud occurs when a publisher or third parties click (manually or through automated means) on a CPC ad with no legitimate buying intent. For example, click fraud can occur when a competitor clicks on ads to deplete its rival's advertising budget, or when publishers attempt to manufacture revenue.

Click fraud is especially associated with pornography sites. In 2011, certain scamming porn websites launched dozens of hidden pages on each visitor's computer, forcing the visitor's computer to click on hundreds of paid links without the visitor's knowledge.

As with offline publications, online impression fraud can occur when publishers over-state the number of ad impressions they have delivered to their advertisers. To combat impression fraud, several publishing and advertising industry associations are developing ways to count online impressions credibly.

Technological Variations

Heterogeneous Clients

Because users have different operating systems, web browsers and computer hardware (including mobile devices and different screen sizes), online ads may appear to users differently from how the advertiser intended, or the ads may not display properly at all. A 2012 comScore study revealed that, on average, 31% of ads were not "in-view" when rendered, meaning they never had an opportunity to be seen. Rich media ads create even greater compatibility problems, as some developers may use competing (and exclusive) software to render the ads.

Furthermore, advertisers may encounter legal problems if legally required information doesn't actually display to users, even if that failure is due to technological heterogeneity. In the United States, the FTC has released a set of guidelines indicating that it's the advertisers' responsibility to ensure the ads display any required disclosures or disclaimers, irrespective of the users' technology.

Ad-blocking

Ad-blocking, or ad filtering, means the ads do not appear to the user because the user uses technology to screen out ads. Many browsers block unsolicited pop-up ads by default. Other software programs or browser add-ons may also block the loading of ads, or block elements on a page with behaviors characteristic of ads (e.g. HTML autoplay of both audio and video). Approximately 9% of all online page views come from browsers with ad-blocking software installed, and some publishers have 40%+ of their visitors using ad-blockers.

Anti-targeting Technologies

Some web browsers offer privacy modes where users can hide information about themselves from publishers and advertisers. Among other consequences, advertisers can't use cookies to serve targeted ads to private browsers. Most major browsers have incorporated Do Not Track options into their browser headers, but the regulations currently are only enforced by the honor system.

Privacy Concerns

The collection of user information by publishers and advertisers has raised consumer concerns about their privacy. Sixty percent of Internet users would use Do Not Track technology to block all collection of information if given an opportunity. Over half of all Google and Facebook users are concerned about their privacy when using Google and Facebook, according to *Gallup*.

Many consumers have reservations about online behavioral targeting. By tracking users' online activities, advertisers are able to understand consumers quite well. Advertisers often use technology, such as web bugs and respawning cookies, to maximizing their abilities to track consumers. According to a 2011 survey conducted by Harris Interactive, over half of Internet users had a negative impression of online behavioral advertising, and forty percent feared that their personally-identifiable information had been shared with advertisers without their consent. Consumers can be especially troubled by advertisers targeting them based on sensitive information, such as financial or health status.

Trustworthiness of Advertisers

Scammers can take advantage of consumers' difficulties verifying an online persona's identity, leading to artifices like phishing (where scam emails look identical to those from a well-known brand owner) and confidence schemes like the Nigerian "419" scam. The Internet Crime Complaint Center received 289,874 complaints in 2012, totaling over half a billion dollars in losses, most of which originated with scam ads.

Consumers also face malware risks, i.e. malvertising, when interacting with online advertising. Cisco's 2013 Annual Security Report revealed that clicking on ads was 182 times more likely to install a virus on a user's computer than surfing the Internet for porn. For example, in August 2014 Yahoo's advertising network reportedly saw cases of infection of a variant of Cryptolocker ransomware.

Spam

The Internet's low cost of disseminating advertising contributes to spam, especially by large-scale spammers. Numerous efforts have been undertaken to combat spam, ranging from blacklists to regulatorily-required labeling to content filters, but most of those efforts have adverse collateral effects, such as mistaken filtering.

Regulation

In general, consumer protection laws apply equally to online and offline activities.[i] However, there are questions over which jurisdiction's laws apply and which regulatory agencies have enforcement authority over transborder activity.

As with offline advertising, industry participants have undertaken numerous efforts to self-regulate and develop industry standards or codes of conduct. Several United States advertising industry organizations jointly published *Self-Regulatory Principles for Online Behavioral Advertising* based on standards proposed by the FTC in 2009.

European ad associations published a similar document in 2011. Primary tenets of both documents include consumer control of data transfer to third parties, data security, and consent for collection of certain health and financial data. Neither framework, however, penalizes violators of the codes of conduct.

Privacy and Data Collection

Privacy regulation can require users' consent before an advertiser can track the user or communicate with the user. However, affirmative consent ("opt in") can be difficult and expensive to obtain. Industry participants often prefer other regulatory schemes.

Different jurisdictions have taken different approaches to privacy issues with advertising. The United States has specific restrictions on online tracking of children in the Children's Online Privacy Protection Act (COPPA), and the FTC has recently expanded its interpretation of COPPA to include requiring ad networks to obtain parental consent before knowingly tracking kids. Otherwise, the U.S. Federal Trade Commission frequently supports industry self-regulation, although increasingly it has been undertaking enforcement actions related to online privacy and security. The FTC has also been pushing for industry consensus about possible Do Not Track legislation.

In contrast, the European Union's "Privacy and Electronic Communications Directive" restricts websites' ability to use consumer data much more comprehensively. The EU limitations restrict targeting by online advertisers; researchers have estimated online advertising effectiveness decreases on average by around 65% in Europe relative to the rest of the world.

Delivery Methods

Many laws specifically regulate the ways online ads are delivered. For example, online advertising delivered via email is more regulated than the same ad content delivered via banner ads. Among other restrictions, the U.S. CAN-SPAM Act of 2003 requires that any commercial email provide an opt-out mechanism. Similarly, mobile advertising is governed by the Telephone Consumer Protection Act of 1991 (TCPA), which (among other restrictions) requires user opt-in before sending advertising via text messaging.

Electronic Publishing

Electronic publishing (also referred to as e-publishing or digital publishing or online publishing) includes the digital publication of e-books, digital magazines, and the development of digital libraries and catalogues. Electronic publishing has become common in scientific publishing where it has been argued that peer-reviewed scientific journals are in the process of being replaced by electronic publishing. It is also becoming common to distribute books, magazines, and newspapers to consumers through tablet reading devices, a market that is growing by millions each year, generated by online vendors such as Apple's iTunes bookstore, Amazon's bookstore for Kindle, and books in the Google Play Bookstore. Market research suggests that half of all magazine and newspaper circulation will be via digital delivery by the end of 2015 and that half of all reading in the United States will be done without paper by 2015.

Although distribution via the Internet (also known as online publishing or web publishing when in the form of a website) is nowadays strongly associated with electronic publishing, there are many non network electronic publications such as Encyclopedias on CD and DVD, as well as technical and reference publications relied on by mobile users and others without reliable and high speed access to a network. Electronic publishing is also being used in the field of test-preparation in developed as well as in developing economies for student education (thus partly replacing conventional books) - for it enables content and analytics combined - for the benefit of students. The use of electronic publishing for textbooks may become more prevalent with iBooks from Apple Inc. and Apple's negotiation with the three largest textbook suppliers in the U.S. Electronic publishing is increasingly popular in works of fiction. Electronic publishers are able to respond quickly to changing market demand, because the companies do not have to order printed books and have them delivered. E-publishing is also making a wider range of books available, including books that customers would not find in standard book retailers, due to insufficient demand for a traditional "print run". As well, e-publication is enabling new authors to release books that would be unlikely to be profitable for traditional publishers. While the term "electronic publishing" is primarily used in the 2010s to refer to online and web-based publishers, the term has a history of being used to describe the development of new forms of production, distribution, and user interaction in regards to computer-based production of text and other interactive media.

Process

The electronic publishing process follows some aspects of the traditional paper-based publishing process but differs from traditional publishing in two ways: 1) it does not include using an offset printing press to print the final product and 2) it avoids the distribution of a physical product (e.g., paper books, paper magazines, or paper newspapers). Because the content is electronic, it may be distributed over the Internet and through electronic bookstores, and users can read the material on a range of electronic and digital devices, including desktop computers, laptops, tablet computers, smartphones or e-reader tablets. The consumer may read the published content online a website, in an application on a tablet device, or in a PDF document on a computer. In some cases, the reader may print the content onto paper using a consumer-grade ink-jet or laser printer or via a print on demand system. Some users download digital content to their devices, enabling them to read the content even when their device is not connected to the Internet (e.g., on an airplane flight).

Distributing content electronically as software applications ("apps") has become popular in the 2010s, due to the rapid consumer adoption of smartphones and tablets. At first, native apps for each mobile platform were required to reach all audiences, but in an effort toward universal device compatibility, attention has turned to using HTML5 to create web apps that can run on any browser and function on many devices. The benefit of electronic publishing comes from using three attributes of digital technology: XML tags to define content, style sheets to define the look of content, and metadata (data about data) to describe the content for search engines, thus helping users to find and locate the content (a common example of metadata is the information about a song's songwriter, composer, genre that is electronically encoded along with most CDs and digital audio files; this metadata makes it easier for music lovers to find the songs they are looking for). With the use of tags, style sheets, and metadata, this enables "reflowable" content that adapts to various reading devices (tablet, smartphone, e-reader, etc.) or electronic delivery methods.

Because electronic publishing often requires text mark-up (e.g., Hyper Text Markup Language or some other markup language) to develop online delivery methods, the traditional roles of typesetters and book designers, who created the printing set-ups for paper books, have changed. Designers of digitally published content must have a strong knowledge of mark-up languages, the variety of reading devices and computers available, and the ways in which consumers read, view or access the content. However, in the 2010s, new user friendly design software is becoming available for designers to publish content in this standard without needing to know detailed programming techniques, such as Adobe Systems' Digital Publishing Suite and Apple's iBooks Author. The most common file format is .epub, used in many e-book formats. .epub is a free and open standard available in many publishing programs. Another common format is .folio, which is used by the Adobe Digital Publishing Suite to create content for Apple's iPad tablets and apps.

Academic Publishing

After an article is submitted to an academic journal for consideration, there can be a delay ranging from several months to more than two years before it is published in a journal, rendering journals a less than ideal format for disseminating current research. In some fields such as astronomy and some parts of physics, the role of the journal in disseminating the latest research has largely been replaced by preprint repositories such as arXiv.org. However, scholarly journals still play an important role in quality control and establishing scientific credit. In many instances, the electronic materials uploaded to preprint repositories are still intended for eventual publication in a peer-reviewed journal. There is statistical evidence that electronic publishing provides wider dissemination, because when a journal is available online, a larger number of researchers can access the journal. Even if a professor is working in a university that does not have a certain journal in its library, she may still be able to access the journal online. A number of journals have, while retaining their longstanding peer review process to ensure that the research is done properly, established electronic versions or even moved entirely to electronic publication.

Copyright

In the early 2000s, many of the existing copyright laws were designed around printed books, magazines and newspapers. For example, copyright laws often set out limits on how much of a book can be mechanically reproduced or copied. Electronic publishing raises new questions in relation to copyright, because if an e-book or e-journal is available online, millions of Internet users may be able to view a single electronic copy of the document, without any "copies" being made. Emerging evidence suggests that e-publishing may be more collaborative than traditional paper-based publishing; e-publishing often involves more than one author, and the resulting works are more accessible, since they is published online. At the same time, the availability of published material online opens up more doors for plagiarism or unauthorized use or re-use of the material. Some publishers are trying to address these concerns. For example, in 2011, HarperCollins limited the number of times that one of its e-books can be lent in a public library. Other publishers, such as Penguin, are attempting to incorporate e-book elements into their regular paper publications.

Examples

Electronic versions of traditional media:

- CD-ROM
- E-book
- Electronic journal
- Online magazine
- Online newspaper
- PDF

New media:

- Blog
- Collaborative software
- Digital publication app
- File sharing
- Mobile apps
- Podcast
- Enhanced publication

Business Models

- Digital distribution
- Online advertising
- Open access (publishing)
- Pay-per-view
- Print on demand
- Subscriptions
- Self-publishing
- Non-subsidy publishing

Online Marketplace

An online marketplace (or online e-commerce marketplace) is a type of e-commerce site where product or service information is provided by multiple third parties, whereas transactions are processed by the marketplace operator. Online marketplaces are the primary type of multichannel ecommerce and can be described as a "simple and convenient portal" to streamline the production process.

In an online marketplace, consumer transactions are processed by the marketplace operator and then delivered and fulfilled by the participating retailers or wholesalers (often called drop shipping). Other capabilities might include auctioning (forward or reverse), catalogs, ordering, wanted advertisement, trading exchange functionality and capabilities like RFQ, RFI or RFP. These type of sites allow users to register and sell single items to a large number of items for a "post-selling" fee.

In general, because marketplaces aggregate products from a wide array of providers, selection is usually more wide, and availability is higher than in vendor-specific online retail stores. Also prices may be more competetive.

Since 2014, online marketplaces are abundant since organized marketplaces are sought after. Some have a wide variety of general interest products that cater to almost all the needs of the consumers, however, some are consumer specific and cater to a particular segment only. Not only is the platform for selling online, but the user interface and user experience matters. People tend to log on to online marketplaces that are organized and products are much more accessible to them.

For Services and Outsourcing

There are marketplaces for the online outsourcing of professional services like IT services, search engine optimization, marketing, crowdsourcing, and skilled crafts & trades work.

Criticism

Many service related online marketplaces have been criticized for taking jobs that would go to local industries that can't compete on price against outsourced providers.

Another criticism is that the laws and regulations surrounding online marketplaces are quite underdeveloped. As of consequence, there is a discrepancy between the responsibility, accountability and liability of the marketplace and third parties. Online marketplaces and platforms have faced much criticism in recent years for their lack of consumer protections.

NetMarket

NetMarket is an online marketplace owned by Trilegiant that sells various goods ranging from electronics to jewelry. It was founded in 1994 by Daniel Kohn and Roger Lee, both former London School of Economics students and by Guy H. T. Haskin and Eiji Hirai from Swarthmore College. The *New York Times* has credited the company with performing the first secure retail transaction on the Internet.

History

NetMarket was initially conceived by Daniel Kohn while he was studying at the London School of Economics after finishing an honors degree in economics from Swarthmore College. He recruited classmate and Yale graduate Roger Lee to become president of the company. The company's management team was rounded out by Guy H. T. Haskin and Eiji Hirai, both from Swarthmore, and both hired for their technical skills. The firm's initial headquarters was a house in Nashua, New Hampshire. It started out selling goods such as CDs and books for various offline stores using non-digital payments.

On August 11, 1994, NetMarket sold *Ten Summoner's Tales*, a CD by Sting, to Phil Brandenberger of Philadelphia using a credit card over the Internet. The *New York Times* characterized this as "...apparently the first retail transaction on the Internet using a readily available version of powerful data encryption software designed to guarantee privacy." The encryption used in the transaction was provided by the Pretty Good Privacy (PGP) program, incorporated into the X Mosiac browser. The author of PGP, Phil Zimmermann, called the transaction an important step towards the creation of digital cash.

NetMarket was soon purchased by CUC International and despite expectations to the contrary, continued to be successful. While general online malls were superseded by specialty shops and forced to close, NetMarket continued to expand the range of its inventory. In 1997 the chairman of CUC estimated the company could fill approximately

20% of a family's retail needs with that number going up to 95% in three years. The company was also profitable, estimating doing more than $1 billion in sales in 1998. *The Economist* called NetMarket's business model the third wave of online retailing - one site providing goods found in an entire mall, but focused on the efficiency and low prices provided by specialized retailers. Also in 1997, CUC paid America Online $50 million to set up and promote NetMarket's services on AOL's Shopping Channel.

In 1999, NetMarket, now owned by Cendant, had its ordering system breached due to a bug in its software. Customer names, addresses, and phone numbers could have been shown publicly along with order details for as many as 983,000 orders stretching back to June 1998.

NetMarket was spun off by Cendant in 2001 under a new parent company, Trilegiant.

Online Shopping

A screenshot from an online store's website.

Online shopping is a form of electronic commerce which allows consumers to directly buy goods or services from a seller over the Internet using a web browser. Consumers find a product of interest by visiting the website of the retailer directly or by searching among alternative vendors using a shopping search engine, which displays the same product's availability and pricing at different e-retailers. As of 2016, customers can shop online using a range of different computers and devices, including desktop computers, laptops, tablet computers and smartphones.

An online shop evokes the physical analogy of buying products or services at a regular "bricks-and-mortar" retailer or shopping center; the process is called business-to-consumer (B2C) online shopping. When an online store is set up to enable businesses to buy from another businesses, the process is called business-to-business (B2B) online shopping. A typical online store enables the customer to browse the firm's range of products and services, view photos or images of the products, along with information about the product specifications, features and prices.

Online stores typically enable shoppers to use "search" features to find specific models, brands or items. Online customers must have access to the Internet and a valid method of payment in order to complete a transaction, such as a credit card, an Interac-enabled debit card, or a service such as PayPal. For physical products (e.g., paperback books or clothes), the e-tailer ships the products to the customer; for digital products, such as digital audio files of songs or software, the e-tailer typically sends the file to the customer over the Internet. The largest of these online retailing corporations are Alibaba, Amazon.com, and eBay.

Terminology

Alternative names for the activity are "e-tailing", a shortened form of "electronic retail" or "e-shopping", a shortened form of "electronic shopping". An online store may also be called an e-web-store, e-shop, e-store, Internet shop, web-shop, web-store, online store, online storefront and virtual store. Mobile commerce (or m-commerce) describes purchasing from an online retailer's mobile device-optimized website or software application ("app"). These websites or apps are designed to enable customers to browse through a companies' products and services on tablet computers and smartphones.

History

Michael Aldrich, pioneer of online shopping in the 1980s.

English entrepreneur Michael Aldrich was a pioneer of online shopping in 1979. His system connected a modified domestic TV to a real-time transaction processing computer via a domestic telephone line. He believed that videotex, the modified domestic TV technology with a simple menu-driven human–computer interface, was a 'new, universally applicable, participative communication medium — the first since the invention of the telephone.' This enabled 'closed' corporate information systems to be opened to 'outside' correspondents not just for transaction processing but also for e-messaging and information retrieval and dissemination, later known as e-business. His definition of the new mass communications medium as 'participative' [interactive, many-to-many] was fundamentally different from the traditional definitions of mass communication and mass media and a precursor to the social networking on the Internet 25 years later. In March 1980 he launched Redifon's Office Revolution, which allowed consumers, customers, agents, distributors, suppliers and service companies to be connected on-line to the corporate systems and allow business transactions to be completed electronically in real-time. During the 1980s he designed, manufactured, sold, installed, maintained and supported many online shopping systems, using videotex technology. These systems which also provided voice response and handprint processing pre-date the Internet and the World Wide Web, the IBM PC, and Microsoft MS-DOS, and were installed mainly in the UK by large corporations.

The first World Wide Web server and browser, created by Tim Berners-Lee in 1990, opened for commercial use in 1991. Thereafter, subsequent technological innovations emerged in 1994: online banking, the opening of an online pizza shop by Pizza Hut, Netscape's SSL v2 encryption standard for secure data transfer, and Intershop's first online shopping system. The first secure retail transaction over the Web was either by NetMarket or Internet Shopping Network in 1994. Immediately after, Amazon.com launched its online shopping site in 1995 and eBay was also introduced in 1995. Alibaba's sites Taobao and Tmall were launched in 2003 and 2008, respectively. Retailers are increasingly selling goods and services prior to availability through "pretail" for testing, building, and managing demand.

International Statistics

Statistics show that in 2012, Asia-Pacific increased their international sales over 30% giving them over $433 billion in revenue. That is a $69 billion difference between the U.S. revenue of $364.66 billion. It is estimated that Asia-Pacific will increase by another 30% in the year 2013 putting them ahead by more than one-third of all global ecommerce sales.The largest online shopping day in the world is Singles Day, with sales just in Alibaba's sites at US$9.3 billion in 2014.

Customers

Online customers must have access to the Internet and a valid method of payment in order to complete a transaction. Generally, higher levels of education and personal income correspond to more favorable perceptions of shopping online. Increased exposure to technology also increases the probability of developing favorable attitudes towards new shopping channels. In a December 2011 study, Equation Research surveyed 1,500 online shoppers and found that 87% of tablet owners made online transactions with their tablet devices during the early Christmas shopping season.

Product Selection

Consumers find a product of interest by visiting the website of the retailer directly or by searching among alternative vendors using a shopping search engine. Once a particular product has been found on the website of the seller, most online retailers use shopping cart software to allow the consumer to accumulate multiple items and to adjust quantities, like filling a physical shopping cart or basket in a conventional store. A "checkout" process follows (continuing the physical-store analogy) in which payment and delivery information is collected, if necessary. Some stores allow consumers to sign up for a permanent online account so that some or all of this information only needs to be entered once. The consumer often receives an e-mail confirmation once the transaction is complete. Less sophisticated stores may rely on consumers to phone or e-mail their orders (although full credit card numbers, expiry date, and Card Security Code, or bank account and routing number should not be accepted by e-mail, for reasons of security).

Payment

Online shoppers commonly use a credit card or a PayPal account in order to make payments. However, some systems enable users to create accounts and pay by alternative means, such as:

- Billing to mobile phones and landlines

- Cash on delivery (C.O.D.)

- Cheque/ Check

- Debit card

- Direct debit in some countries

- Electronic money of various types

- Gift cards

- Postal money order

- Wire transfer/delivery on payment

- Invoice, especially popular in some markets/countries, such as Switzerland

- Bitcoin or other cryptocurrencies

Some online shops will not accept international credit cards. Some require both the purchaser's billing and shipping address to be in the same country as the online shop's base of operation. Other online shops allow customers from any country to send gifts anywhere. The financial part of a transaction may be processed in real time (e.g. letting the consumer know their credit card was declined before they log off), or may be done later as part of the fulfillment process.

Product Delivery

Once a payment has been accepted, the goods or services can be delivered in the following ways. For physical items:

- Shipping: The product is shipped to a customer-designated address. Retail package delivery is typically done by the public postal system or a retail courier such as FedEx, UPS, DHL, or TNT.

- Drop shipping: The order is passed to the manufacturer or third-party distributor, who then ships the item directly to the consumer, bypassing the retailer's physical location to save time, money, and space.

- In-store pick-up: The customer selects a local store using a locator software and picks up the delivered product at the selected location. This is the method often used in the bricks and clicks business model.

For digital items or tickets:

- Downloading/Digital distribution: The method often used for digital media products such as software, music, movies, or images.

- Printing out, provision of a code for, or e-mailing of such items as admission tickets and scrip (e.g., gift certificates and coupons). The tickets, codes, or coupons may be redeemed at the appropriate physical or online premises and their content reviewed to verify their eligibility (e.g., assurances that the right of admission or use is redeemed at the correct time and place, for the correct dollar amount, and for the correct number of uses).

- Will call, COBO (in Care Of Box Office), or "at the door" pickup: The patron picks up pre-purchased tickets for an event, such as a play, sporting event, or concert, either just before the event or in advance. With the onset of the Internet and e-commerce sites, which allow customers to buy tickets online, the popularity of this service has increased.

Shopping Cart Systems

Simple shopping cart systems allow the off-line administration of products and categories. The shop is then generated as HTML files and graphics that can be uploaded to a webspace. The systems do not use an online database. A high-end solution can be bought or rented as a stand-alone program or as an addition to an enterprise resource planning program. It is usually installed on the company's web server and may integrate into the existing supply chain so that ordering, payment, delivery, accounting and warehousing can be automated to a large extent. Other solutions allow the user to register and create an online shop on a portal that hosts multiple shops simultaneously from one back office. Examples are Big Commerce, Shopify and FlickRocket. Open source shopping cart packages include advanced platforms such as Interchange, and off-the-shelf solutions such as Magento, osCommerce, Shopgate, PrestaShop, and Zen Cart. Commercial systems can also be tailored so the shop does not have to be created from scratch. By using an existing framework, software modules for various functionalities required by a web shop can be adapted and combined.

Design

Customers are attracted to online shopping not only because of high levels of convenience, but also because of broader selections, competitive pricing, and greater access to information. Business organizations seek to offer online shopping not only because it is of much lower cost compared to bricks and mortar stores, but also because it offers access to a worldwide market, increases customer value, and builds sustainable capabilities.

Information Load

Designers of online shops are concerned with the effects of information load. Information load is a product of the spatial and temporal arrangements of stimuli in the web store. Compared with conventional retail shopping, the information environment of virtual shopping is enhanced by providing additional product information such as comparative products and services, as well as various alternatives and attributes of each alternative, etc. Two major dimensions of information load are complexity and novelty. Complexity refers to the number of different elements or features of a site, often the result of increased information diversity. Novelty involves the unexpected, suppressed, new, or unfamiliar aspects of the site. The novelty dimension may keep consumers exploring a shopping site, whereas the complexity dimension may induce impulse purchases.

Consumer Needs and Expectations

According to the output of a research report by Western Michigan University published in 2005, an e-commerce website does not have to be good looking with listing on a lot of search engines. It must build relationships with customers to make money. The report also suggests that a website must leave a positive impression on the customers, giving them a reason to come back.

Dyn, an Internet performance management company conducted a survey on more than 1400 consumers across 11 countries in North America, Europe, Middle-East and Asia and the results of the survey are as follows:

- Online retailers must improve the website speed
- Online retailers must ease consumers fear around security

These concerns majorly affect the decisions of almost two thirds of the consumers.

User Interface

The most important factors determining whether customers return to a website are ease of use and the presence of user-friendly features. Usability testing is important for finding problems and improvements in a web site. Methods for evaluating usability include heuristic evaluation, cognitive walkthrough, and user testing. Each technique has its own characteristics and emphasizes different aspects of the user experience.

Market Share

E-commerce B2C product sales totaled $142.5 billion, representing about 8% of retail product sales in the United States. The $26 billion worth of clothes sold online represented about 13% of the domestic market, and with 72% of women looking online for apparel, it has become one of the most popular cross-shopping categories. Forrester Research estimates that the United States online retail industry will be worth $279 billion in 2015. The popularity of online shopping continues to erode sales of conventional retailers. For example, Best Buy, the largest retailer of electronics in the U.S. in August 2014 reported its tenth consecutive quarterly dip in sales, citing an increasing shift by consumers to online shopping. There were 242 million people shopping online in China in 2012. For developing countries and low-income households in developed countries, adoption of e-commerce in place of or in addition to conventional methods is limited by a lack of affordable Internet access.

Advantages

Convenience

Online stores are usually available 24 hours a day, and many consumers in Western countries have Internet access both at work and at home. Other establishments such as Internet cafes, community centers and schools provide internet access as well. In contrast, visiting a conventional retail store requires travel or commuting and costs such as gas, parking, or bus tickets, and must typically take place during business hours. In the event of a problem with the item (e.g., the product was not what the consumer ordered or the product was not satisfactory), consumers are concerned with the ease of returning an item in exchange for the correct product or a refund. Consumers may need to contact the retailer, visit the post office and pay return shipping, and then wait for a replacement or refund. Some online companies have more generous return policies to compensate for the traditional advantage of physical stores. For example, the online shoe retailer Zappos.com includes labels for free return shipping, and does not charge a restocking fee, even for returns which are not the result of merchant error. (Note: In the United Kingdom, online shops are prohibited from charging a restocking fee if the consumer cancels their order in accordance with the Consumer Protection (Distance Selling) Act 2000).

Information and Reviews

Online stores must describe products for sale with text, photos, and multimedia files, whereas in a physical retail store, the actual product and the manufacturer's packaging will be available for direct inspection (which might involve a test drive, fitting, or other experimentation). Some online stores provide or link to supplemental product information, such as instructions, safety procedures, demonstrations, or manufacturer specifications. Some provide background information, advice, or how-to guides designed to help consumers decide which product to buy. Some stores even allow customers to comment or rate their items. There are also dedicated review sites that host user reviews for different products. Reviews and even some blogs give customers the option of shopping for cheaper purchases from all over the world without having to depend on local retailers. In a conventional retail store, clerks are generally available to answer questions. Some online stores have real-time chat features, but most rely on e-mails or phone calls to handle customer questions. Even if an online store is open 24 hours a day, seven days a week, the customer service team may only be available during regular business hours.

Price and Selection

One advantage of shopping online is being able to quickly seek out deals for items or services provided by many different vendors (though some local search engines do exist to help consumers locate products for sale in nearby stores). Search engines, online price comparison services and discovery shopping engines can be used to look up sellers of a particular product or service. Shipping costs (if applicable) reduce the price advantage of online merchandise, though depending on the jurisdiction, a lack of sales tax may compensate for this. Shipping a small number of items, especially from another country, is much more expensive than making the larger shipments bricks-and-mortar retailers order. Some retailers (especially those selling small, high-value items like electronics) offer free shipping on sufficiently large orders. Another major advantage for retailers is the ability to rapidly switch suppliers and vendors without disrupting users' shopping experience.

Disadvantages

Fraud and Security Concerns

Given the lack of ability to inspect merchandise before purchase, consumers are at higher risk of fraud than face-to-face transactions. When ordering merchandise online, the item may not work properly, it may have defects, or it might not be the same item pictured in the online photo. Merchants also risk fraudulent purchases if customers are using stolen credit cards or fraudulent repudiation of the online purchase. However, merchants face less risk from physical theft by using a warehouse instead of a retail storefront. Secure Sockets Layer (SSL) encryption has generally solved the problem of credit card numbers being intercepted in transit between the consumer and the merchant. However, one must still trust the merchant (and employees) not to use the credit card information subsequently for their own purchases, and not to pass the information to others. Also, hackers might break into a merchant's web site and steal names, addresses and credit card numbers, although the Payment Card Industry Data Security Standard is intended to minimize the impact of such breaches. Identity theft is still a concern for consumers. A number of high-profile break-ins in the 2000s has prompted some U.S. states to require disclosure to consumers when this happens. Computer security has thus become a major concern for merchants and e-commerce service providers, who deploy countermeasures such as firewalls and anti-virus software to protect their networks. Phishing is another danger, where consumers are fooled into thinking they are dealing with a reputable retailer, when they have actually been manipulated into feeding private information to a system operated by a malicious party. Denial of service attacks are a minor risk for merchants, as are server and network outages.

Quality seals can be placed on the Shop web page if it has undergone an independent assessment and meets all requirements of the company issuing the seal. The purpose of these seals is to increase the confidence of online shoppers. However, the existence of many different seals, or seals unfamiliar to consumers, may foil this effort to a certain extent.

A number of resources offer advice on how consumers can protect themselves when using online retailer services. These include:

- Sticking with well-known stores, or attempting to find independent consumer reviews of their experiences; also ensuring that there is comprehensive contact information on the website before using the service, and noting if the retailer has enrolled in industry oversight programs such as a trust mark or a trust seal.

- Before buying from a new company, evaluating the website by considering issues such as: the professionalism and user-friendliness of the site; whether or not the company lists a telephone number and/or street address along with e-contact information; whether a fair and reasonable refund and return policy is clearly stated; and whether there are hidden price inflators, such as excessive shipping and handling charges.

- Ensuring that the retailer has an acceptable privacy policy posted. For example, note if the retailer does not explicitly state that it will not share private information with others without consent.

- Ensuring that the vendor address is protected with SSL when entering credit card information. If it does the address on the credit card information entry screen will start with "HTTPS".

- Using strong passwords which do not contain personal information such as the user's name or birthdate. Another option is a "pass phrase," which might be something along the lines: "I shop 4 good a buy!!" These are difficult to hack, since they do not consist of words found in a dictionary, and provides a variety of upper, lower, and special characters. These passwords can be site specific and may be easy to remember.

Although the benefits of online shopping are considerable, when the process goes poorly it can create a thorny situation. A few problems that shoppers potentially face include identity theft, faulty products, and the accumulation of spyware. If users are required to put in their credit card information and billing/shipping address and the website is not secure, customer information can be accessible to anyone who knows how to obtain it. Most large online corporations are inventing new ways to make fraud more difficult. However, criminals are constantly responding to these developments with new ways to manipulate the system. Even though online retailers are making efforts to protect consumer information, it is a constant fight to maintain the lead. It is advisable to be aware of the most current technology and scams to protect consumer identity and finances. Product delivery is also a main concern of online shopping. Most companies offer shipping insurance in case the product is lost or damaged. Some shipping companies will offer refunds or compensation for the damage, but this is up to their discretion.

Lack of Full Cost Disclosure

The lack of full cost disclosure may also be problematic. While it may be easy to compare the base price of an item online, it may not be easy to see the total cost up front. Additional fees such as shipping are often not be visible until the final step in the checkout process. The problem is especially evident with cross-border purchases, where the cost indicated at the final checkout screen may not include additional fees that must be paid upon delivery such as duties and brokerage. Some services such as the Canadian-based Wishabi attempts to include estimates of these additional cost, but nevertheless, the lack of general full cost disclosure remains a concern.

Privacy

Privacy of personal information is a significant issue for some consumers. Many consumers wish to avoid spam and telemarketing which could result from supplying contact information to an online merchant. In response, many merchants promise to not use consumer information for these purposes, Many websites keep track of consumer shopping habits in order to suggest items and other websites to view. Brick-and-mortar stores also collect consumer information. Some ask for a shopper's address and phone number at checkout, though consumers may refuse to provide it. Many larger stores use the address information encoded on consumers' credit cards (often without their knowledge) to add them to a catalog mailing list. This information is obviously not accessible to the merchant when paying in cash or through a bank (money transfer, in which case there is also proof of payment).

Product Suitability

Many successful purely virtual companies deal with digital products, (including information storage, retrieval, and modification), music, movies, office supplies, education, communication, software, photography, and financial transactions. Other successful marketers use drop shipping or affiliate marketing techniques to facilitate transactions of tangible goods without maintaining real inventory. Some non-digital products have been more successful than others for online stores. Profitable items often have a high value-to-weight ratio, they may involve embarrassing purchases, they may typically go to people in remote locations, and they may have shut-ins as their typical purchasers. Items which can fit in a standard mailbox—such as music CDs, DVDs and books—are particularly suitable for a virtual marketer.

Products such as spare parts, both for consumer items like washing machines and for industrial equipment like centrifugal pumps, also seem good candidates for selling online. Retailers often need to order spare parts specially, since they typically do not stock them at consumer outlets—in such cases, e-commerce solutions in spares do not compete with retail stores, only with other ordering systems. A factor for success in this niche can consist of providing customers with exact, reliable information about which part number their particular version of a product needs, for example by providing parts lists keyed by serial number. Products less suitable for e-commerce include products that have a low value-to-weight ratio, products that have a smell, taste, or touch component, products that need trial fittings—most notably clothing—and products where colour integrity appears important. Nonetheless, some web sites have had success delivering groceries and clothing sold through the internet is big business in the U.S.

Aggregation

High-volume websites, such as Yahoo!, Amazon.com, and eBay, offer hosting services for online stores to all size retailers. These stores are presented within an integrated navigation framework, sometimes known as virtual shopping malls or online mar-ketplaces.

Impact of Reviews on Consumer Behaviour

One of the great benefits of online shopping is the ability to read product reviews, written either by experts or fellow online shoppers. The Nielsen Company conducted a survey in March 2010 and polled more than 27,000 Internet users in 55 markets from the Asia-Pacific, Europe, Middle East, North America, and South America to look at questions such as "How do consumers shop online?", "What do they intend to buy?", "How do they use various online shopping web pages?", and the impact of social media and other factors that come into play when consumers are trying to decide how to spend their money on which product or service. According to the research, reviews on electronics (57%) such as DVD players, cellphones, or PlayStations, and so on, reviews on cars (45%), and reviews on software (37%) play an important role in influencing consumers who tend to make purchases online. Furthermore, 40% of online shoppers indicate that they would not even buy electronics without consulting online reviews first.

In addition to online reviews, peer recommendations on online shopping pages or social media websites play a key role for online shoppers when they are researching future purchases. 90% of all purchases made are influenced by social media. Each day, over two million buyers are shopping online for jewelry.

Electronic Trading

Electronic trading, sometimes called etrading, is a method of trading securities (such as stocks, and bonds), foreign exchange or financial derivatives electronically. Information technology is used to bring together buyers and sellers through an electronic trading platform and network to create virtual market places. They can include various exchange-based systems, such as NASDAQ, NYSE Arca and Globex, as well as other types of trading platforms, such as electronic communication networks (ECNs), alternative trading systems, crossing networks and "dark pools". Electronic trading is rapidly replacing human trading in global securities markets.

Electronic trading is in contrast to older floor trading and phone trading and has a number of advantages, but glitches and cancelled trades do still occur.

History

For many years stock exchanges were physical locations where buyers and sellers met and negotiated. Exchange trading would typically happen on the floor of an exchange, where traders in brightly colored jackets (to identify which firm they worked for) would shout and gesticulate at one another – a process known as open outcry or pit trading (the exchange floors were often pit-shaped – circular, sloping downwards to the centre, so that the traders could see one another). With the improvement in communications technology in the late 20th century, the need for a physical location became less important and traders started to transact from remote locations in what became known as electronic trading. Electronic trading made transactions easier to complete, monitor, clear, and settle and this helped spur on its development.

One of the earliest examples of widespread electronic trading was on Globex, the CME Group's electronic trading platform conceived in 1987 and launched fully in 1992. This allowed access to a variety of financial markets such as treasuries, foreign exchange and commodities. The Chicago Board of Trade (CBOT) produced a rival system that was based on Oak Trading Systems' Oak platform branded 'E Open Outcry,' an electronic trading platform that allowed for trading to take place alongside that took place in the CBOT pits.

Set up in 1971, NASDAQ was the world's first electronic stock market, though it originally operated as an electronic bulletin board, rather than offering straight-through processing (STP).

By 2011 investment firms on both the buy side and sell side were increasing their spending on technology for electronic trading. With the result that many floor traders and brokers were removed from the trading process. Traders also increasingly started to rely on algorithms to analyze market conditions and then execute their orders automatically.

The move to electronic trading compared to floor trading continued to increase with many of the major exchanges around the world moving from floor trading to completely electronic trading.

Trading in the financial markets can broadly be split into two groups:

- Business-to-business (B2B) trading, often conducted on exchanges, where large investment banks and brokers trade directly with one another, transacting large amounts of securities, and

- Business-to-consumer (B2C) trading, where retail (e.g. individuals buying and selling relatively small amounts of stocks and shares) and institutional clients (e.g. hedge funds, fund managers or insurance companies, trading far larger amounts of securities) buy and sell from brokers or "dealers", who act as middle-men between the clients and the B2B markets.

While the majority of retail trading in the United States happens over the Internet, retail trading volumes are dwarfed by institutional, inter-dealer and exchange trading. However, in developing economies, especially in Asia, retail trading constitutes a significant portion of overall trading volume.

For instruments which are not exchange-traded (e.g. US treasury bonds), the inter-dealer market substitutes for the exchange. This is where dealers trade directly with one another or through inter-dealer brokers (i.e. companies like GFI Group, ICAP and BGC Partners. They acted as middle-men between dealers such as investment banks). This type of trading traditionally took place over the phone but brokers moved to offering electronic trading services instead.

Similarly, B2C trading traditionally happened over the phone and, while some still does, more brokers are allowing their clients to place orders using electronic systems. Many retail (or "discount") brokers (e.g. Charles Schwab, E-Trade) went online during the late 1990s and most retail stock-broking probably takes place over the web now.

Larger institutional clients, however, will generally place electronic orders via proprietary electronic trading platforms such as Bloomberg Terminal, Reuters 3000 Xtra, Thomson Reuters Eikon, BondsPro, Thomson TradeWeb or CanDeal (which connect institutional clients to several dealers), or using their brokers' proprietary software.

For stock trading, the process of connecting counterparties through electronic trading is supported by the Financial Information eXchange (FIX) Protocol. Used by the vast majority of exchanges and traders, the FIX Protocol is the industry standard for pre-trade messaging and trade execution. While the FIX Protocol was developed for trading stocks, it has been further developed to accommodate commodities, foreign exchange, derivatives, and fixed income trading.

Impact

The increase of electronic trading has had some important implications:

- Reduced cost of transactions – By automating as much of the process as possible (often referred to as "straight-through processing" or STP), costs are brought down. The goal is to reduce the incremental cost of trades as close to zero as possible, so that increased trading volumes don't lead to significantly increased costs. This has translated to lower costs for investors.

- Greater liquidity – electronic systems make it easier to allow different companies to trade with one another, no matter where they are located. This leads to greater liquidity (i.e. there are more buyers and sellers) which increases the efficiency of the markets.

- Greater competition – While electronic trading hasn't necessarily lowered the cost of entry to the financial services industry, it has removed barriers within the industry and had a globalisation-style competition effect. For example, a trader can trade futures on Eurex, Globex or LIFFE at the click of a button – he or she doesn't need to go through a broker or pass orders to a trader on the exchange floor.

- Increased transparency – Electronic trading has meant that the markets are less opaque. It's easier to find out the price of securities when that information is flowing around the world electronically.

- Tighter spreads – The "spread" on an instrument is the difference between the best buying and selling prices being quoted; it represents the profit being made by the market makers. The increased liquidity, competition and transparency means that spreads have tightened, especially for commoditised, exchange-traded instruments.

For retail investors, financial services on the web offer great benefits. The primary benefit is the reduced cost of transactions for all concerned as well as the ease and the convenience. Web-driven financial transactions bypass traditional hurdles such as logistics.

Technology and Systems

Electronic trading systems are typically proprietary software (*etrading platforms* or electronic trading platforms), running on COTS hardware and operating systems, often using common underlying protocols, such as TCP/IP.

Exchanges typically develop their own systems (sometimes referred to as matching engines), although sometimes an exchange will use another exchange's technology (e.g. e-cbot, the Chicago Board of Trade's electronic trading platform, uses LIFFE's Connect system), and some newer electronic exchanges use 3rd-party specialist software providers (e.g. the Budapest stock exchange and the Moscow Interbank Currency Exchange use automated trading system originally written and implemented by FMSC, an Australian technology company that was acquired by Computershare, and whose intellectual property rights are now owned by OMX).

Exchanges and ECNs generally offer two methods of accessing their systems –

- an exchange-provided GUI, which the trader runs on his or her desktop and connects directly to the exchange/ECN, and

- an API which allows dealers to plug their own in-house systems directly into the exchange/ECN's.

From an infrastructure point of view, most exchanges will provide "gateways" which sit on a company's network, acting in a manner similar to a proxy, connecting back to the exchange's central system.

ECNs will generally forego the gateway/proxy, and their GUI or the API will connect directly to a central system, across a leased line.

Many brokers develop their own systems, although there are some third-party solutions providers specializing in this area. Like ECNs, brokers will often offer both a GUI and an API (although it's likely that a slightly smaller proportion of brokers offer an API, as compared with ECNs), and connectivity is typically direct to the broker's systems, rather than through a gateway.

Investment banks and other dealers have far more complex technology requirements, as they have to interface with multiple exchanges, brokers and multi-dealer platforms, as well as their own pricing, P&L, trade processing and position-keeping systems. Some banks will develop their own electronic trading systems in-house, but this can be costly, especially when they need to connect to many exchanges, ECNs and brokers. There are a number of companies offering solutions in this area.

Algorithmic Trading

Some electronic trades are not planned or executed by human traders, but by complex algorithms.

Many types of algorithmic or automated trading activities can be described as high-frequency trading (HFT), which is a specialized form of algorithmic trading characterized by high turnover and high order-to-trade ratios

Online Food Ordering

Online food ordering is a process of ordering food from a local restaurant or food cooperative through a web page or app. Much like ordering consumer goods online, many of these allow customers to keep accounts with them in order to make frequent ordering convenient. A customer will search for a favorite restaurant, usually filtered via type of cuisine and choose from available items, and choose delivery or pick-up. Payment can be amongst others either by credit card or cash, with the restaurant returning a percentage to the online food company.

In May 2015, TechCrunch reported that "of the $70 billion [takeout and delivery market], only about $9 billion (roughly 13 percent) is online."

Service Types

Restaurant-controlled

The preexisting delivery infrastructure of these franchises was well suited for an online ordering system, so much so that, in 2008, Papa John's International announced that its online sales were growing on average more than 50 percent each year and neared $400 million in 2007 alone.

Local companies have teamed up with e-commerce companies to make ordering quicker and more precise. Annie Maver, director of operations for The Original Pizza Pan, Inc. of Cleveland, Ohio comments that "the system is good for customers who don't speak English."

Some restaurants have adopted online ordering despite their lack of delivery systems, using it to manage pick-up orders or to take reservations.

Independent

Independent online food ordering companies offer two solutions. One is a software service whereby restaurants purchase database and account management software from the company and manage the online ordering themselves. The other solution is an Web-based service whereby restaurants sign contracts with an online food ordering website that may handle orders from many restaurants in a regional or national area.

One difference between the systems is how the online menu is created and later updated. Managed services do this via phone or email, while unmanaged services require the customer to do it. Some websites use wizards to find the best-suited menu for the customer.

Food Cooperatives

Food cooperatives also allow consumers the ability to place an order of locally grown and/or produced food online. Consumers place an order online based on what is available for the ordering cycle (month, week) and then pick up and pay for their orders at a central location.

Apps

Many restaurants offer the technology to place an order with an app, and may offer a discount or bonus item when the order is placed.

Online Menus

Advantages for Online Ordering

Customers are turning more towards online food services options for the convenience its offers, the variety of options and affordable food choices.

Disadvantage for Online Ordering

Customers are not able to ask about quality of food or ask for any specialized diet foods. It is more difficult to ask for gluten free or allergy free foods with online ordering. Also, it is more possible for a customer to place an order but never pick up the order which can lead to waste of food and possibly a loss of profits.

Timeline of Online Food Delivery

This is a timeline of online food delivery.

Streaming Media

Streaming media is multimedia that is constantly received by and presented to an end-user while being delivered by a provider. The verb "to stream" refers to the process of delivering or obtaining media in this manner; the term refers to the delivery method of the medium, rather than the medium itself, and is an alternative to file downloading, a process in which the end-user obtains the entire file for the content before watching or listening to it.

A typical webcast, streaming in an embedded media player

A live stream from a camera pointed at a fish tank, Schou FishCam

A client end-user can use their media player to begin to play the data file (such as a digital file of a movie or song) before the entire file has been transmitted. Distinguishing delivery method from the media distributed applies specifically to telecommunications networks, as most of the delivery systems are either inherently streaming (e.g. radio, television) or inherently non-streaming (e.g. books, video cassettes, audio CDs). For example, in the 1930s, elevator music was among the earliest popularly available streaming media; nowadays Internet television is a common form of streamed media. The term "streaming media" can apply to media other than video and audio such as live closed captioning, ticker tape, and real-time text, which are all considered "streaming text". The term "streaming" was first used in the early 1990s as a better description for video on demand on IP networks; at the time such video was usually referred to as "store and forward video", which was misleading nomenclature.

As of 2016, streaming is generally taken to refer to cases where a user watches digital video content and/or listens to digital audio content on a computer screen and speakers (ranging from a desktop computer to a smartphone) over the Internet. With streaming content, the user does not have to download the entire digital video or digital audio file before they start to watch/listen to it. There are challenges with streaming content on the Internet. If the user does not have enough bandwidth in their Internet connection, they may experience stops in the content and some users may not be able to stream certain content due to not having compatible computer or software systems. As of 2016, two popular streaming services are the video sharing website YouTube, which contains video and audio files on a huge range of topics and Netflix, which streams movies and TV shows.

Live streaming refers to Internet content delivered in real-time, as events happen, much as live television broadcasts its contents over the airwaves via a television signal. An example of live streaming is Metropolitan Opera Live in HD, a program in which the Metropolitan Opera streams an opera performance "live", as the performance is taking place; in 2013–2014, 10 operas were transmitted via satellite into at least 2,000 theaters in 66 countries. Live internet streaming requires a form of source media (e.g. a video camera, an audio interface, screen capture software), an encoder to digitize the content, a media publisher, and a content delivery network to distribute and deliver the content. Live streaming does not need to be recorded at the origination point, although it frequently is.

History

In the early 1920s, George O. Squier was granted patents for a system for the transmission and distribution of signals over electrical lines which was the technical basis for what later became *Muzak*, a technology streaming continuous music to commercial customers without the use of radio. Attempts to display media on computers date back to the earliest days of computing in the mid-20th century. However, little progress was made for several decades, primarily due to the high cost and limited capabilities of computer hardware. From the late 1980s through the 1990s, consumer-grade personal computers became powerful enough to display various media. The primary technical issues related to streaming were: having enough CPU power and bus bandwidth to support the required data rates and creating low-latency interrupt paths in the operating system to prevent buffer underrun and thus enable skip-free streaming of the content. However, computer networks were still limited in the mid-1990s, and audio and video media were usually delivered over non-streaming channels, such as by downloading a digital file from a remote server and then saving it to a local drive on the end user's computer or storing it as a digital file and playing it back from CD-ROMs.

Late 1990s – Early 2000s

During the late 1990s and early 2000s, users had increased access to computer networks, especially the Internet, and especially during the early 2000s, users had access to increased network bandwidth, especially in the "last mile". These technological improvement facilitated the streaming of audio and video content to computer users in their homes and workplaces. As well, there was an increasing use of standard protocols and formats, such as TCP/IP, HTTP, HTML and the Internet became increasingly commercialized, which led to an infusion of investment into the sector. The band Severe Tire Damage was the first group to perform live on the Internet. On June 24, 1993, the band was playing a gig at Xerox PARC while elsewhere in the building, scientists were discussing new technology (the Mbone) for broadcasting on the Internet using multicasting. As proof of PARC's technology, the band's performance was broadcast and could be seen live in Australia and elsewhere.

Microsoft Research developed Microsoft TV application which was compiled under MS Windows Studio Suite and tested in conjunction with Connectix QuickCam. RealNetworks was also a pioneer in the streaming media markets, when it broadcast a baseball game between the New York Yankees and the Seattle Mariners over the Internet in 1995. The first symphonic concert on the Internet took place at the Paramount Theater in Seattle, Washington on November 10, 1995. The concert was a collaboration between The Seattle Symphony and various guest musicians such as Slash (Guns 'n Roses, Velvet Revolver), Matt Cameron (Soundgarden, Pearl Jam), and Barrett Martin (Screaming Trees). When *Word Magazine* launched in 1995, they featured the first-ever streaming soundtracks on the Internet. Using local downtown musicians the first music stream was "Big Wheel" by Karthik Swaminathan and the second being "When We Were Poor" by Karthik Swaminathan with Marc Ribot and Christine Bard.

Business Developments

Microsoft developed a media player known as ActiveMovie in 1995 that allowed streaming media and included a proprietary streaming format, which was the precursor to the streaming feature later in Windows Media Player 6.4 in 1999. In June 1999 Apple also introduced a streaming media format in its QuickTime 4 application. It was later also widely adopted on websites along with RealPlayer and Windows Media streaming formats. The competing formats on websites required each user to download the respective applications for streaming and resulted in many users having to have all three applications on their computer for general compatibility. Around 2002, the interest in a single, unified, streaming format and the widespread adoption of Adobe Flash prompted the development of a video streaming format through Flash, which is the format used in Flash-based players on many popular video hosting sites today such as YouTube. Increasing consumer demand for live streaming has prompted YouTube to implement a new live streaming service to users. Presently the company also offers a (secured) link returning the available connection speed of the user.

Use by Consumers

These advances in computer networking, combined with powerful home computers and modern operating systems, made streaming media practical and affordable for ordinary consumers. Stand-alone Internet radio devices emerged to offer listeners a no-computer option for listening to audio streams. These audio streaming services have become increasingly popular over recent years, as streaming music hit a record of 118.1 billion streams in 2013. In general, multimedia content has a large volume, so media storage and transmission costs are still significant. To offset this somewhat, media are generally compressed for both storage and streaming. Increasing consumer demand for streaming of high definition (HD) content has led the industry to develop a number of technologies such as WirelessHD or ITU-T G.hn, which are optimized for streaming HD content without forcing the user to install new networking cables. In 1996, digital pioneer Marc Scarpa produced the first large-scale, online, live broadcast in history, the Adam Yauch-led Tibetan Freedom Concert, an event that would define the format of social change broadcasts. Scarpa continued to pioneer in the streaming media world with projects such as Woodstock '99, Townhall with President Clinton, and more recently Covered CA's campaign "Tell a Friend Get Covered" which was live streamed on YouTube.

As of 2016, a media stream can be streamed either "live" or "on demand". Live streams are generally provided by a means called "true streaming". True streaming sends the information straight to the computer or device without saving the file to a hard disk. On-demand streaming is provided by a means called *progressive streaming* or *progressive download.* Progressive streaming saves the file to a hard disk and then is played from that location. On-demand streams are often saved to hard disks and servers for extended amounts of time; while the live streams are only available at one time only (e.g., during the football game). Streaming media is increasingly being coupled with use of social media. For example, sites such as YouTube encourage social interaction in webcasts through features such as live chat, online surveys, user posting of comments online and more. Furthermore, streaming media is increasingly being used for social business and e-learning. Due the popularity of the streaming medias, many developers have introduced free HD movie streaming apps for the people who use smaller devices such as tablets and smartphones for everyday purposes.

Bandwidth and Storage

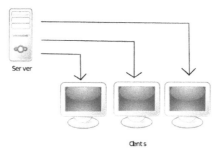

Unicast connections require multiple connections from the same streaming server even when it streams the same content

A broadband speed of 2 Mbit/s or more is recommended for streaming standard definition video without experiencing buffering or skips, especially live video, for example to a Roku, Apple TV, Google TV or a Sony TV Blu-ray Disc Player. 5 Mbit/s is recommended for High Definition content and 9 Mbit/s for Ultra-High Definition content. Streaming media storage size is calculated from the streaming bandwidth and length of the media using the following formula (for a single user and file) requires a storage size in megabytes which is equal to length (in seconds) × bit rate (in bit/s) / (8 × 1024 × 1024). For example, one hour of digital video encoded at 300 kbit/s (this was a typical broadband video in 2005 and it was usually encoded in a 320 × 240 pixels window size) will be: (3,600 s × 300,000 bit/s) / (8×1024×1024) requires around 128 MB of storage.

If the file is stored on a server for on-demand streaming and this stream is viewed by 1,000 people at the same time using a Unicast protocol, the requirement is 300 kbit/s × 1,000 = 300,000 kbit/s = 300 Mbit/s of bandwidth. This is equivalent to around 135 GB per hour. Using a multicast protocol the server sends out only a single stream that is common to all users. Therefore, such a stream would only use 300 kbit/s of serving bandwidth. The calcula-tion for live streaming is similar. Assuming that the seed at the encoder is 500 kbit/s and if the show lasts for 3 hours with 3,000 viewers, then the calculation is number of MBs transferred = encoder speed (in bit/s) × number of seconds × number of viewers

/ (8*1024*1024). The results of this calculation are as follows: number of MBs transferred = 500 x 1024 (bit/s) × 3 × 3,600 (= 3 hours) × 3,000 (number of viewers) / (8*1024*1024) = 1,977,539 MB

Protocols

The audio stream is compressed to make the file size smaller using an audio coding format such as MP3, Vorbis, AAC or Opus. The video stream is compressed using a video coding format to make the file size smaller. Video coding formats include H.264, HEVC, VP8 or VP9. Encoded audio and video streams are assembled in a container "bitstream" such as MP4, FLV, WebM, ASF or ISMA. The bitstream is delivered from a streaming server to a streaming client (e.g., the computer user with their Internet-connected laptop) using a transport protocol, such as Adobe's RTMP or RTP. In the 2010s, technologies such as Apple's HLS, Microsoft's Smooth Streaming, Adobe's HDS and non-proprietary formats such as MPEG-DASH have emerged to enable adaptive bitrate streaming over HTTP as an alternative to using proprietary transport protocols. Often, a streaming transport protocol is used to send video from an event venue to a "cloud" transcoding service and CDN, which then uses HTTP-based transport protocols to distribute the video to individual homes and users. The streaming client (the end user) may interact with the streaming server using a control protocol, such as MMS or RTSP.

Protocol Challenges

Designing a network protocol to support streaming media raises many problems. Datagram protocols, such as the User Datagram Protocol (UDP), send the media stream as a series of small packets. This is simple and efficient; however, there is no mechanism within the protocol to guarantee delivery. It is up to the receiving application to detect loss or corruption and recover data using error correction techniques. If data is lost, the stream may suffer a dropout. The Real-time Streaming Protocol (RTSP), Real-time Transport Protocol (RTP) and the Real-time Transport Control Protocol (RTCP) were specifically designed to stream media over networks. RTSP runs over a variety of transport protocols, while the latter two are built on top of UDP.

Another approach that seems to incorporate both the advantages of using a standard web protocol and the ability to be used for streaming even live content is adaptive bitrate streaming. HTTP adaptive bitrate streaming is based on HTTP progressive download, but contrary to the previous approach, here the files are very small, so that they can be compared to the streaming of packets, much like the case of using RTSP and RTP. Reliable protocols, such as the Transmission Control Protocol (TCP), guarantee correct delivery of each bit in the media stream. However, they accomplish this with a system of timeouts and retries, which makes them more complex to implement. It also means that when there is data loss on the network, the media stream stalls while the protocol handlers detect the loss and retransmit the missing data. Clients can minimize this effect by buffering data for display. While delay due to buffering is acceptable in video on demand scenarios, users of interactive applications such as video conferencing will experience a loss of fidelity if the delay caused by buffering exceeds 200 ms.

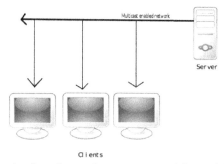

Multicasting broadcasts the same copy of the multimedia
over the entire network to a group of clients

Unicast protocols send a separate copy of the media stream from the server to each recipient. Unicast is the norm for most Internet connections, but does not scale well when many users want to view the same television program concurrently. Multicast protocols were developed to reduce the server/network loads resulting from duplicate data streams that occur when many recipients receive unicast content streams independently. These protocols send a single stream from the source to a group of recipients. Depending on the network infrastructure and type, multicast transmission may or may not be feasible. One potential disadvantage of multicasting is the loss of video on demand functionality. Continuous streaming of radio or television material usually precludes the recipient's ability to control playback. However, this problem can be mitigated by elements such as caching servers, digital set-top boxes, and buffered media players.

IP Multicast provides a means to send a single media stream to a group of recipients on a computer network. A multicast protocol, usually Internet Group Management Protocol, is used to manage delivery of multicast streams to the groups of recipients on a LAN. One of the challenges in deploying IP multicast is that routers and firewalls between LANs must allow the passage of packets destined to multicast groups. If the organization that is serving the content has control over the network between server and recipients (i.e., educational, government, and corporate intranets), then routing protocols such as Protocol Independent Multicast can be used to deliver stream content to multiple Local Area Network segments. As in mass delivery of content, multicast protocols need much less energy and other resources, widespread introduction of reliable multicast (broadcast-like) protocols and their preferential use, wherever possible, is a significant ecological and economic challenge. Peer-to-peer (P2P) protocols arrange for prerecorded streams to be sent between computers. This prevents the server and its network connections from becoming a bottleneck. However, it raises technical, performance, security, quality, and business issues.

Applications and Marketing

Useful – and typical – applications of the "streaming" concept are, for example, long video lectures performed "online" on the Internet. An advantage of this presentation is that these lectures can be very long, indeed, although they can always be interrupted or repeated at arbitrary places. There are also new marketing concepts. For example, the Berlin Philharmonic Orchestra sells Internet live streams of whole concerts, instead of several CDs or similar fixed media, by their so-called "Digital Concert Hall" using YouTube for "trailing" purposes only. These "online concerts" are also spread over a lot of different places – cinemas – at various places on the globe. A similar concept is used by the Metropolitan Opera in New York. Many successful startup ventures have based their business on streaming media. Some of the most popular live streaming app services are Periscope, Stringwire, Meerkat, Hang w/, Nichestreem and Facebook. Popular investors in media streaming are Accel, Benchmark, Balderton, Lakestar, Klaus Hommels, Marc Andreessen, Sina Afra, Nikolaus Zemanek, Daniel Ek.

Recording

It is possible to record any streamed media through certain media players, for instance VLC player.

Copyright

Streaming copyrighted content can involve making infringing copies of the works in question. Streaming, or looking at content on the Internet, is legal in Europe, even if that material is copyrighted.

E-governance

Electronic governance or e-governance is the application of information and communication technology (ICT) for delivering government services, exchange of information, communication transactions, integration of various stand-alone systems and services between government-to-customer (G2C), government-to-business (G2B), government-to-government (G2G) as well as back office processes and interactions within the entire government framework. Through e-governance, government services will be made available to citizens in a convenient, efficient and transparent manner. The three main target groups that can be distinguished in governance concepts are government, citizens and businesses/interest groups. In e-governance there are no distinct boundaries.

Generally four basic models are available – government-to-citizen (customer), government-to-employees, government-to-government and government-to-business.

Distinction from E-government

Both terms are treated to be the same; however, there is a difference between the two. "E-government" is the use of the ICTs in public administration – combined with organizational change and new skills – to improve public services and democratic processes and to strengthen support to public. The problem in this definition to be congruence definition of e-governance is that there is no provision for governance of ICTs. As a matter of fact, the governance of ICTs requires most probably a substantial increase in regulation and policy-making capabilities, with all the expertise and opinion-shaping processes along the various social stakeholders of these concerns. So, the perspective of the e-governance is "the use of the technologies that both help governing and have to be governed". The public–private partnership (PPP) based e-governance projects are hugely successful in India.

Many countries are looking forward to a corruption-free government. E-government is one-way communication protocol whereas e-governance is two-way communication protocol. The essence of e-governance is to reach the beneficiary and ensure that the services intended to reach the desired individual has been met with. There should be an auto-response to support the essence of e-governance, whereby the Government realizes the efficacy of its governance. E-governance is by the governed, for the governed and of the governed.

Establishing the identity of the end beneficiary is a challenge in all citizen-centric services. Statistical information published by governments and world bodies does not always reveal the facts. The best form of e-governance cuts down on unwanted interference of too many layers while delivering governmental services. It depends on good infrastructural setup with the support of local processes and parameters for governments to reach their citizens or end beneficiaries. Budget for planning, development and growth can be derived from well laid out e-governance systems

Government to Citizen

The goal of government-to-customer (G2C) e-governance is to offer a variety of ICT services to citizens in an efficient and economical manner, and to strengthen the relationship between government and citizens using technology.

There are several methods of government-to-customer e-governance. Two-way communication allows citizens to instant message directly with public administrators, and cast remote electronic votes (electronic voting) and instant opinion voting. Transactions such as payment of services, such as city utilities, can be completed online or over the phone. Mundane services such as name or address changes, applying for services or grants, or transferring existing services are more convenient and no longer have to be completed face to face.

By Country

G2C e-Governance is unbalanced across the globe as not everyone has Internet access and computing skills, but the United States, European Union, and Asia are ranked the top three in development.

The Federal Government of the United States has a broad framework of G2C technology to enhance citizen access to Government information and services. Benefits.Gov is an official US government website that informs citizens of benefits they are eligible for and provides information of how to apply assistance. US State Governments also engage in G2C interaction through the Department of Transportation, Department of Public Safety, United States Department of Health and Human Services, United States Department of Education, and others. As with e-Governance on the global level, G2C services vary from state to state. The Digital States Survey ranks states on social measures, digital democracy, e-commerce, taxation, and revenue. The 2012 report shows Michigan and Utah in the lead and Florida and Idaho with the lowest scores. Municipal governments in the United States also use government-to-customer technology to complete transactions and inform the public. Much like states, cities are awarded for innovative technology. Government Technology's "Best of the Web 2012" named Louisville, KY, Arvada, CO, Raleigh, NC, Riverside, CA, and Austin, TX the top five G2C city portals.

European countries were ranked second among all geographic regions. The Single Point of Access for Citizens of Europe supports travel within Europe and eEurope is a 1999 initiative supporting online government. Main focuses are to provide public information, allow customers to have access to basic public services, simplify online procedures, and promote electronic signatures.

Asia is ranked third in comparison, and there are diverse G2C programs between countries. Singapore's eCitizen Portal is an organized single access point to government information and services. South Korea's Home Tax Service (HTS) provides citizens with 24/7 online services such as tax declaration. Taiwan has top ranking G2C technology including an online motor vehicle services system, which provides 21 applications and payment services to citizens.

Government-to-Citizen is the communication link between a government and private individuals or residents. Such G2C communication most often refers to that which takes place through Information and Communication Technologies (ICTs), but can also include direct mail and media campaigns. G2C can take place at the federal, state, and local levels. G2C stands in contrast to G2B, or Government-to-Business networks.

One such Federal G2C network is USA.gov: the United States' official web portal, though there are many other examples from governments around the world.

Concerns

A full switch to government-to-customer e-governance will cost a large amount of money in development and implementation. In addition, Government agencies do not always engage citizens in the development of their e-Gov services or accept feedback. Customers identified the following barriers to government-to-customer e-governance: not everyone has Internet access, especially in rural or low income areas, G2C technology can be problematic for citizens who lack computing skills. some G2C sites have technology requirements (such as browser requirements and plug-ins) that won't allow access to certain services, language barriers, the necessity for an e-mail address to access certain services, and a lack of privacy.

Government to Employees

E-Governance to Employee partnership (G2E) Is one of four main primary interactions in the delivery model of E-Governance. It is the relationship between online tools, sources, and articles that help employees maintain communication with the government and their own companies. E-Governance relationship with Employees allows new learning technology in one simple place as the computer. Documents can now be stored and shared with other colleagues online. E-governance makes it possible for employees to become paperless and makes it easy for employees to send important documents back and forth to colleagues all over the world instead of having to print out these records or fax G2E services also include software for maintaining personal information and records of employees. Some of the benefits of G2E expansion include:

- E-payroll – maintaining the online sources to view paychecks, pay stubs, pay bills, and keep records for tax information.

- E-benefits – be able to look up what benefits an employee is receiving and what benefits they have a right to.

- E-training – allows for new and current employees to regularly maintain the training they have through the development of new technology and to allow new employees to train and learn over new materials in one convenient location. E-learning is another way to keep employees informed on the important materials they need to know through the use of visuals, animation, videos, etc. It is usually a computer based learning tool, although not always. It is also a way for employees to learn at their own pace (distance learning), although it can be instructor-led.

- Maintaining records of personal information – Allows the system to keep all records in one easy location to update with every single bit of information that is relevant to a personal file. Examples being social security numbers, tax information, current address, and other information

Government-to-employees (abbreviated G2E) is the online interactions through instantaneous communication tools between government units and their employees. G2E is one out of the four primary delivery models of e-Government.

G2E is an effective way to provide e-learning to the employees, bring them together and to promote knowledge sharing among them. It also gives employees the possibility of accessing information in regard to compensation and benefit policies, training and learning opportunities and civil rights laws. G2E services also includes software for maintaining personnel information and records of employees.

G2E is adopted in many countries including the United States, Hong Kong and New Zealand.

Government to Government

E-government

From the start of 1990s e-commerce and e-product, there has rampant integration of e-forms of government process. Governments have now tried to use their efficiencies of their techniques to cut down on waste. E-government is a fairly broad subject matter, but all relate to how the services and representation are now delivered and how they are now being implemented.

Many governments around the world have gradually turned to Information technologies (IT) in an effort to keep up with today's demands. Historically, many governments in this sphere have only been reactive but up until recently there has been a more proactive approach in developing comparable services such things as e-commerce and e-business.

Before, the structure emulated private-like business techniques. Recently that has all changed as e-government begins to make its own plan. Not only does e-government introduce a new form of record keeping, it also continues to become more interactive to better the process of delivering services and promoting constituency participation.

The framework of such organization is now expected to increase more than ever by becoming efficient and reducing the time it takes to complete an objective. Some examples include paying utilities, tickets, and applying for permits. So far, the biggest concern is accessibility to Internet technologies for the average citizen. In an effort to help, administrations are now trying to aid those who do not have the skills to fully participate in this new medium of governance, especially now as e-government progressing to more e-governance terms

An overhaul of structure is now required as every pre-existing sub-entity must now merge under one concept of e- government. As a result, Public Policy has also seen changes due to the emerging of constituent participation and the Internet. Many governments such as Canada's have begun to invest in developing new mediums of communication of issues and information through virtual communication and participation. In practice this has led to several responses and adaptations by interest groups, activist, and lobbying groups. This new medium has changed the way the polis interacts with government.

Municipal

The purpose to include e-governance to government is to means more efficient in various aspects. Whether it means to reduce cost by reducing paper clutter, staffing cost, or communicating with private citizens or public government. E-government brings many advantages into play such as facilitating information delivery, application process/renewal between both business and private citizen, and participation with constituency. There are both internal and external advantages to the emergence of IT in government, though not all municipalities are alike in size and participation.

In theory, there are currently 4 major levels of E-government in municipal governments:

- the establishment of a secure and cooperative interaction among governmental agencies;

- Web-based service delivery;

- the application of e-commerce for more efficient government transactions activities,;

- and digital democracy.

These, along with 5 degrees of technical integration and interaction of users include:

- simple information dissemination (one-way communication);

- two- way communication (request and response);

- service and financial transactions;

- integration (horizontal and vertical integration);

- political participation

The adoption of e-government in municipalities evokes greater innovation in e- governance by being specialized and localized. The level success and feedback depends greatly on the city size and government type. A council-manager government municipality typically works the best with this method, as opposed to mayor-council government positions, which tend to be more political. Therefore, they have greater barriers towards its application. Council-Manager governments are also more inclined to be effective here by bringing innovation and reinvention of governance to e- governance.

The International City/County Management Association and Public Technology Inc. have done surveys over the effectiveness of this method. The results are indicating that most governments are still in either the primary stages (1 or stage 2), which revolves around public service requests. Though application of integration is now accelerating, there has been little to no instigating research to see its progression as e-governance to government. We can only theorize it's still within the primitive stages of e-governance.

Overview

Government-to-Government (abbreviated G2G) is the online non-commercial interaction between Government organisations, departments, and authorities and other Government organisations, departments, and authorities. Its use is common in the UK, along with G2C, the online non-commercial interaction of local and central Government and private individuals, and G2B the online non-commercial interaction of local and central Government and the commercial business sector.

G2G systems generally come in one of two types: Internal facing - joining up a single Governments departments, agencies, organisations and authorities - examples include the integration aspect of the Government Gateway, and the UK NHS Connecting for Health Data SPINE. External facing - joining up multiple Governments IS systems - an example would include the integration aspect of the Schengen Information System (SIS), developed to meet the requirements of the Schengen Agreement.

Objective

The strategic objective of e-governance, or in this case G2G is to support and simplify governance for government, citizens and businesses. The use of ICT can connect all parties and support processes and activities. Other objectives are to make government administration more transparent, speedy and accountable, while addressing the society's needs and expectations through efficient public services and effective interaction between the people, businesses and government.

Government-to-government model

Delivery Model

Within every of those interaction domains, four sorts of activities take place:

Pushing data over the internet, e.g.: regulative services, general holidays, public hearing schedules, issue briefs, notifications, etc. two-way communications between one governmental department and another, users will interact in dialogue with agencies and post issues, comments, or requests to the agency. Conducting transactions, e.g.: Lodging tax returns, applying for services and grants. Governance, e.g.: To alter the national transition from passive info access to individual participation by:

- Informing the individual

- Representing an individual

- Consulting an individual

- Involving the individual

Internal G2G (UK)

In the field of networking, the Government Secure Intranet (GSI) puts in place a secure link between central government departments. It is an IP based Virtual Private Network based on broadband technology introduced in April 1998 and further upgraded in February 2004. Among other things it offers a variety of advanced services including file transfer and search facilities, directory services, email exchange facilities (both between network members and over the Internet) as well as voice and video services. An additional network is currently also under development: the Public Sector Network (PSN) will be the network to interconnect public authorities (including departments and agencies in England; devolved administrations and local governments) and facilitate in particular sharing of information and services among each other.

Government to Business

Government-to-Business (G2B) is the online non-commercial interaction between local and central government and the commercial business sector with the purpose of providing businesses information and advice on e-business 'best practices'. G2B:Refers to the conduction through the Internet between government agencies and trading companies. B2G:Professional transactions between the company and the district, city, or federal regulatory agencies. B2G usually include recommendations to complete the measurement and evaluation of books and contracts.

Objective

The objective of G2B is to reduce difficulties for business, provide immediate information and enable digital communication by e-business (XML).In addition, the government should re-use the data in the report proper, and take advantage of commercial electronic transaction protocol. Government services are concentrated to the following groups: human services; community services; judicial services; transport services; land resources; business services; financial services and other. Each of the components listed above for each cluster of related services to the enterprise.

Benefits for Business

E-government reduce costs, carry out all companies to interact with the government. Electronic trading saves time compared to human doing business. No need for driving to government and no waiting time. If the transaction is not completed, you can use the mouse to click on the return trip rather than drive to the office. As more and more companies are doing online conduct government business, and their transaction costs will be reduced. More technology and less workers needed reduce the business cost.

E-Government provides a greater amount of information that business needed, also it makes those information more clear. A key factor in business success is the ability to plan for the future. Planning and forecasting through data-driven future. The government collected a lot of economic, demographic and other trends in the data. This makes the data more accessible to companies which may increase the chance of economic prosperity.

In addition, E-Government can help businesses navigate through government regulations by providing an intuitive site organization with a wealth of useful applications. The electronic filings of applications for environmental permits gives an example of it. Companies often do not know how, when, and what they must apply. Therefore, failure to comply with environmental regulations up to 70%, a staggering figure most likely to confusion about the requirements, rather than the product of willful disregard of the law.

Disadvantages

The government should concern that not all people are able to access to the internet to gain on-line government services. The network reliability, as well as information on government bodies can influence public opinion and prejudice hidden agenda. There are many considerations and implementation, designing e-government, including the potential impact of government and citizens of disintermediation, the impact on economic, social and political factors, vulnerable to cyber attacks, and disturbances to the status quo in these areas.

G2B rises the connection between government and businesses. Once the e-government began to develop, become more sophisticated, people will be forced to interact with e-government in the larger area. This may result in a lack of privacy for businesses as their government get their more and more information. In the worst case, there is so much information in the electron transfer between the government and business, a system which is like totalitarian could be developed. As government can access more information, the loss privacy could be a cost.

The government site does not consider about "potential to reach many users including those who live in remote areas, are homebound, have low literacy levels, exist on poverty line incomes."

Examples

- e-Tender Box (ETB) system – ETB system was developed by Government Logistics Department (GLD) to replace Electronic Tendering System. Users can use ETB system to download the resources and gain the service from the GLD.

- e-Procurement Programme – e-Procurement Programme provide a simple, convenient on-line ways for suppliers of the participating bureaux/departments (B/Ds) and suppliers of Government Logistics Department and agree to provide the low-valued goods and service.

- Finance and support for your business – UK Government provide the on-line financial help for business including grants,loans,business guide,what's more,it also offer the funding for the sunrise businesses(just start) or small scale firms.

Overview

The Main Goal of Government to Business – is to increase productivity by giving business more access to information in a more organize manner while lowering the cost of doing business as well as the ability to cut "red tape", save time, reduce operational cost and to create a more transparent business environment when dealing with government.

- Lowering cost of doing business – electronic transaction save time compared to conducting business in person.

- Cutting red tape – rules and regulation placed upon business normally take time and are most likely to cause a delay- in (G2B) will allow a much faster process with less delays and decreasing the number of rules and regulations

- Transparency – More information will be available, making G2B easier to communicate.

Government to Business Key Points:

1. Reduce the burden on business by adopting a process that enables collecting data once for multiple uses and streamlining redundant data.

2. Key lines of business: regulations, economic development, trade, permits/licenses, grants/loans, and asset management.

Difference Between G2B and B2G

- *Government to business (G2B)* – Refers to the conducting of transactions between government bodies and business via internet.

- *Business to government (B2G)* – Professional affairs conducted between companies and regional, municipal, or federal governing bodies. B2G typically encompasses the determination and evaluation of proposal and completion of contract.

Conclusion:

The overall benefit of e-governance when dealing with business is that it enables business to perform more efficiently.

Challenges – International Position

E-governance is facing numerous challenges world over. These challenges are arising from administrative, legal, institutional and technological factors.

Print on Demand

An on demand book printer at the Internet Archive headquarters in San Francisco, California. Two large printers print the pages (left) and the cover (right) and feed them into the rest of the machine for collating and binding. Depending on the number of pages in a given book, it might take from 5 to 20 minutes to print

Print on demand (POD) is a printing technology and business process in which copies of a book (or other document) are not printed until an order has been received, allowing books to be printed singly, or in small quantities. While build to order has been an established business model in many other industries, "print on demand" developed only after digital printing began, because it was not economical to print single copies using traditional printing technology such as letterpress and offset printing.

Many traditional small presses have replaced their traditional printing equipment with POD equipment or contract their printing out to POD service providers. Many academic publishers, including university presses, use POD services to maintain a large backlist; some even use POD for all of their publications. Larger publishers may use POD in special circumstances, such as reprinting older titles that are out of print or for performing test marketing.

Predecessors

Before digital printing technology was introduced, production of small numbers of publications had many limitations. Before the introduction of printing, hand-copying was the only way; each copy required as much effort as the original. After the introduction of the printing press large print runs were not a problem, but small numbers of printed pages were typically produced using stencils and reproducing on a mimeograph or similar machine. These produced printed pages of inferior quality to a book, cheaply and reasonably fast. In about 1950 electrostatic copiers were available to make paper master plates for offset duplicating machines; from about 1960 copying onto plain paper became possible to make multiple good-quality copies of a monochrome original. As technology advanced it became possible to store text in digital form—paper tape, punched cards readable on a digital computer, magnetic mass storage, etc.—and to print on a teletypewriter, line printer or other computer printer, but the software and hardware to produce original good-quality printed colour text and graphics and to print short runs fast and cheaply was not available.

Book Publishing

Print on demand with digital technology is used as a way of printing items for a fixed cost per copy, regardless of the size of the order. While the unit price of each physical copy printed is higher than with offset printing, the average cost is lower for very small print runs, because setup costs are much higher for offset printing.

POD has other business benefits besides lower costs (for small runs):

- Technical set-up is usually quicker than for offset printing.

- Large inventories of a book or print material do not need to be kept in stock, reducing storage, handling costs, and inventory accounting costs.

- There is little or no waste from unsold products.

These advantages reduce the risks associated with publishing books and prints and can lead to increased choice for consumers. However, the reduced risks for the publisher can also mean that quality control is less rigorous than usual.

Other Publishing

King and McGaw art prints are made on demand at their warehouse in Newhaven, England

Digital technology is ideally suited to publish small print runs of posters (often as a single copy) when they are needed. The introduction of UV-curable inks and media for large format inkjet printers has allowed artists, photographers and owners of image collections to take advantage of print on demand.

For example, UK art retailer King and McGaw fulfils many of its art print orders by printing on demand rather than pre-printing and storing them until they are sold, requiring less space and reducing overheads to the business. This was brought about after a fire destroyed £3 million worth of stock and damage to their warehouse.

Service Providers

The introduction of POD technologies and business-models has fueled a range of new book-creation and publishing opportunities. The innovation in this space is currently clustered around three categories of offerings

Self-publishing Authors

POD fuels a new category of publishing (or printing) company that offers services, usually for a fee, directly to authors who wish to self-publish. These services generally include printing and shipping each individual book ordered, handling royalties, and getting listings in online bookstores. The initial investment required for POD services is lower than for print runs. Other services may also be available, including formatting, proofreading, and editing, but such companies typically do not spend money on marketing, unlike the conventional publishers they disintermediate. Such companies are suitable for authors prepared to design and promote their work themselves, with minimal support and at minimal cost. POD publishing gives authors editorial independence, speed to market, ability to revise content, and greater financial return per copy than royalties paid by conventional publishers.

POD Enablement Platforms

While amateur/professional writers are targeted as early adopters by players like Infinity Publishing and Trafford Publishing, there is an effort now to make POD more mass-market. A class of horizontal technology platforms like Lulu, Picaboo, Blurb, Peecho and QooP have chosen to be "author agnostic" and drive POD technology across the chasm, extending from its early adopter writers, to a broad mass-market of ordinary citizens who may want to express, record and print keepsake copies of memories and personal writing (diaries, travelogues, wedding journals, baby books, family reunion reports etc.). Instead of tailoring themselves to the classic book format (100+ pages, mostly text, complex rules around copyrights and royalties), these new platforms strive to make POD more mass-market by creating tools/APIs within which a range of different text and picture entry systems can be transferred into a POD paradigm, and delivered back to the consumer as finished books. The management of copyrights and royalties is often less important in this market, as the books themselves have a narrow audience (close family and friends, for instance), and the real value proposition is around the ability to get a physical copy of a digital journal, blog, or picture-collection.

The major photo storage services (e.g. Kodak's Ofoto and Shutterfly and HP's Snapfish) have included the ability to produce picture books and calendars. However, they focus on monetizing digital photography. Blurb and Lulu bring this paradigm to a larger volume of creative work (primarily text, as written in personal blogs), and include the capability to embed photographs, and other media. QooP and Peecho take on the role of an infrastructure service provider, allowing any partner website to leverage its pre-designed payment and printing functions. Next to an API, Peecho provides an embeddable print button, very similar to a "Facebook Like".

Publisher Use

Print-on-demand services that offer printing and distributing services to publishing companies (instead of directly to self-publishing authors) are also growing in popularity within the industry.

Maintaining Availability

Among traditional publishers, POD services can be used to make sure that books remain available when one print run has sold out, but another has not yet become available. This maintains the availability of older titles whose future sales may not be great enough to justify a further conventional print run. This can be useful for publishers with large backlists, where sales for individual titles may be low, but where cumulative sales may be significant.

Managing Uncertainty

Print on demand can be used to reduce risk when dealing with "surge" titles that are expected to have large sales but a short sales life (such as celebrity biographies or event tie-ins): these titles represent high profitability but also high risk owing to the danger of inadvertently printing many more copies than are necessary, and the associated costs of maintaining excess inventory or pulping. POD allows a publisher to exploit a short "sales window" with minimized risk exposure by "guessing low" - using cheaper conventional printing to produce enough copies to satisfy a more pessimistic forecast of the title's sales, and then relying on POD to make up the difference.

Niche Publications

Print on demand is also used to print and reprint "niche" books that may have a high retail price but limited sales opportunities, such as specialist academic works. An academic publisher may be expected to keep these specialist titles in print even though the target market is almost saturated, making further conventional print runs uneconomic.

The detailed local history of a small community is one "niche" well adapted to print-on-demand, as these books are invaluable to libraries, museums and archives in that small community but are limited in their marketability outside their home region. Public libraries which normally avoid print-on-demand tomes due to their lower quality will readily make exceptions if content fits a local niche which cannot be addressed by more conventional means.

Many of the smallest small presses, often called micro-presses because they have inconsequential profits, have become heavily reliant on POD technology and ebooks. This is either because they serve such a small market that print runs would be unprofitable or because they are too small to absorb much financial risk.

Variable Formats

Print on demand also allows for books to be printed in a variety of formats. This process, known as accessible publishing, allows books to be printed in a variety of larger fonts, special formats for those with vision impairment or reading disabilities, as well as personalised fonts and formats that suit the individuals needs. This has been championed by a variety of new companies.

Economics

Profits from print on demand publishing are on a per-sale basis, and royalties vary depending on the route by which the item is sold. Highest profits are usually generated from sales direct from the print-on-demand service's website or by the author buying copies from the service at a discount, as the publisher, and then selling them personally. Lower royalties come from traditional "bricks and mortar" bookshops and online retailers both of which buy at high discount, although some POD companies allow the publisher or author to set their own discount level. Unless the publisher or author has fixed their discount rate, the higher the volume sold the lower the royalty becomes, as the retailer is able to buy at greater discount.

Because the per-unit cost is typically greater with POD than with a print run of thousands of copies, it is common for POD books to be more expensive than similar books that come from conventional print runs, especially if that book is produced exclusively with POD instead of using POD as a supplemental technology between print runs.

Book stores order books through a wholesaler or distributor, usually at high discount of anything up to 70 percent. Wholesalers obtain their books in two ways; either as a special order where the book is ordered direct from the publisher when a book store requests a copy, or as a stocked title which they keep in their own warehouse as part of their inventory. Stocked titles are usually also available via sale or return, meaning that the book store can return unsold stock for full credit at anything up to one year after the initial sale.

POD books are rarely if ever available on such terms because for the publishing provider it is considered too much of a risk. However, wholesalers keep a careful eye on what titles they are selling, and if authors work hard to promote their work and achieve a reasonable number of orders from book stores or online retailers (who use the same wholesalers as the bricks and mortar stores), then there is a reasonable chance of their work becoming available on such terms.

Although returnability lessens the risk for book stores and helps POD authors get through the door, only a certain proportion of such stock can be returned. Non-returnability can make bookstores less enthusiastic about POD books.

Many print-on-demand titles are debut works; many bookstores are reluctant to take a risk on an author's first, untested work without the endorsement of a commercial publisher.

References

- Cronin, Mary J. (1997). Banking and Finance on the Internet, John Wiley and Sons. ISBN 0-471-29219-2 page 41 from Banking and Finance on the Internet. Retrieved 2008-07-10.

- Tapscott, Don (1997). The digital economy : promise and peril in the age of networked intelligence. New York: McGraw-Hill. ISBN 0-07-063342-8.

- Tulloch, Mitch (2003). Koch, Jeff; Haynes, Sandra, eds. Microsoft Encyclopedia of Security. Redmond, Washington: Microsoft Press. p. 16. ISBN 0-7356-1877-1.

- Pieters, Rik (2008). "A Review of Eye-Tracking Research in Marketing". Review of Marketing Research. 4: 123–147. doi:10.1108/s1548-6435(2008)0000004009. ISBN 978-0-7656-2092-7.

- Mary Maureen Brown. "Electronic Government" Jack Rabin (ed.). Encyclopedia of Public Administration and Public Policy, Marcel Dekker, 2003, pp. 427–432 ISBN 0824742400.

- JA, Ashiq. "Recommendations for Providing Digital Signature Services". Cryptomathic. Retrieved 7 January 2016.

- "FIPS PUB 186-4: Digital Signature Standard (DSS)" (PDF). National Institute of Standards and Technology. Retrieved 7 January 2016.

- Turner, Dawn. "What is a digital signature - what it does, how it work". Cryptomathic. Retrieved 7 June 2016.

- "Streaming the London Olympic Games with the "Go Live Package" from iStreamPlanet and Haivision | iStreamPlanet". www.istreamplanet.com. Retrieved 2015-11-11.

- Secoder 2.0-Standard in StarMoney starmoney.de, Star Finanz-Software Entwicklung und Vertriebs GmbH, Retrieved on November 18, 2015.

- "Now, SMS from IRCTC is equivalent to e-ticket". Hubli: The Hindu. 27 February 2012. Retrieved Dec 21, 2014.

- "IAB internet advertising revenue report 2013 first six months' results" (PDF). Internet Advertising Bureau. October 2013. Retrieved 4 March 2014.

- Lucian Constantin (2014-05-15). "Online advertising poses significant security, privacy risks to users, US Senate report says". Network World. Retrieved 2015-12-24.

- "CryptoWall! crooks! 'turn! to! Yahoo! ads! to! spread! ransomware!'". The Register. 11 August 2014. Retrieved 4 January 2015.

- Lewis, Peter (August 12, 1994). "Attention Shoppers: Internet Is Open". New York Times. Retrieved November 29, 2014.

- Wolverton, Troy (May 10, 1999). "Netmarket exposes customer order data". CNET. Retrieved November 29, 2014.

- Peters, Kurt (July 24, 2001). "Trilegiant reduces unfilled and back orders with web ordering system". Internet Retailers. Retrieved November 29, 2014.

- Gilber, Alorie (11 August 2004). "E-commerce turns 10". CNet. Archived from the original on 29 October 2014. Retrieved 29 October 2014.

Open Source E-commerce: An Integrated Study

The chapter on open source e-commerce offers an insightful focus, keeping in mind the complex subject matter. Various free and open-source software are available online that help to maintain store inventory and other databases. OsCommerce, drupal commerce, magenoto, nopCommerce, spree commerce and woocommerce are some softwares related to open source E-commerce.

OsCommerce

OsCommerce (styled "osCommerce" - "open source Commerce") is an e-commerce and online store-management software program. It can be used on any web server that has PHP and MySQL installed. It is available as free software under the GNU General Public License.

History

OsCommerce was started in March 2000 in Germany by project founder and leader Harald Ponce de Leon as *The Exchange Project*. In its infancy, OsCommerce was referred to by Ponce de Leon as "a side thing" and "an example research study". By late 2001, a team formed for its development and in the words of HPDL, this was the point the team started taking the project seriously.

As of August 2008, OsCommerce reported over 14,000 'live' websites using the program. This number is almost certainly conservative, given the inclusion of OsCommerce in hosting panel application installers such as Fantastico and Softaculous.

In November 2010 the development of OsCommerce v2.2 was met with another stable release. Version 2.3, as it was branded, takes advantage of the benefits of tableless web design, and includes a number of social networking tools.

The current iteration is version 3.x (in development) and is a major re-write of the program to incorporate an object-oriented backend, a template system to allow easy layout changes, and inclusion of an administration-area username and password definition during installation. The latest development version is 3.0.2, and was released on 6 August 2011.

Versions

There are currently two releases of OsCommerce. Versions 2.3 (stable) and 3.0 (in development) are developed as two independent programs, and as such do not share code. Contributions, the official name for the open-source community developed plugins, are developed for either 2.x or 3.0, and are incompatible with one another.

Release date	Release name
12 March 2000	The Exchange Project Preview Release 1.0
14 May 2000	The Exchange Project Preview Release 1.1
2 December 2000	The Exchange Project Preview Release 2.0
13 December 2000	The Exchange Project Preview Release 2.0a
6 March 2001	The Exchange Project Preview Release 2.1
17 February 2003	OsCommerce 2.2 Milestone 1
7 December 2003	OsCommerce 2.2 Milestone 2
12 November 2005	OsCommerce 2.2 Milestone 2 Update 051112
13 November 2005	OsCommerce 2.2 Milestone 2 Update 051113
17 August 2006	OsCommerce 2.2 Milestone 2 Update 060817
3 July 2007	OsCommerce Online Merchant 2.2 RC1
16 January 2008	OsCommerce Online Merchant 2.2 RC2
30 January 2008	OsCommerce Online Merchant 2.2 RC2a
12 November 2010	OsCommerce Online Merchant 2.3
14 November 2010	OsCommerce Online Merchant 2.3.1
31 March 2011	OsCommerce Online Merchant 3.0 (development)
6 August 2011	OsCommerce Online Merchant 3.0.2 (development)
18 July 2012	OsCommerce Online Merchant 2.3.2
15 August 2012	OsCommerce Online Merchant 2.3.3
26 September 2013	OsCommerce Online Merchant 2.3.3.4
5 June 2014	OsCommerce Online Merchant 2.3.4

Branches

Distributed under the GNU General Public License, OsCommerce is one of the earliest PHP based Open Source shopping cart software distributions. As such, it has spawned a number of forks, such as Zen Cart (2003).

Publicised Vulnerabilities

In August 2011 three vulnerabilities in version 2.2 of the OsCommerce system were exploited, allowing the addition of an iframe and JavaScript code to infect visitors to websites. Armorize reports this allowed infected web pages to hit 90,000 in a very short time until it was noticed and increasing further to 4.5 million pages within the space of a week. OsCommerce 2.3 was made available in November 2011 and patched the exploited security holes.

Drupal Commerce

Drupal Commerce is open-source eCommerce software that augments the content management system Drupal. Within the context of a Drupal-based site, Drupal Commerce presents products for purchase; walks customers through the checkout process; keeps track of invoices, receipts, orders, and payments; facilitates shipping and payment; and performs other functions needed by online merchants.

History

Drupal Commerce was created by Commerce Guys under the leadership of Ryan Szrama, the author of shopping-cart software Übercart. It was originally born as a rearchitecture project of Übercart, and was called "Übercore" until January 14, 2010, when Mr. Szrama renamed it "Drupal Commerce". Version 1.0 was released on August 23, 2011.

Drupal Commerce has had steady growth since its introduction. Over 53,000 active sites use it, including U.K. postal service Royal Mail, international language school Eurocentres, McDonalds (France), and hundreds of consumer brands. The Drupal Commerce market has also supported publication of several instructional books and video courses.

Extending Drupal Commerce

Like Drupal itself, Drupal Commerce can be extended through the use of modules that add functionality and themes that define visual presentation. There are more than 300 Drupal Commerce-specific modules available for free in such categories as payment gateways, shipping service providers, and administrative and development tools.

Magento

Magento is an open-source e-commerce platform written in PHP. The software was originally developed by Varien Inc., a US private company headquartered in Culver City, California, with assistance from volunteers.

Varien published the first general-availability release of the software on March 31, 2008. Roy Rubin, former CEO of Varien, later sold a substantial share of the company to eBay, which eventually completely acquired and then spun off the company.

According to the research conducted by aheadWorks in May 2015, Magento's market share among the 30 most popular e-commerce platforms is about 29.8%.

On November 17, 2015, Magento 2.0 was released, with an aim to provide new ways to heighten user engagement, smooth navigation, conversion rates and overall revenue generation, it has well-organized business user tools speed up build up time and enhances productivity. Table locking issues have purportedly been considerably reduced, Improved Page Caching and also allows in streamlining Guest checkout process for existing users, Enterprise-grade scalability, improved performance and better code base are some of the touted benefits of newer Magento version.

Magento employs the MySQL/MariaDB relational database management system, the PHP programming language, and elements of the Zend Framework. It applies the conventions of object-oriented programming and model–view–controller architecture. Magento also uses the entity–attribute–value model to store data. On top of that, Magento 2 introduced the Model-View-ViewModel pattern to its front-end code using the JavaScript library Knockout.js.

History

Magento officially started development in early 2007. Seven months later, on August 31, 2007, the first public beta version was released.

Varien, the company owning Magento, formerly worked with osCommerce. It had originally planned to fork osCommerce but later decided to rewrite it as Magento.

In February 2011, eBay announced it had made an investment in Magento in 2010, worth a 49% ownership share of the company.

On June 6, 2011, eBay announced that it would be acquiring the rest of Magento, which would join its new X.Commerce initiative. Magento's CEO and co-founder Roy Rubin wrote on the Magento blog that "Magento will continue to operate out of Los Angeles, with Yoav Kutner and me as its leaders.".

Yoav Kutner left Magento in April 2012 citing the vision for Magento having changed since the time of acquisition due to high level staff changes.

As a result of the breakup of eBay following Carl Icahn's raid, Magento was spun out as an independent company by the new owner Permira private equity fund on November 3, 2015.

Overview

Magento is the provider of three distinct platforms, Magento Community Edition, Magento Enterprise Edition and Magento Enterprise Cloud Edition. There were also two former platforms, Magento Professional Edition and Magento Go.

Magento Community Edition

Magento Community Edition is an open-source eCommerce platform. Developers can implement the core files and extend its functionality by adding new plug-in modules provided by other developers. Since the first public beta version was released in 2007,

Community Edition has been developed and customized in order to provide a basic eCommerce platform.

The current release and each of the previous historical release versions of the 1.X and 2.X version branches of Magento Community Edition are available on the Magento Commerce, Inc. website for download as singe-file downloads Development of the 2.X version branch of Magento CE is coordinated publicly on GitHub.

The latest actively supported versions of Magento Community Edition are CE 1.9.2.4 and 2.0.4 released on March 31, 2016.

Magento Enterprise Edition

Magento Enterprise Edition is derived from the Magento Community Edition and has the same core files. Unlike Community Edition, this is not free, but has more features and functionality. This edition is designed for large businesses that require technical support with installation, usage, configuration, and troubleshooting. Although Magento Enterprise has annual maintenance fees, neither Community nor Enterprise Editions include hosting. The Magento team develops Enterprise Edition by cooperating with users and third parties. Development on the 2.X branch of Magento EE is coordinated publicly on GitHub.

The latest actively supported versions of Magento Enterprise Edition are EE 1.14.2.4 and EE 2.0.4 released on March 31, 2016.

Magento Go

Magento Go was a cloud-based eCommerce solution that included web hosting by Magento Inc. It was launched in February 2011 to support small businesses by providing an option that did not require software installation. Magento Go was the least customizable platform, though it still had built-in modules and could have Magento extensions enabled for more functionality. On July 1, 2014, Magento Inc. announced that they would be shutting down the Magento Go platform on February 1, 2015.

Magento 2

new release of this eCommerce platform. It has many new and improved features, and its architecture is quite different from all the previous versions. Magento 2 was announced in 2010. It was planned for release in 2011, and its merchant beta version was released in July 2015. Since then Magento 1 and Magento 2 have existed simultaneously, but only the latter has new updates.

Features

Magento supports a Web template system which generates multiple similar-looking pages and customizes theme.

Magento provides a basic theme which sets up an eCommerce website. The theme is designed for customizing all pages by adding or editing the PHP, HTML and CSS. Magento users may install themes which change the display of the website or its functionality. Without loss of content or layout of pages, themes are interchangeable with Magento installations. Themes are installed by uploading theme folders via FTP or SSH and applying them using the backend admin system.

Magento developers have created Magento plugins that extend its basic built-in functionality. Magento users can install modules by downloading them, and uploading them to their server, or applying a module's Extension Key through Magento Connect Manager.

Magento allows users to integrate several different domain names into one control panel and manage more than one storefront at a time from a single admin panel.

"Imagine eCommerce" Conference

"Imagine eCommerce" is the annual Magento eCommerce conference that has run since 2011. The first event was held in February 2011 in Los Angeles with more than 600 Magento merchants, partners, and developers. The goals of the "Imagine eCommerce" are sharing ecommerce ideas and providing networking opportunity sessions.

Certification

There are four different Magento certifications. Three of them aim to prove developers' competency in implementing modules; one (Certified Solution Specialist) targets business users (consultants, analysts, project managers). Magento Front End Developer Certification is mainly focused on improving the user interface (UI) of built-in applications. This certification is related with templates, layouts, Javascript, and CSS. Magento Developer certification is geared toward back end developers who implement the core modules. The Plus certification tests deep understanding of Magento Enterprise modules and the entire architecture.

NopCommerce

NopCommerce is an open-source E-commerce solution based on ASP.NET MVC 4.0 and MS SQL Server 2008 (or higher) backend Database. It is available under the nopCommerce Public License V3 and officially launched in October 2008 for small to medium-sized businesses.

History

Nopcommerce development started in 2008 by Andrei Mazulnitsyn in Yaroslavl, Russia. In 2009, the Nop Solutions were founded and expanded to a company of two. Later that year, Microsoft recognized nopCommerce as significant and included it to Microsoft Web platform Installer. The company has its offices in Yaroslavl, Russia.

The first versions introduced basic functionality and main features such as order processing, attributes, plugins, discounts, tier pricing, news, blogs, private messages, forums, tax and shipping support . In June 2010, a new data access layer was introduced in version 1.70. Version 2.00 (August 2011) launched nopCommerce as an ASP.NET MVC based solution. Later in 2011 nopCommerce moved to ASP.NET MVC 4. Versions 3.00 and 3.10 was extended to include multi-store and multi-vendor features and to simplify the product logic. In versions 3.5 and 3.6 and 3.7 a new modern and responsive template were included. The version release cycle is 5–6 months.

Usage

As for December 2015, Builtwith.com reports that 25,511 websites that have used nopCommerce and that the market share for nopCommerce among top sites is 2.5%. The installation package was downloaded more than 1.7 million times.

Business Model

nopCommerce can be downloaded, installed and used free of charge. The community forum provides free support. There is an optional fee for white-labeling. Until 2014, the documentation was downloaded on a paid basis and now is available free of charge.

Community

nopCommerce has an active community of users and developers, which provides assistance to other users contributes with code, plugins and other extensions and helps to the planning of the roadmap. It has 107 solution partners in 37 countries providing custom development, graphic theme creation, and other services. The stackoverflow.com has more than 750 questions tagged "nopCommerce". Current marketplace offers more than thousand plug-ins and themes. As for December 2015, the program had been translated to 30 languages. On the 30th of October 2015, the first conference of the nopCommerce community #NopDevDays took place in Amsterdam, Netherlands, attracting more than 65 delegates from 14 countries.

Awards and Recognitions

In 2010 and 2011 nopCommerce had reached the final in Packt Open Source E-Commerce Award. nopCommerce is in the featured and top 5 most downloaded applications provided by Microsoft Web Platform Installer. In 2013, nopCommerce was chosen as the best finance app by Russian WebReady awards. In January 2016, nopCommerce won CMScritic's "Best eCommerce for SMB" award.

Spree Commerce

Spree Commerce (also known as Spree) is an open source e-commerce solution based on Ruby on Rails. It was created by Sean Schofield in 2007 and has since had over 740 contributors.

On July 1, 2011, Spree received $1.5 million in seed funding from AOL and True Ventures. On February 25, 2014 Spree raised an additional $5M in Series A funding led by Thrive Capital. Also participating were Vegas Tech Fund (led by Zappos CEO Tony Hsieh), Red Swan (led by Bonobos CEO Andy Dunn) as well as existing investors True Ventures and AOL Ventures.

Companies using Spree include Chipotle Mexican Grill (NYSE: CMG), Second Life, Bonobos (apparel), Fortnum and Mason.

Spree has been downloaded 429,501 times as of January 29, 2016.

On September 21, 2015 it was acquired by First Data

After the First Data acquisition, developers from Spark Solutions and VinSol now maintain the Spree Commerce Open Source project.

WooCommerce

WooCommerce is an open source e-commerce plugin for WordPress. It is designed for small to large-sized online merchants using WordPress. Launched on September 27, 2011, the plugin quickly became popular for its simplicity to install and customize and free base product.

History

WooCommerce was first developed by WordPress theme developer WooThemes, who hired Mike Jolley and James Koster, developers at Jigowatt, to work on a fork of Jigoshop that became WooCommerce. In August 2014, WooCommerce powered 381,187 sites (or 17.77% of e-commerce sites online).

In November 2014, the first WooConf, a conference focusing on eCommerce using WooCommerce was held in San Francisco, California. It attracted 300 attendees.

In May 2015, WooThemes and WooCommerce were acquired by Automattic, operator of WordPress.com and core contributor to the WordPress software.

Usage

WooCommerce has been adopted by over 380,000 online retailers. It is used by a number of high-traffic websites, among them are Internet Systems Consortium and Small Press Expo. For the 3rd week of September 2015, Trends indicated that WooCommerce ran on 30% of e-commerce sites and millions of active installs.

WooCommerce has attracted significant popularity as the base product, in addition to many extensions and plugins, is free and open source. In addition, there are thousands of paid add-ons for fixed prices. However, web developers have listed compatibility issues with WordPress, a steeper learning curve, lack of live support, and dependence on large numbers of plugins (which can decrease performance) as disadvantages.

References

- Jones, Richard (September 2013). Getting Started with Drupal Commerce. Packt Publishing. p. 152. ISBN 9781783280230. Retrieved 10 June 2014.

- Carter, Richard (June 2013). Building E-commerce Sites with Drupal Commerce Cookbook. Packt Publishing. p. 206. ISBN 9781782161226. Retrieved 10 June 2014.

- "Magento 2 Migration. Is it worth it?". Magento Developers & Designers - MavenEcommerce. Retrieved 2016-02-19.

- "Open Source Ecommerce Software & Solutions | Magento". www.magentocommerce.com. Retrieved 2016-03-14.

- Perez, Sarah (27 September 2011). "WooThemes Launches WooCommerce To Turn WordPress Sites Into Online Shops". TechCrunch. Retrieved 17 January 2015.

- Imel, Ryan (28 August 2011). "Jigoshop team and WordPress community members share thoughts on forking". WPCandy. Retrieved 17 January 2015.

- Imel, Ryan (25 August 2011). "WooThemes forks Jigoshop into WooCommerce, launches WooLabs". WPCandy. Retrieved 17 January 2015.

- "WordPress Parent Automattic Buys WooCommerce, a Shopping Tool for Web Publishers". Re/code. Retrieved 19 May 2015.

- "Statistics for websites using Ecommerce technologies (The Entire Internet Tab)". builtwith.com. Retrieved 21 September 2015.

- Geller, Tom (November 17, 2011). Create Your First Online Store with Drupal Commerce. lynda.com. Retrieved 10 June 2014.

- Rao, Leena (12 April 2012). "Recently Departed Magento CTO And Co-Founder: eBay Doesn't Understand The Meaning Of Open". TechCrunch. Retrieved 17 January 2015.

- Spree Raises $1.5 Million From True Ventures, Aol For Open Source eCommerce Platform techcrunch.com. Retrieved October 1, 2012.

- Ponce de Leon, Harald. "osCommerce Online Merchant v2.3". osCommerce Development Blog. Retrieved 20 March 2011.

- Warren, Christina (6 June 2011). "eBay Acquires Open Source Ecommerce Company Magento". Mashable. Retrieved 17 January 2015.

Darknet Market: A Comprehensive Overview

Websites that operate on darknets or the deep web are known as a darknet market. Darknet markets basically function as black-markets and they deal in illicit substances such as drugs, weapons and steroids. This chapter incorporates the types of darknet markets which are as agora, evolution and Silk Road.

Darknet Market

A darknet market or cryptomarket is a commercial website on the dark web that operates via darknets such as Tor or I2P. They function primarily as black markets, selling or brokering transactions involving drugs, cyber-arms, weapons, counterfeit currency, stolen credit card details, forged documents, unlicensed pharmaceuticals, steroids, other illicit goods as well as the sale of legal products. In December 2014, a study by Gareth Owen from the University of Portsmouth suggested the second most popular content on Tor were darknet markets.

Following on from the model developed by Silk Road, contemporary markets are characterised by their use of darknet anonymised access (typically Tor), bitcoin payment with escrow services, and eBay-like vendor feedback systems.

History

1970s to 2011

Though e-commerce on the dark web only started around 2006, illicit goods were among the first items to be transacted using the internet, when in the early 1970s students at Stanford University and Massachusetts Institute of Technology used what was then called the ARPANET to coordinate the purchase of cannabis. By the end of the 1980s, newsgroups like alt.drugs would become online centres of drug discussion and information; however, any related deals were arranged entirely off-site directly between individuals. With the development and popularization of the World Wide Web and e-commerce in the 1990s, the tools to discuss or conduct illicit transactions became more widely available. One of the better-known web-based drug forums, The Hive, launched in 1997, serving as an information sharing forum for practical drug synthesis and legal discussion. The Hive was featured in a Dateline NBC special called *The*

"X" Files in 2001, bringing the subject into public discourse. From 2003, the "Research Chemical Mailing List" (RCML) would discuss sourcing "Research Chemicals" from legal and grey sources as an alternative to forums such as alt.drugs.psychedelics. However Operation Web Tryp let to a series of website shut downs and arrests in this area.

Since the year 2000, some of the emerging cyber-arms industry operates online, including the Eastern European "Cyber-arms Bazaar", trafficking in the most powerful crimeware and hacking tools. In the 2000s, early cybercrime and carding forums such as ShadowCrew experimented with drug wholesaling on a limited scale.

The Farmer's Market was launched in 2006 and moved onto Tor in 2010. It was closed and several operators and users arrested in April 2012 as a result of Operation Adam Bomb, a two-year investigation led by the U.S. Drug Enforcement Administration. It has been considered a "proto-Silk Road" but the use of payment services such as PayPal and Western Union allowed law enforcement to trace payments and it was subsequently shut down by the FBI in 2012.

Silk Road and Early Markets

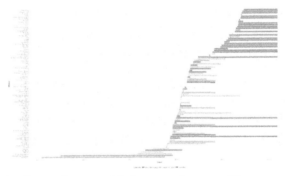

Timeline and status of darknet markets, as of June 7, 2015

The first pioneering marketplace to use both Tor and bitcoin escrow was Silk Road, founded by Ross Ulbricht under pseudonym "Dread Pirate Roberts" in February 2011. In June 2011, Gawker published an article about the site, which led to "Internet buzz" and an increase in website traffic. This in turn led to political pressure from Senator Chuck Schumer on the US DEA and Department of Justice to shut it down which they finally did in October 2013 following a lengthy investigation. Silk Road's use of both Tor, bitcoin escrow and feedback systems would set the standard for new darknet markets for the coming years. The shutdown was described by news site DeepDotWeb as "the best advertising the dark net markets could have hoped for" following the proliferation of competing sites this caused, and *The Guardian* predicted others would take over the market that Silk Road previously dominated.

The months and years following Silk Road's closure would be marked by a greatly increased number of shorter-lived markets as well as semi-regular law enforcement take downs, hacks, scams and voluntary closures.

Atlantis, the first site to accept Litecoin as well as bitcoin, closed in September 2013, just prior to the Silk Road raid, leaving users just 1 week to withdraw any coins. In October 2013 *Project Black Flag*, closed and stole their users' bitcoins in the panic shortly following Silk Road's shut down. Black Market Reloaded's popularity increased dramatically after the closure of Silk Road and Sheep Marketplace however in late November 2013, the owner of Black Market Reloaded announced that the website would be taken offline due to the unmanageable influx of new customers this caused. Sheep Marketplace which launched in March 2013 was one of the lesser known sites to gain popularity with Silk Road's closure. Not long after those events it ceased operation in December 2013, when it announced it was shutting down after two Florida men stole $6 million worth of users' bitcoins.

Post-silk Road to Present

From late 2013 through to 2014, new markets started launching with regularity, such as the Silk Road 2.0, run by the former Silk Road site administrators as well as the Agora marketplace. Such launches were not always a success, in February 2014 the highly anticipated market based on Black Market Reloaded, Utopia opened only to shut down 8 days later following rapid actions by Dutch law enforcement. February 2014 also marked the short lifespans of Black Goblin Market and CannabisRoad, two sites which closed after being deanonymised without much effort.

November 2014 briefly shook the darknet market ecosystem, when Operation Onymous executed by the FBI and UK's National Crime Agency led to the seizure of 27 hidden sites, including one of the largest markets at the time Silk Road 2.0 as well 12 smaller markets and individual vendor sites. By September 2014, Agora was reported to be the largest market, avoiding Operation Onymous and as of April 2015 has gone on to be the largest overall marketplace with more listings than the Silk Road at its height.

2015 would feature market diversification and further developments around escrow and decentralisation.

In March 2015 the Evolution marketplace performed an 'exit scam', stealing escrowed bitcoins worth $12 million, half of the ecosystem's listing market share at that time. The closure of Evolution led to a users redistributing to Black Bank and Agora. However Black Bank, which as of April 2015 captured 5% of the darknet market's listings, announced on May 18, 2015 its closure for 'maintenance' before disappearing in a similar scam. Following these events commentators suggested that further market decentralization could be required, such as the service OpenBazaar in order to protect buyers and vendors from this risk in the future as well as more widespread support from 'multi-sig' cryptocurrency payments.

In April, TheRealDeal, the first open cyber-arms market for software exploits as well as drugs launched to the interest of computer security experts. In May varied DDOS attacks were performed against different markets including TheRealDeal. The market owners set up a phishing website to get the attacker's password, and subsequently revealed collaboration between the attacker and the administrator of Mr Nice Guy's market who was also planning to scam his users. This information was revealed to news site DeepDotWeb.

On July 31, the Italian police in conjunction with Europol shut down the Italian language Babylon darknet market seizing 11,000 bitcoin wallet addresses and 1 million euros.

At the end of August, the leading marketplace Agora announced its imminent temporary closure after reporting 'suspicious activity' on their server, suspecting some kind of deanonymisation bug in Tor.

Since October 2015, AlphaBay is recognized as the largest market. From then on, through to 2016 there was a period of extended stability for the markets, until in April when the large Nucleus marketplace collapsed for unknown reasons, taking escrowed coins with it.

Market Features

Search and Discussion

One of the central discussion forums is Reddit's /r/DarkNetMarkets/, which have been the subject of legal investigation, as well as the Tor-based discussion forum, The Hub. Many market places maintain their own dedicated discussion forums and subreddits. The majority of the marketplaces are in English, but some are opening up in Chinese, Russian, and Ukrainian.

The dedicated market search engine 'Grams' allows the searching of multiple markets directly without login or registration.

Dark web news and review sites such as DeepDotWeb. and All Things Vice provide exclusive interviews and commentary into the dynamic markets. Uptime and comparison services such as DNStats provide sources of information about active markets as well as suspected scams and law enforcement activity. Due to the decentralized nature of these markets, phishing and scam site are often maliciously or accidentally referenced.

After discovering the location of a market, a user must register on the site, sometimes with a referral link after which they can browse listings. A further PIN may be required to perform transactions, better protecting users against login credential compromise.

Customer Payments

Transactions typically use bitcoin for payment, sometimes combined with tumblers for added anonymity and PGP to secure communications between buyers and vendors from being stored on the site itself. Many sites use bitcoin multisig transactions to improve security and reduce dependency on the site's escrow. The Helix bitcoin tumbler offers direct anonymized marketplace payment integrations.

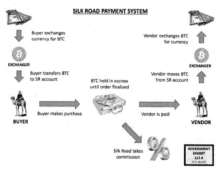

Flowchart of The Silk Road's payment system, produced
to serve as evidence in the trial of its owner.

On making a purchase, the buyer must transfer cryptocurrency into the site's escrow, after which a vendor dispatches their goods then claims the payment from the site. On receipt or non-receipt of the item users may leave feedback against the vendor's account. Buyers may "finalize early" (FE), releasing funds from escrow to the vendor prior to receiving their goods in order to expedite a transaction, but leave themselves vulnerable to fraud if they choose to do so.

Market Types

Items on a typical centralized darknet market are listed from a range of vendors in an eBay like marketplace format. Virtually all such markets have advanced reputation, search and shipping features similar to Amazon.com.

Some of the most popular vendors are now opening up dedicated own online shops separate from the large market places. Individual sites have even returned to operating on the clearnet, with mixed success.

Some internet forums such as the defunct Tor Carding Forum and the Russian Anonymous Marketplace function as markets with trusted members providing escrow services and users engaging in off-forum messaging. In May 2014 the "Deepify" service attempted to automate the process of setting up markets with a SAAS solution, however this closed a short time later.

Following repeated failures of centralised infrastructure, a number of decentralised marketplace software alternatives have arisen using blockchain technology, including OpenBazaar, Syscoin, Shadow, BitBay, Bitmarkets, and Nxt.

Vendors

To list on a market, a vendor may have undergone an application process via referral, proof of reputation from another market or given a cash deposit to the market.

Many vendors list their wares of multiple markets, ensuring they retain their reputation even should a single market place close. Grams have launched "InfoDesk" to allow central content and identity management for vendors.

Meanwhile, individual law enforcement operations regularly investigate and arrest individual vendors and those purchasing significant quantities for personal use.

A February 2016 report suggested that 1/4 of all DNM purchases were for resale.

Products

Whilst a great many products are sold, drugs dominate the numbers of listings. Due to the increased law enforcement attention, many markets will refuse to list weapons or poisons. Markets such as the original Silk Road would refuse to list anything where the *"purpose is to harm or defraud, such as stolen credit cards, assassinations, and weapons of mass destruction"*.

Later markets such as Evolution would ban 'child pornography, services related to murder/assassination/terrorism, prostitution, ponzi schemes, and lotteries' but allow the wholesaling of credit card data. Such markets as AlphaBay Market would go on to host a significant share of the commercial fraud market, featuring carding, counterfeiting and many related services. Loyalty card information is also sold as it is easy to launder.

The weapons market appears to attract extra attention from law enforcement as well as certain items that bear an association with weapons such as certain types of knives and blades .

Market Operations

Nachash, former proprietor of Doxbin wrote a guide in early 2015 entitled *So, You Want To Be a Darknet Drug Lord ....*

Background research tasks included learning from past drug lords, researching legal matters, studying law enforcement agency tactics and obtaining legal representation. With regards to the prospective market's hosting, he recommends identifying a hosting country with gaps in their mutual legal assistance treaty with one's country of residence, avoiding overpriced bulletproof hosting and choosing a web host with Tor support that accepts suitably hard to trace payment. Patterns recommend to avoid include hiring hitmen like Dread Pirate Roberts and sharing handles for software questions on sites like Stackexchange.

He advises on running a secured server operating system with a server-side transparent Tor proxy server, hardening web application configurations, Tor-based server administration, automated server configuration management rebuild and secure destruction with frequent server relocation rather than a darknet managed hosting service. Obfuscating traffic by investing in Tor relays which the market site will exclusively use he recommends to protect against guard node deanonymisation.

For a local machine configuration he recommends a computer purchased in cash running Linux using a local Tor transparent proxy. For OPSEC he suggests avoiding storing conversation logs, varying writing styles, avoiding mobile phone based tracking and leaking false personal details to further obfuscate one's identity. Use of OTR and PGP are recommended.

He recommends verifying market employees carefully and to weed out law enforcement infiltration through barium meal tests.

Fraudulent Markets

A large amount of services pretend to a legitimate vendor shop, or marketplace of some kind in order to defraud people. These include the notoriously unreliable gun stores, or even fake assassination websites.

Commentary

In December 2014, "The Darknet: From Memes to Onionland" Carmen Weisskopf and Domagoj Smoljo explored Darknet culture in an exhibition. This featured the "Random Darknet Shopper" which spent $100 BTC per week from Agora. Their aim was to explore the ethical and philosophical implications of these markets, which, despite high-profile internationally co-ordinated raids persist and flourish.

James Martin's 2014 book *Drugs on the Dark Net: How Cryptomarkets are Transforming the Global Trade in Illicit Drugs* discusses some vendors are even branding their opium or cocaine as "fair trade", "organic" or sourced from conflict-free zones. In June 2015 journalist Jamie Bartlett gave a TED talk about the state of the darknet market ecosystem as it stands today.

According to 2014 studies by Martin, Aldridge & Décary-Hétu and a January 2015 report from the Global Drug Policy Observatory, many harm reduction trends have been spotted. These include the reduced risks associated with street dealing such as being offered hard drugs. The vendor feedback system provides accountability for risks of mixing and side effects and protection against scammers. Online forum communities provide information about safe drug use in an environment where users can anonymously ask questions. Some users report the online element having a moderating affect on their consumption due to the increased lead time ordering from the sites compared to street dealing.

Professor for addiction research Heino Stöver notes that the shops can be seen as a political statement - advancing drug legalization "from below". The result of these markets are higher quality and lower prices of the psychoactive substances as well as a lower risk of violent incidents. A number of studies suggest that markets such as Silk Road may have helped users reduce the harm caused by illicit drug use, particularly compared with street-based drug marketplaces. Examples include the sale of high-quality products with low risk for contamination, vendor-tested products, sharing of trip reports and online discussion of harm reduction practices. Some health professionals such as "DoctorX" provide information, advice and drug-testing services on the darknet. The quality of the products is attributed to the competition and transparency of darknet markets which involve user feedback and reputation features.

Europol reported in December 2014, "We have lately seen a large amount of physical crime move online, at least the "marketing" and delivery part of the business ... [Buyers can] get the illegal commodity delivered risk-free to a place of their choice by the mailman or a courier, or maybe by drone in the future, and can pay with virtual currency and in full anonymity, without the police being able to identify either the buyer or the seller."

In June 2015 the European Monitoring Centre for Drugs and Drug Addiction (EMCD-DA) produced a report citing difficulties controlling virtual market places via darknet markets, social media and mobile apps. In August 2015 it was announced that Interpol now offers a dedicated Dark Web training program featuring technical information on Tor, cybersecurity and simulated darknet market take downs.

In October 2015 the UK's National Crime Agency and GCHQ announced the formation of a "Joint Operations Cell" to focus on cybercrime. In November 2015 this team would be tasked with tacking child exploitation on the dark web as well as other cybercrime.

In February 2015, the EMCDDA produced another report citing the increased importance of customer service and reputation management in the marketplace, the reduced risk of violence and increased product purity. It estimated 1/4 of all purchases were for resale and that the trend towards decentralisation meant they are unlikely to be eliminated any time soon.

A June 2016 report from the Global Drug Survey described how the markets are increasing in popularity, despite ongoing law enforcement action and scams. Other findings include consumers making purchases via friends operating Tor browser and Bitcoin payments, rather than directly. Access to markets in 79% of respondent's cases led to users trying a new type of drug.

Size of Listings

The size of the darknet markets economy can be problematic to estimate. A study based on a combination of listing scrapes and feedback to estimate sales volume by researchers at Carnegie Mellon University captured some of the best data. A reviewed 2013 analysis put the Silk Road grossing $300,000 a day, extrapolating to over $100 million over a year. Subsequent data from later markets has significant gaps as well as complexities associated with analysing multiple marketplaces.

- 18,174 - October 2013, Digital Citizens Alliance, 13,472 of which were on Silk Road in November 2013

- 41,207 - April 2014 Digital Citizens Alliance

- 33,985 - May 2014 The Guardian via Reddit

- 43,175 - July 2014 a report by the BBC

- 65,595 - August 2014 Digital Citizens Alliance

- 51,755 - December 2014 Digital Citizens Alliance

- 68,835 - March 2015 (pre Evolution scam), Digital Citizens Alliance

- 68,322 - April 2015 (post Evolution scam)

In Fiction

In the episode "eps2.3_logic-b0mb.hc" (ep. 5 of season 2) of the drama–thriller television series *Mr. Robot* the protagonist Elliot is supposed to be repairing a Tor hidden site which turns out to be a darknet market called "Midland City" styled after the Silk Road for the sale of guns, sex trafficked women, rocket launchers, drugs and hitmen for hire. When he learns about this his conscience shows. Later he is dragged out of bed and beaten up by two goons and reminded by Ray, the site's administrator, that he was told not to look at the site's content.

Types of Darknet Market

Agora (Online Marketplace)

Agora is a darknet market operating in the Tor network. It launched in 2013. All transactions on Agora are conducted in bitcoin.

Agora was unaffected by Operation Onymous, the November 2014 seizure of several darknet websites (most notably Silk Road 2.0). After Evolution closed in an exit scam in March 2015, Agora replaced it as the largest darknet market.

In October 2014 to January 2015, the art collective !Mediengruppe Bitnik explored darknet culture in an exhibition in Switzerland entitled *The Darknet: From Memes to Onionland*, displaying the purchases of the Random Darknet Shopper, an automated online shopping bot which spent $100 in Bitcoins per week on Agora. The aim was to examine philosophical questions surrounding the darknet, such as the legal culpability of a piece of software or robot. The exhibition of the robot's purchases, a landscape of traded goods that included a bag of ten 120mg Ecstasy pills "with no bullshit inside" (containing 90mg of MDMA), was staged next-door to a police station near Zürich.

In August 2015 Agora's admins released a PGP signed message announcing a pause of operations to protect the site against potential attacks that they believe might be used to deanonymize server locations:

Recently research had come [*sic*] that shed some light on vulnerabilities in Tor Hidden Services protocol which could help to deanonymize server locations. Most of the new and previously known methods do require substantial resources to be executed, but the new research shows that the amount of resources could be much lower than expected, and in our case we do believe we have interested parties who possess such resources. We have a solution in the works which will require big changes into our software stack which we believe will mitigate such problems, but unfortunately it will take time to implement. Additionally, we have recently been discovering suspicious activity around our servers which led us to believe that some of the attacks described in the research could be going on and we decided to move servers once again, however this is only a temporary solution.

At this point, while we don't have a solution ready it would be unsafe to keep our users using the service, since they would be in jeopardy. Thus, and to our great sadness we have to take the market offline for a while, until we can develop a better solution. This is the best course of action for everyone involved.

Evolution (Marketplace)

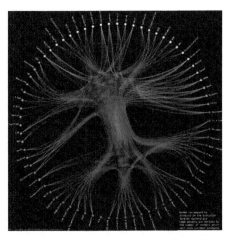

An analysis of the defunct Evolution marketplace shows
the different types of products and vendors on a market

Evolution was a darknet market operating on the Tor network. The site was founded by an individual known as 'Verto' who also founded the now defunct Tor Carding Forum.

Launched January 14, 2014, it saw rapid growth within its first several months, helped in part by law enforcement seizures of some of its competitors during the six-month-long investigation codenamed Operation Onymous. Speaking about why Evolution was not part of Operation Onymous, head of European police cybercrimes division said it was "because there's only so much we can do on one day." *Wired* estimated that as of October 11 it was one of the two largest drug markets.

Evolution was similar to other darknet markets in its prohibitions, disallowing "child pornography, services related to murder/assassination/terrorism, prostitution, ponzi schemes, and lotteries". Where it most prominently differed was in its more lax rules concerning stolen credit cards and others kinds of fraud, permitting, for example, the wholesaling of credit card data.

In mid-March 2015, administrators froze its users escrow accounts, disallowing withdrawals, citing technical difficulties. Evolution had earned a reputation not just for its security, but also for its professionalism and reliability, with an uptime rate much higher than its competition. Partly for that reason, when the site went offline a few days later, on March 18, the user community panicked. The shut down was discovered to be an exit scam, with the operators of the site shutting down abruptly in order to steal the approximately $12 million in bitcoins it was holding as escrow.

Silk Road (Marketplace)

Silk Road was an online black market and the first modern darknet market, best known as a platform for selling illegal drugs. As part of the dark web, it was operated as a Tor hidden service, such that online users were able to browse it anonymously and securely without potential traffic monitoring. The website was launched in February 2011; development had begun six months prior. Initially there were a limited number of new seller accounts available; new sellers had to purchase an account in an auction. Later, a fixed fee was charged for each new seller account.

In October 2013, the Federal Bureau of Investigation (FBI) shut down the website and arrested Ross William Ulbricht under charges of being the site's pseudonymous founder "Dread Pirate Roberts". On 6 November 2013, Silk Road 2.0 came online, run by former administrators of Silk Road. It too was shut down and the alleged operator was arrested on 6 November 2014 as part of the so-called "Operation Onymous".

Ulbricht was convicted of seven charges related to Silk Road in U.S. Federal Court in Manhattan and was sentenced to life in prison without possibility of parole. Further charges alleging murder-for-hire remain pending in Maryland.

History

Operations

Silk Road was founded in February 2011. The name "Silk Road" comes from a historical network of trade routes started during the Han Dynasty (206 BC – 220 AD) between

Europe, India, China, and many other countries on the Afro-Eurasian landmass. Silk Road was operated by the pseudonymous "Dread Pirate Roberts" (named after the fictional character from *The Princess Bride*), who was known for espousing libertarian ideals and criticizing regulation. Two other individuals were also closely involved in the site's growth and success, known as Variety Jones and Smedley.

In June 2011, Gawker published an article about the site which led to "Internet buzz" and an increase in website traffic. Once the site was known publicly, U.S. Senator Charles Schumer asked federal law enforcement authorities to shut it down, including the Drug Enforcement Administration (DEA) and Department of Justice.

In February 2013, an Australian cocaine and MDMA ("ecstasy") dealer became the first person to be convicted of crimes directly related to Silk Road, after authorities intercepted drugs that he was importing through the mail, searched his premises, and discovered his Silk Road alias in an image file on his personal computer. Australian police and the DEA have targeted Silk Road users and made arrests, albeit with limited success at reaching convictions. In December 2013, a New Zealand man was sentenced to two years and four months in jail after being convicted of importing 15 grams of methamphetamine that he had bought on Silk Road.

In May 2013, Silk Road was taken down for a short period of time by a sustained DDoS attack. On 23 June 2013, it was first reported that the DEA seized 11.02 bitcoins, then worth $814, which the media suspected was a result of a Silk Road honeypot sting.

The FBI have claimed that the real IP address of the Silk Road server was found via data leaked directly from the site's CAPTCHA, but security researchers believe that the PHP login page was manipulated to output its $_SERVER variable and real IP following site maintenance reconfiguration.

Arrest and Trial of Ross Ulbricht

Image placed on original Silk Road after seizure of property by the FBI

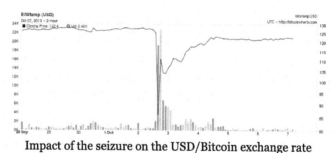

Impact of the seizure on the USD/Bitcoin exchange rate

Ross Ulbricht was alleged by the FBI to be the founder and owner of Silk Road and the person behind the pseudonym "Dread Pirate Roberts". He was arrested on 2 October 2013 in San Francisco at 3:15 p.m. PST in Glen Park Library, a branch of the San Francisco Public Library.

Ulbricht was indicted on charges of money laundering, computer hacking, conspiracy to traffic narcotics, and attempting to have six people killed. Prosecutors alleged that Ulbricht paid $730,000 to others to commit the murders, although none of the murders actually occurred. Ulbricht ultimately was not prosecuted for any of the alleged murder attempts.

The FBI initially seized 26,000 bitcoins from accounts on Silk Road, worth approximately $3.6 million at the time. An FBI spokesperson said that the agency would hold the bitcoins until Ulbricht's trial finished, after which the bitcoins would be liquidated. In October 2013, the FBI reported that it had seized 144,000 bitcoins, worth $28.5 million, and that the bitcoins belonged to Ulbricht. On 27 June 2014, the U.S. Marshals Service sold 29,657 bitcoins in 10 blocks in an online auction, estimated to be worth $18 million at current rates and only about a quarter of the seized bitcoins. Another 144,342 bitcoins were kept which had been found on Ulbricht's computer, roughly $87 million. Tim Draper bought the bitcoins at the auction with an estimated worth of $17 million, to lend them to a bitcoin start-up called Vaurum which is working in developing economies of emerging markets.

Ulbricht's trial began on 13 January 2015 in Federal Court in Manhattan. At the start of the trial, Ulbricht admitted to founding the Silk Road website, but claimed to have transferred control of the site to other people soon after he founded it. Ulbricht's lawyers contended that Dread Pirate Roberts was really Mark Karpelès, and that Karpelès set up Ulbricht as a fall guy. However, Judge Katherine B. Forrest ruled that any speculative statements regarding whether Karpelès or anyone else ran Silk Road would not be allowed, and statements already made would be stricken from the record.

In the second week of the trial, prosecutors presented documents and chat logs from Ulbricht's computer that, they said, demonstrated how Ulbricht had administered the site for many months, which contradicted the defense's claim that Ulbricht had relinquished control of Silk Road. Ulbricht's attorney suggested that the documents and chat logs were planted there by way of BitTorrent, which was running on Ulbricht's computer at the time of his arrest.

On 4 February 2015, the jury convicted Ulbricht of seven charges, including charges of engaging in a continuing criminal enterprise, narcotics trafficking, money laundering, and computer hacking. He faced 30 years to life in prison. The government also accused Ulbricht of paying for the murders of at least five people, but there is no evidence that the murders were actually carried out, and the accusations never became formal charges against Ulbricht.

During the trial, Judge Forrest received death threats. Users of an underground site called The Hidden Wiki posted her personal information there, including her address and Social Security number. Ulbricht's lawyer Joshua Dratel said that he and his client "obviously, and as strongly as possible, condemn" the anonymous postings against the judge. "They do not in any way have anything to do with Ross Ulbricht or anyone associated with him or reflect his views or those of anyone associated with him", Dratel said.

In late March 2015, a criminal complaint issued by the United States District Court for the Northern District of California led to the arrest of two former federal agents who had worked undercover in the Baltimore Silk Road investigation of Ulbricht, former Drug Enforcement Administration agent Carl Mark Force IV and Secret Service agent Shaun Bridges. The agents are alleged to have kept funds that Ulbricht transferred to them in exchange for purported information about the investigation. The agents were charged with wire fraud and money laundering.

On March 15, 2015, director/screenwriter Alex Winter debuted at the South by Southwest Film Festival a movie based on Silk Road. *Deep Web* gives the inside story of the arrest of Ross Ulbricht.

In a letter to Judge Forrest before his sentencing, Ulbricht stated that his actions through Silk Road were committed through libertarian idealism and that "Silk Road was supposed to be about giving people the freedom to make their own choices" and admitted that he made a "terrible mistake" that "ruined his life". On May 29, 2015, Ulbricht was given five sentences to be served concurrently, including two for life imprisonment without the possibility of parole. He was also ordered to forfeit $183 million. Ulbricht's lawyer Joshua Dratel said that he would appeal the sentencing and the original guilty verdict.

Other Trials

Dutch drug dealer 23-year-old Cornelis Jan "Maikel" Slomp pled guilty for large scale selling of drugs through the Silk Road website and was sentenced in Chicago to only 10 years in prison on 29 May 2015 with his attorney, Paul Petruzzi, present. Dealer Steven Sadler was sentenced to five years in prison.

Products

In March 2013, the site had 10,000 products for sale by vendors, 70% of which were drugs. In October 2014, there were 13,756 listings for drugs, grouped under the headings stimulants, psychedelics, prescription, precursors, other, opioids, ecstasy, dissociatives, cannabis and steroids/PEDs. Fake driver's licenses were also offered for sale. The site's terms of service prohibited the sale of certain items. This included child pornography, stolen credit cards, assassinations, and weapons of any type; other darknet markets such as Black Market Reloaded gained user notoriety because they were not as restrictive on these items as the Silk Road incarnations were. There were also legal goods and services for sale, such as apparel, art, books, cigarettes, erotica, jewellery, and writing services. A sister site, called "The Armory", sold weapons (primarily guns) during 2012, but was shut down because of a lack of demand.

Buyers were able to leave reviews of sellers' products on the site, and in an associated forum where crowdsourcing provided information about the best sellers and worst scammers. Most products were delivered through the mail, with the site's seller's guide instructing sellers how to vacuum-seal their products to escape detection.

Sales

Based on data from 3 February 2012 to 24 July 2012, an estimated $15 million in transactions were made annually on Silk Road. Twelve months later, Nicolas Christin, the study's author, said in an interview that a major increase in volume to "somewhere between $30 million and $45 million" would not surprise him. Buyers and sellers conducted all transactions with bitcoins (BTC), a cryptocurrency that provides a certain degree of anonymity. Silk Road held buyers' bitcoins in escrow until the order had been received and a hedging mechanism allowed sellers to opt for the value of bitcoins held in escrow to be fixed to their value in US$ at the time of the sale to mitigate against Bitcoin's volatility. Any changes in the price of bitcoins during transit were covered by Dread Pirate Roberts.

The complaint published when Ulbricht was arrested included information the FBI gained from a system image of the Silk Road server collected on 23 July 2013. It noted that, "From February 6, 2011 to July 23, 2013 there were approximately 1,229,465 transactions completed on the site. The total revenue generated from these sales was 9,519,664 Bitcoins, and the total commissions collected by Silk Road from the sales amounted to 614,305 Bitcoins. These figures are equivalent to roughly $1.2 billion in revenue and $79.8 million in commissions, at current Bitcoin exchange rates...", according to the September 2013 complaint, and involved 146,946 buyers and 3,877 vendors. This statement was made to emphasize the importance of the operation, because in the years 2011-2013 the value of 9,519,664 Bitcoins was $0.2 billion. According to information users provided upon registering, 30 percent were from the United States, 27 percent chose to be "undeclared", and beyond that, in descending order of prevalence: the United Kingdom, Australia, Germany, Canada, Sweden, France, Russia, Italy, and the Netherlands. During the 60-day period from 24 May to 23 July, there were 1,217,218 messages sent over Silk Road's private messaging system.

Similar Sites

The Farmer's Market was a Tor site similar to Silk Road, but which did not use bit-coins. It has been considered a 'proto-Silk Road' but the use of payment services such as PayPal and Western Union allowed law enforcement to trace payments and it was subsequently shut down by the FBI in 2012. Other sites already existed when Silk Road was shut down and *The Guardian* predicted that these would take over the market that Silk Road previously dominated. Sites named 'Atlantis', closing in September 2013, and *Project Black Flag*, closing in October 2013, each stole their users' bitcoins. In October 2013, the site named *Black Market Reloaded* closed down temporarily after the site's source code was leaked. The market shares of various Silk Road successor sites were described by *The Economist* in May 2015.

Book Club

The Silk Road has a Tor-based book club that continued to operate following the initial site's closure and even following an arrest of one of its members. Reading material in-cluded conspiracy theories and computer hacking.

Direct Successors

Silk Road 2.0

Alert placed on the Silk Road's homepage following its being seized by
the U.S. government and European law enforcement

On 6 November 2013, administrators from the closed Silk Road relaunched the site, led by a new pseudonymous Dread Pirate Roberts, and dubbed it "Silk Road 2.0". It recreated the original site's setup and promised improved security. The new DPR took the precaution of distributing encrypted copies of the site's source code to allow the site to be quickly recreated in the event of another shutdown.

On 20 December 2013, it was announced that three alleged Silk Road 2.0 administra-tors had been arrested; two of these suspects, Andrew Michael Jones and Gary Davis, were named as the administrators "Inigo" and "Libertas" who had continued their work on Silk Road 2.0. Around this time, the new Dread Pirate Roberts abruptly surrendered control of the site and froze its activity, including its escrow system. A new temporary administrator under the screenname "Defcon" took over and promised to bring the site back to working order.

On 13 February 2014, Defcon announced that Silk Road 2.0's escrow accounts had been compromised through a vulnerability in Bitcoin's protocol called "transaction malleability". While the site remained online, all the bitcoins in its escrow accounts, valued at $2.7 million, were reported stolen. It was later reported that the vulnerability was in the site's "Refresh Deposits" function, and that the Silk Road administrators had used their commissions on sales since 15 February to refund users who lost money, with 50 percent of the hack victims being completely repaid as of 8 April.

On 6 November 2014, authorities with the Federal Bureau of Investigation, Europol, and Eurojust announced the arrest of Blake Benthall, allegedly the owner and operator of Silk Road 2.0 under the pseudonym "Defcon", the previous day in San Francisco as part of Operation Onymous.

Others

Following the closure of Silk Road 2.0 in November 2014, Diabolus Market renamed itself to 'Silk Road 3 Reloaded' in order to capitalise on the brand.

In January 2015 'Silk Road Reloaded' launched on I2P with multiple cryptocurrency support and similar listing restrictions to the original Silk Road market.

References

- Mike Power (2 May 2013). "Your Crack's in the Post". Drugs 2.0: The Web Revolution That's Changing How the World Gets High. Granta Publications. pp. 211–237. ISBN 978-1-84627-461-9.

- Shin, Laura (30 May 2016). "Mystery Solved: $6.6 Million Bitcoin Theft That Brought Down Dark Web Site Tied To 2 Florida Men". Retrieved 1 June 2016.

- DeepDotWeb (9 February 2014). "Another Two Bites The Dust (Black Goblin Marketplace & CannabisRoad)". Retrieved 17 September 2016.

- Cox, Joseph (19 April 2016). "Dark Web Market Disappears, Users Migrate in Panic, Circle of Life Continues". Retrieved 23 April 2016.

- Howell O'Neill, Patrick (9 November 2015). "The Dark Net drug market that survived Ukraine's civil war". Retrieved 22 February 2016.

- "Cheltenham drug user who bought cannabis on 'dark web' with Bitcoin was caught by Home Office". Gloucestershire Echo. 21 May 2016. Retrieved 28 May 2016.

- Cox, Joseph (18 May 2016). "This Fake Hitman Site Is the Most Elaborate, Twisted Dark Web Scam Yet". Retrieved 20 May 2016.

- Cox, Joseph (14 June 2016). "More People Than Ever Say They Get Their Drugs on the Dark Web". Retrieved 15 June 2016.

- Kyle Soska and Nicolas Christin (13 August 2015). "Measuring the Longitudinal Evolution of the Online Anonymous Marketplace Ecosystem" (PDF). Retrieved 9 June 2016.

- Mullin, Joe (13 January 2015). "Silk Road stunner: Ulbricht admits founding the site, but says he isn't DPR". Ars Technica. Retrieved 2015-11-07.

- Jon Seidel (28 May 2015). "World's most prolific online drug dealer 'Supertrips' gets 10 years". Chicago Sun-Times. Retrieved 30 May 2015.

- Isaacson, Betsy (31 January 2014). "The Deep Web Is Filled With Drugs, Porn And ... Book Lovers(!)". Retrieved 18 October 2015.

- Brandom, Russell (13 February 2014). "The Silk Road 2 has been hacked for $2.7 million". The Verge. Retrieved 14 February 2014.

- Pepitone, Julianne (6 November 2014). "FBI Arrests Alleged 'Silk Road 2.0' Operator Blake Benthall". NBC News. Retrieved 6 November 2014.

- "Sealed Complaint 13 MAG 2328: United States of America v. Ross William Ulbricht" (PDF). 27 September 2014. Retrieved 27 January 2014.

Various Electronic Payment System

The systems used to settle financial transactions such as the transfer of money are known as payment system. A number of electronic payment systems have emerged such as debit cards, credit cards, direct credits and Internet banking. The various electronic payment systems discussed in this section are digital wallets, giropay, Google wallet and comparison of payment systems.

Payment System

A payment system is any system used to settle financial transactions through the transfer of monetary value, and includes the institutions, instruments, people, rules, procedures, standards, and technologies that make such an exchange possible. A common type of payment system is the operational network that links bank accounts and provides for monetary exchange using bank deposits.

What makes a payment system a system is the use of cash-substitutes; traditional payment systems are negotiable instruments such as drafts (e.g., checks) and documentary credits such as letters of credit. With the advent of computers and electronic communications a large number of alternative electronic payment systems have emerged. These include debit cards, credit cards, electronic funds transfers, direct credits, direct debits, internet banking and e-commerce payment systems. Some payment systems include credit mechanisms, but that is essentially a different aspect of payment. Payment systems are used in lieu of tendering cash in domestic and international transactions and consist of a major service provided by banks and other financial institutions.

Payment systems may be physical or electronic and each has its own procedures and protocols. Standardization has allowed some of these systems and networks to grow to a global scale, but there are still many country- and product-specific systems. Examples of payment systems that have become globally available are credit card and automated teller machine networks. Specific forms of payment systems are also used to settle financial transactions for products in the equity markets, bond markets, currency markets, futures markets, derivatives markets, options markets and to transfer funds between financial institutions both domestically using clearing and real-time gross settlement (RTGS) systems and internationally using the SWIFT network.

The term electronic payment can refer narrowly to e-commerce—a payment for buying and selling goods or services offered through the Internet, or broadly to any type of electronic funds transfer.

National

An efficient national payment system reduces the cost of exchanging goods, services, and assets and is indispensable to the functioning of the interbank, money, and capital markets. A weak payment system may severely drag on the stability and developmental capacity of a national economy; its failures can result in inefficient use of financial resources, inequitable risk-sharing among agents, actual losses for participants, and loss of confidence in the financial system and in the very use of money The technical efficiency of payment system is important for a development of economy. Real-time gross settlement systems (RTGS) are funds transfer systems where transfer of money or securities takes place from one bank to another on a "real-time" and on "gross" basis. Settlement in "real time" means that payment transaction does not require any waiting period. The transactions are settled as soon as they are processed. "Gross settlement" means the transaction is settled on one to one basis without bunching or netting with any other transaction. Once processed, payments are final and irrevocable.

TARGET2 is a RTGS system that covers the European Union member states that use the euro, and is part of the Eurosystem, which comprises the European Central Bank and the national central banks of those countries that have adopted the euro. TARGET2 is used for the settlement of central bank operations, large-value Euro interbank transfers as well as other euro payments. TARGET 2 provides real-time financial transfers, debt settlement at central banks which is immediate and irreversible.

International

Globalization is driving corporations to transact more frequently across borders. Consumers are also transacting more on a global basis—buying from foreign eCommerce sites; traveling, living, and working abroad. For the payments industry, the result is higher volumes of payments—in terms of both currency value and number of transactions. This is also leading to a consequent shift downwards in the average value of these payments.

The ways these payments are made can be cumbersome, error prone, and expensive. Growth, after all, is often messy. Payments systems set up decades ago continue to be used sometimes retrofitted, sometimes force-fitted—to meet the needs of modern corporations. And, not infrequently, the systems creak and groan as they bear the strain.

For users of these systems, on both the paying and receiving sides, it can be difficult and time-consuming to learn how to use cross-border payments tools, and how to set up processes to make optimal use of them. Solution providers (both banks and non-banks) also face challenges, struggling to cobble together old systems to meet new demands.

But for these providers, cross-border payments are both lucrative (especially given foreign exchange conversion revenue) and rewarding, in terms of the overall financial relationship created with the end customer.

The challenges for global payments are not simply those resulting from volume increases. A number of economic, political, and technical forces are changing the types of cross-border transactions conducted. Consider these factors:

- Corporations are making more cross-border purchases of services (as opposed to goods), as well as more purchases of complex fabricated parts rather than simple raw materials.

- Enterprises are purchasing from more countries, in more regions.

- Increased outsourcing is leading to new in-country and new cross-border intra-company transactions.

- More enterprises are participating in complex, automated supply chains, which in some cases drive automatic ordering and fulfillment. Online purchasing continues to grow, both by large enterprises as part of an automated procurement systems and by smaller enterprises purchasing directly.

- There is continued growth in the use of cross-border labor.

- Individuals are increasingly taking their investments abroad.

E-commerce Payment System

An e-commerce payment system facilitates the acceptance of electronic payment for online transactions. Also known as a sample of Electronic Data Interchange (EDI), e-commerce payment systems have become increasingly popular due to the widespread use of the internet-based shopping and banking.

Over the years, credit cards have become one of the most common forms of payment for e-commerce transactions. In North America almost 90% of online retail transactions were made with this payment type. Turban et al. goes on to explain that it would be difficult for an online retailer to operate without supporting credit and debit cards due to their widespread use. Increased security measures include use of the card verification number (CVN) which detects fraud by comparing the verification number printed on the signature strip on the back of the card with the information on file with the cardholder's issuing bank. Also online merchants have to comply with stringent rules stipulated by the credit and debit card issuers (Visa and MasterCard) this means that merchants must have security protocol and procedures in place to ensure transactions are more secure. This can also include having a certificate from an authorized certification authority (CA) who provides PKI(Public-Key infrastructure) for securing credit and debit card transactions.

Despite widespread use in North America, there are still a large number of countries such as China, India and Pakistan that have some problems to overcome in regard to credit card security. In the meantime, the use of smartcards has become extremely popular. A Smartcard is similar to a credit card; however it contains an embedded 8-bit microprocessor and uses electronic cash which transfers from the consumers' card to the sellers' device. A popular smartcard initiative is the VISA Smartcard. Using the VISA Smartcard you can transfer electronic cash to your card from your bank account, and you can then use your card at various retailers and on the internet.

There are companies that enable financial transactions to take place over the internet, such as PayPal. Many of the mediaries permit consumers to establish an account quickly, and to transfer funds into their on-line accounts from a traditional bank account (typically via ACH transactions), and *vice versa*, after verification of the consumer's identity and authority to access such bank accounts. Also, the larger mediaries further allow transactions to and from credit card accounts, although such credit card transactions are usually assessed a fee (either to the recipient or the sender) to recoup the transaction fees charged to the mediary.

The speed and simplicity with which cyber-mediary accounts can be established and used have contributed to their widespread use, although the risk of abuse, theft and other problems—with disgruntled users frequently accusing the mediaries themselves of wrongful behavior—is associated with them.

Methods of Online Payment

Credit cards constitute a popular method of online payment but can be expensive for the merchant to accept because of transaction fees primarily. Debit cards constitute an excellent alternative with similar security but usually much cheaper charges. Besides card-based payments, other forms of payment have emerged and sometimes even claimed market leadership. Wallets like PayPal and Alipay are playing major roles in the ecosystem. Bitcoin payment processors are a cheaper alternative for accepting payments online which also offer better protection from fraud.

Net Banking

This is a system, well known in India, that does not involve any sort of physical card. It is used by customers who have accounts enabled with Internet banking. Instead of entering card details on the purchaser's site, in this system the payment gateway allows one to specify which bank they wish to pay from. Then the user is redirected to the bank's website, where one can authenticate oneself and then approve the payment. Typically there will also be some form of two-factor authentication.

It is typically seen as being safer than using credit cards, with the result that nearly all merchant accounts in India offer it as an option.

A very similar system, known as iDEAL, is popular in the Netherlands.

PayPal

PayPal is a global e-commerce business allowing payments and money transfers to be made through the Internet. Online money transfers serve as electronic alternatives to paying with traditional paper methods, such as cheques and money orders. It is subject to the US economic sanction list and other rules and interventions required by US laws or government. PayPal is an acquirer, a performing payment processing for online vendors, auction sites, and other commercial users, for which it charges a fee. It may also charge a fee for receiving money, proportional to the amount received. The fees depend on the currency used, the payment option used, the country of the sender, the country of the recipient, the amount sent and the recipient's account type. In addition, eBay purchases made by credit card through PayPal may incur extra fees if the buyer and seller use different currencies. On October 3, 2002, PayPal became a wholly owned subsidiary of eBay. Its corporate headquarters are in San Jose, California, United States at eBay's North First Street satellite office campus. The company also has significant operations in Omaha, Scottsdale, Charlotte and Austin in the United States; Chennai in India; Dublin in Ireland; Berlin in Germany; and Tel Aviv in Israel. From July 2007, PayPal has operated across the European Union as a Luxembourg-based bank

Paymentwall

Paymentwall, an e-commerce solutions providing company launched in 2010, offers a wide range of online payment methods that its clients can integrate on their website.

Google Wallet

Google Wallet was launched in 2011, serving a similar function as PayPal to facilitate payments and transfer money online. It also features a security that has not been cracked to date, and the ability to send payments as attachments via email.

Mobile Money Wallets

In undeveloped countries the banked population is very less, especially in tier II and tier III cities. Taking the example of India, there are more mobile phone users than there are people with active bank accounts. Telecom operators, in such geographies, have started offering mobile money wallets which allows adding funds easily through their existing mobile subscription number, by visiting physical recharge points close to their homes and offices and converting their cash into mobile wallet currency. This can be used for online transaction and eCommerce purchases. Many payment options such as Airtel Money and M-Pesa in Kenya , ATW are being accepted as alternate payment options on various eCommerce websites.

E-commerce Credit Card Payment System

Electronic commerce, commonly known as e-commerce or eCommerce, or e-business consists of the buying and selling of products or services over electronic systems such as the Internet and other computer networks. The amount of trade conducted electronically has grown extraordinarily with widespread Internet usage. The use of commerce is conducted in this way, spurring and drawing on innovations in electronic funds transfer, supply chain management, Internet marketing, online transaction processing, electronic data interchange (EDI), inventory management systems, and automated data collection systems. Modern electronic commerce typically uses the World Wide Web at least at some point in the transaction's lifecycle, although it can encompass a wider range of technologies such as e-mail as well.

A large percentage of electronic commerce is conducted entirely electronically for virtual items such as access to premium content on a website, but most electronic commerce involves the transportation of physical items in some way. Online retailers are sometimes known as e-tailers and online retail is sometimes known as e-tail. Almost all big retailers have electronic commerce presence on the World Wide Web.

Electronic commerce that is conducted between businesses is referred to as business-to-business or B2B. B2B can be open to all interested parties (e.g. commodity market) or limited to specific, pre-qualified participants (private electronic market). Electronic commerce that is conducted between businesses and consumers, on the other hand, is referred to as business-to-consumer or B2C. This is the type of electronic commerce conducted by companies such as Amazon.com. Online shopping is a form of electronic commerce where the buyer is connected directly online to the seller's computer usually via the Internet. There is no specific intermediary service. The sale and purchase transaction is completed electronically and interactively in real-time, such as when buying a new book on Amazon.com. If an intermediary is present, then the sale and purchase transaction is called consumer-to-consumer, such as an online auction conducted on eBay.com.

This payment system has been widely accepted by consumers and merchants throughout the world, and is by far the most popular method of payments especially in the retail markets. Some of the most important advantages over the traditional modes of payment are: privacy, integrity, compatibility, good transaction efficiency, acceptability, convenience, mobility, low financial risk and anonymity.

This flow of ecommerce payment system can be better understood from the flow of the system below.

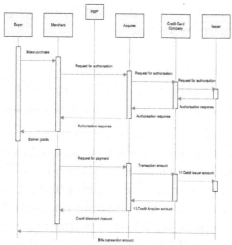

Figure: Online Credit Card (VISA) Transaction Process

Electronic Payment Services

Electronic Payment Services (Chinese: 易辦事), commonly known as EPS, is the largest electronic payment system in Hong Kong, Macau and Shenzhen starting from 1985. The service is provided by EPS Company (Hong Kong) Limited. Currently there are over 25,000 acceptance locations.

Provider

Established in 1984, EPS Company (Hong Kong) Limited (formerly Electronic Payment Services Company) is currently a consortium of 21 major banks in Hong Kong.

System

In each retail location, a terminal is installed and is usually connected to the POS system of the retailer. The terminal may also be independently connected to banks through the public phone system.

Transactions approved before the cut-off time are batched into a payment made directly to the retailer's account by the end of the business day.

Service at Consumer Level

EPS Service

EPS (易辦事) entails the simple use of an ATM card or a credit card with ATM capability issued by a member bank of the EPS. No application for the service is required.

The EPS device is a dual-unit device consisting of a removable card processor and a stationary base that serves as a charger and data link. This is the flow of a typical transaction by EPS:

Customer:	Hands over the card
Retailer:	Inserts the card into the processor and keys in the transaction amount
	Retailer gives the processor to the customer
Customer:	Confirms the amount, selects the desired account, enters the PIN
	Customer returns the processor to the retailer
Retailer:	Docks the processor to the base unit
	The base communicates with the EPS server and prints out a slip indicating approval or rejection
Retailer:	Hands the receipt to the customer

Some retailers may use an integrated machine. In such situations, the customer inserts the card into the machine directly and waits for the retailer's acknowledgement before proceeding to the rest of the steps.

EPS EasyCash Service

EPS EasyCash (提款易) allows card holders to withdraw cash at over 1,200 locations in Hong Kong upon a regular purchase by EPS. The cash withdrawal amount must be in units of $100, up to $500. EPS EasyCash service is also commonly known as Cashback.

EPS EasyCash service is available at Hong Kong based chain stores such as Gourmet, Great, IKEA, Mannings, MarketPlace, Massimo Dutti, Circle K, Oliver's, Parknshop, Taste, ThreeSixty, Vango, China Resources Vanguard (CRV), V'ole and Wellcome.

EPS Company Member Bank List

- Bank of China (Hong Kong) Limited
- Bank of Communications, HK Branch
- China Construction Bank (Asia)
- China Merchants Bank Company Limited
- Chiyu Banking Corporation Limited
- Chong Hing Bank Limited
- Citibank (Hong Kong) Limited
- Citic Ka Wah Bank Limited

- Dah Sing Bank Limited

- DBS Bank (Hong Kong) Limited

- Fubon Bank (Hong Kong) Limited

- Hang Seng Bank Limited

- The Hongkong and Shanghai Banking Corporation (HSBC)

- ICBC (Asia)

- Mevas Bank Limited

- Nanyang Commercial Bank Limited

- Shanghai Commercial Bank Limited

- Standard Chartered Bank (Hong Kong) Limited

- The Bank of East Asia Limited

- Wing Hang Bank Limited

- Wing Lung Bank Limited

Digital Wallet

A digital wallet refers to an electronic device that allows an individual to make electronic commerce transactions. This can include purchasing items on-line with a computer or using a smartphone to purchase something at a store. An individual's bank account can also be linked to the digital wallet. They might also have their driver's license, health card, loyalty card(s) and other ID documents stored on the phone. The credentials can be passed to a merchant's terminal wirelessly via near field communication (NFC). Increasingly, digital wallets are being made not just for basic financial transactions but to also authenticate the holder's credentials. For example, a digital-wallet could potentially verify the age of the buyer to the store while purchasing alcohol. The system has already gained popularity in Japan, where digital wallets are known as Osaifu-Keitai or "wallet mobiles".

Technology

A digital wallet has both a software and information component. The software provides security and encryption for the personal information and for the actual transaction. Typically, digital wallets are stored on the client side and are easily self-maintained and fully compatible with most e-commerce Web sites. A server-side digital wallet, also known as a thin wallet, is one that an organization creates for and about you and maintains on its servers. Server-side digital wallets are gaining popularity among major retailers due to the security, efficiency, and added utility it provides to the end-user, which increases their satisfaction of their overall purchase. The information component is basically a database of user-input information. This information consists of your shipping address, billing address, payment methods (including credit card numbers, expiry dates, and security numbers), and other information.

The key point to take from digital wallets is that they're composed of both digital wallet devices and digital wallet systems. There are dedicated digital wallet devices such as the biometric wallet by Dunhill, where it's a physical device holding someone's cash and cards along with a Bluetooth mobile connection. Presently there are further explorations for smartphones with NFC digital wallet capabilities, such as the Samsung Galaxy series and the Google Nexus smartphones utilizing Google's Android operating system and the Apple Inc. iPhone 6 and iPhone 6 Plus utilizing Apple Pay.

Digital wallet systems enable the widespread use of digital wallet transactions among various retail vendors in the form of mobile payments systems and digital wallet applications. The M-PESA mobile payments system and microfinancing service has widespread use in Kenya and Tanzania, while the MasterCard PayPass application has been adopted by a number of vendors in the U.S. and worldwide.

Digital wallet is being used more and more in Asian countries as well. One in five consumers in Asia are now using digital wallet representing twofold increase from two years ago. A recent survey by MasterCard's mobile shopping survey shows on 8500 adults aged 18–64 across 14 markets showed, 45% users in China, 36.7% users in India and 23.3% users in Singapore are the biggest adopters of digital wallet. The survey was conducted on between October and December 2015. Also analysis showed (48.5%) consumers in these regions made purchase using smartphones. Indian consumers are leading the way with 76.4% using a smartphone to make purchase which is a drastic increase of 29.3% from previous year. This has made companies like Reliance and Amazon India to come out with its own digital wallet. Flipkart has already introduced its own digital wallet.

Payments for Goods and Services Purchased Online

A client-side digital wallet requires minimal setup and is relatively easy to use. Once the software is installed, the user begins by entering all the pertinent information. The digital wallet is now set up. At the purchase or check-out page of an e-commerce site, the digital wallet software has the ability to automatically enter the user information in the online form. By default, most digital wallets prompt when the software recognizes a form in which it can fill out; if one chooses to fill out the form automatically, the user will be prompted for a password. This keeps unauthorized users away from viewing personal information stored on a particular computer.

ECML

Digital wallets are designed to be accurate when transferring data to retail checkout forms; however, if a particular e-commerce site has a peculiar checkout system, the digital wallet may fail to properly recognize the form's fields. This problem has been eliminated by sites and wallet software that use Electronic Commerce Modeling Language (ECML) technology. Electronic Commerce Modeling Language is a protocol that dictates how online retailers structure and set up their checkout forms. Participating e-commerce vendors who incorporate both digital wallet technology and ECML include: Microsoft, Discover, IBM, Omaha Steaks and Dell Computers.

Application of Digital Wallets

Consumers are not required to fill out order forms on each site when they purchase an item because the information has already been stored and is automatically updated and entered into the order fields across merchant sites when using a digital wallet. Consumers also benefit when using digital wallets because their information is encrypted or protected by a private software code; merchants benefit by receiving protection against fraud.

Digital wallets are available to consumers free of charge, and they're fairly easy to obtain. For example, when a consumer makes a purchase at a merchant site that's set up to handle server-side digital wallets, he types his name and payment and shipping information into the merchant's own form. At the end of the purchase, the consumer is asked to sign up for a wallet of his choice by entering a user name and password for future purchases. Users can also acquire wallets at a wallet vendor's site.

Although a wallet is free for consumers, vendors charge merchants for wallets. Some wallet vendors make arrangements for merchants to pay them a percentage of every successful purchase directed through their wallets. In other cases, digital wallet vendors process the transactions between cardholders and participating merchants and charge merchants a flat fee.

Advantages for E-commerce Sites

Upwards of 25% of online shoppers abandon their order due to frustration in filling in forms. The digital wallet combats this problem by giving users the option to transfer their information securely and accurately. This simplified approach to completing transactions results in better usability and ultimately more utility for the customer.

Digital Wallets can also increase the security of the transaction since the wallet typically does not pass payment card details to the website (a unique transaction identifier or token is shared instead). Increasingly this approach is a feature of online payment gateways, especially if the payment gateway offers a "hosted payment page" integration approach.

Real-time Gross Settlement

Real-time gross settlement systems (RTGS) are specialist funds transfer systems where the transfer of money or securities takes place from one bank to another on a "real time" and on a "gross" basis. Settlement in "real time" means a payment transaction is not subjected to any waiting period, with transactions being settled as soon as they are processed. "Gross settlement" means the transaction is settled on one to one basis without bundling or netting with any other transaction. "Settlement" means that once processed, payments are final and irrevocable.

RTGS systems are typically used for high-value transactions that require and receive immediate clearing. In some countries the RTGS systems may be the only way to get same day cleared funds and so may be used when payments need to be settled urgently. However, most regular payments would not use a RTGS system, but instead would use a national payment system or network that allows participants to batch and net payments.

RTGS systems are usually operated by a country's central bank as it is seen as a critical infrastructure for a country's economy. Economists believe that an efficient national payment system reduces the cost of exchanging goods and services, and is indispensable to the functioning of the interbank, money, and capital markets. A weak payment system may severely drag on the stability and developmental capacity of a national economy; its failures can result in inefficient use of financial resources, inequitable risk-sharing among agents, actual losses for participants, and loss of confidence in the financial system and in the very use of money.

Central Banks and RTGS

The RTGS system is normally maintained or controlled by the central bank of a country. There is no physical exchange of money; the central bank makes adjustments in the electronic accounts of Bank A and Bank B, reducing the balance in Bank A's account by the amount in question and increasing the balance of Bank B's account by the same amount. The RTGS system is suited for low-volume, high-value transactions. It lowers settlement risk, besides giving an accurate picture of an institution's account at any point of time. The objective of RTGS systems by central banks throughout the world is to minimize risk in high-value electronic payment settlement systems. In an RTGS system, transactions are settled across accounts held at a central bank on a continuous gross basis. Settlement is immediate, final and irrevocable. Credit risks due to settlement lags are eliminated. The best RTGS national payment system cover up to 95% of high-value transactions within the national monetary market.

RTGS systems are an alternative to systems of settling transactions at the end of the day, also known as the net settlement system, such as the BACS system in the United Kingdom. In a net settlement system, all the inter-institution transactions during the day are accumulated, and at the end of the day, the central bank adjusts the accounts of the institutions by the net amounts of these transactions.

The World Bank has been paying increasing attention to payment system development as a key component of the financial infrastructure of a country, and has provided various forms of assistance to over 100 countries. Most of the RTGS systems in place are secure and have been designed around international standards and best practices.

There are several reasons for central banks to adopt RTGS. First, a decision to adopt is influenced by competitive pressure from the global financial markets. Second, it is more beneficial to adopt an RTGS system for central bank when this allows access to a broad system of other countries' RTGS systems. Third, it is very likely that the knowledge acquired through experiences with RTGS systems spills over to other central banks and helps them make their adoption decision. Fourth, central banks do not necessarily have to install and develop RTGS themselves. The possibility of sharing development with providers that have built RTGS systems in more than one country (CGI of UK, CMA Small System of Sweden, JV Perago of South Africa and SIA SpA of Italy, Montran of USA) has presumably lowered the cost and hence made it feasible for many countries to adopt.

As at 1985, three central banks had implemented RTGS systems, while by the end of 2005, RTGS systems had been implemented by 90 central banks.

Systems in Europe Covering Multiple Countries

- TARGET2

Existing Systems

Below is a listing of countries and their RTGS systems:

- Albania - AECH, RTGS

- Angola - SPTR, (Sistema de pagamentos em tempo real)

- Azerbaijan - AZIPS (Azerbaijan Interbank Payment System)

- Australia - RITS (Reserve Bank Information and Transfer System)

- Barbados - Central Bank Real Time Gross Settlement System (CBRTGS)

- Bosnia and Herzegovina - RTGS

- Bulgaria - RINGS (Real-time INterbank Gross-settlement System)

- Brazil - STR (Sistema de Transferência de Reservas)

- Canada - LVTS (Large Value Transfer System) (This is actually an RTGS *Equivalent* system. Final settlement happens in the evening.)

- China - China National Advanced Payment System ("CNAPS") (also called "Super Online Banking System)

- Chile - LBTR/CAS (Spanish: *Liquidación Bruta en Tiempo Real*)

- Croatia - HSVP (Croatian: *Hrvatski sustav velikih plaćanja*)

- Czech Republic - CERTIS (Czech Express Real Time Interbank Gross Settlement System)

- Egypt - RTGS

- Eurozone - TARGET2

- Fiji - FIJICLEAR

- Hong Kong - Clearing House Automated Transfer System (CHATS)

- Hungary - VIBER (Hungarian: *Valós Idejű Bruttó Elszámolási Rendszer*)

- Georgia - GPSS (Georgian Payment and Securities System)

- India - RTGS, NEFT, IMPS

- Indonesia - Sistem Bank Indonesia Real Time Gross Settlement (BI-RTGS)

- Iran - SATNA (ساماًه تسوهی خاىلصآًی, Real-Time Gross Settlement System)

- Iraq - RTGS (Real Time Gross Settlement System)

- Japan - BOJ-NET (Bank of Japan Financial Network System)

- Jordan - RTGS-JO

- Kenya - Kenya Electronic Payment and Settlement System (KEPSS)

- Korea - BOK-WIRE+ (The Bank of Korea Financial Wire Network,한은금융망)

- Kuwait - KASSIP (Kuwait's Automated Settlement System for Inter-Participant Payments)

- Lebanon - BDL-RTGS (Real Time Gross Settlement System)

- Macedonia - MIPS (Macedonian Interbank Payment System)

- Malawi - MITASS (Malawi Interbank Settlement System)

- Malaysia - RENTAS (Real Time Electronic Transfer of Funds and Securities)

- Mexico - SPEI (Spanish: *Sistema de Pagos Electrónicos Interbancarios*)

- Morocco - SRBM (Système de règlement brut du Maroc)

- Namibia - NISS (Namibia Inter-bank Settlement System)

- New Zealand - ESAS (Exchange Settlement Account System)
- Nigeria - CIFTS (CBN Inter-Bank Funds Transfer System)
- Peru - LBTR (Spanish: *Liquidación Bruta en Tiempo Real*)
- Philippines - PhilPaSS
- Poland - SORBNET and SORBNET2
- Russia - BESP system (Banking Electronic Speed Payment System)
- Romania - ReGIS system
- Saudi Arabia - (Saudi Arabian Riyal Interbank Express) SARIE
- Singapore - MEPS+ (MAS Electronic Payment System Plus)
- South Africa - SAMOS (The South African Multiple Option Settlement)
- Spain - SLBE (Spanish: Servicio de Liquidación del Banco de España)
- Sri Lanka - LankaSettle (RTGS/SSSS)
- Sweden - RIX (Swedish: *Riksbankens system för överföring av kontoförda pengar*)
- Switzerland - SIC (Swiss Interbank Clearing)
- Taiwan - CIFS (CBC Interbank Funds Transfer System)
- Tanzania - TIS (Tanzania interbank settlement system)
- Thailand - BAHTNET (Bank of Thailand Automated High value Transfer Network)
- Turkey - EFT (Electronic Fund Transfer)
- Ukraine - SEP (System of Electronic Payments of the National Bank of Ukraine)
- United Kingdom - CHAPS (Clearing House Automated Payment System)
- United States - Fedwire
- Zambia - ZIPSS-Zambian Inter-bank Payment and Settlement System
- Zimbabwe - ZETSS-Zimbabwe Electronic Transfer and Settlement System

Online Banking ePayments

Online Banking ePayments (OBeP) is a type of payments network, developed by the banking industry in conjunction with technology providers, specifically designed to address the unique requirements of payments made via the Internet.

Key aspects of OBeP which distinguish it from other online payments systems are:

1. The consumer is authenticated in real-time by the consumer financial institution's online banking infrastructure.

2. The availability of funds is validated in real-time by the consumer's financial institution.

3. The consumer's financial institution provides guarantee of payment to the merchant.

4. Payment is made as a credit transfer (push payment) from the consumer's financial institution to the merchant, as opposed to a debit transfer (pull payment).

5. Payment is made directly from the consumer's account rather than through a third-party account.

Nearly half of the bills paid in the US during 2013 were done via electronic bill payment. Also, during 2014, nearly 48% of all online shopping in North America were made with a credit card. Globally, online payments are expected to exceed 3 trillion Euros (approx. US$3.2 trillion) in the next 5 years.

Privacy and Security Features

OBeP systems protect consumer personal information by not requiring the disclosure of account numbers or other sensitive personal data to online merchants or other third parties. During the checkout process, the merchant redirects the consumer to their financial institution's online banking site where they login and authorize charges. After charges are authorized, the financial institution redirects the consumer back to the merchant site. All network communications are protected using industry standard encryption. Additionally, communications with the OBeP network take place on a virtual private network, not over the public Internet.

In order to be positive that your identity, information and other personal features are truly secure, the following cautions should be taken: Make sure a secure browser is being used. Read all privacy policies provided. Many individuals simply skip over such important information that could spell out potential risks. If a risk seems unnecessary and odd, it would be safer to skip this payment rather than take the risk with one's hard earned money. Keep all personal information private. If phone numbers, social security numbers or other private, important information is asked for one should be cautious. Banking information is important information as it is, asking for unnecessary personal information should be a red flag of suspicious behavior. Selecting businesses that are trustworthy is key. Most companies will email a customer with a transaction receipt upon payment. Keeping a record of these is important in order to have proof of purchase or payment. Lastly, checking bank statements regularly is crucial in keeping up-to-date with transactions.

Costs

Costs associated with fraud, estimated at 1.2% of sales by online retailers in 2009, are reported to be dramatically reduced with OBeP, because the issuer bank is responsible for the authentication of the credit transaction and provides guaranteed funds to the merchant.

Because the merchant is not responsible for storing and protecting confidential consumer information, OBeP systems also reduce costs associated with mitigating fraud, fraud screening, and PCI audits.

Transaction fees on Online Banking ePayments vary by network, but are often fixed, and lower than the average 1.9% merchant fees associated with credit card transactions – especially for larger purchases.

Other Benefits

For Consumers

- use of cash-like payment encourages responsible consumerism
- does not require set-up or registration with a third-party payments entity
- presents familiar interface to facilitate online payment
- awareness of funds availability

For Merchants

- improved sales conversion / reduced abandoned carts
- real time authorization of guaranteed ACH payment (good funds)
- offering preferred payment methods may drive repeat transactions

For Financial Institutions

- recapture revenue being lost to alternative payment providers
- encourages consumers to move to online banking, replacing more costly branch and telephone alternatives

Potential Downfalls

The idea of online payments and transactions has led numerous individuals, corporations and groups to be hesitant. Sharing of personal information to such a vast entity, such as the internet, can lead to potential problems. Remaining cautious and careful with what information is shared and to whom it is shared with is key in remaining safe and secure when using ePayments.

- Identity theft is prevalent with online transactions

- No face-to-face interaction for help, questions, issues

- Website issues can hinder the ability to make payments in a timely manner

- Passwords - sometimes remembering a password can be difficult and with something as important as an ePayment website, it is crucial this information is not lost or forgotten

Types and Implementations

- Multi-Bank – requires that a merchant have a single connection to the OBeP network in order to accept payment from any participating financial institution.

- Mono-Bank – requires that a merchant have a separate connection to each participating financial institution.

- A third category, also known as "overlay payment solutions" provide a similar consumer experience to Online Banking ePayments, but violate a key tenet of the OBeP definition by requiring the consumer to share their online banking credentials with a third party.

- A fourth category requires that a merchant have a single connection to an alternative payment provider. This alternative payment provider has connections to multiple online banks. This does not require the consumer to share their online banking credentials, but still offers the same advantages to the merchants as "overlay payment solutions".

Giropay

Giropay is an Internet payment System in Germany, based on online banking. Introduced in February 2006, this payment method allows customers to buy securely on the Internet using direct online transfers from their bank account. The system is similar to the Dutch iDEAL payment system, the Interac Online service in Canada, pagomiscuentas payment service in Argentina, and Secure Vault payments in the United States. Giropay is owned by giropay GmbH.

Transaction Volume

By May 2007 more than 100 million euro in purchases were made.

In 2008, the system processed 3.2 million transfers, and the products and services paid with this payment method had a combined worth of 185 million Euros.

Over one million transactions are processed every month.

Scope

Most German *Sparkassen* and cooperative banks are participating in Giropay. However, the number of participating banks from the private sector is limited. In this sector, the only major participating bank is Deutsche Postbank. Nevertheless, Giropay has a reach of about 17 million German online banking customers, and about 60% of all commercial bank accounts. That number means the participating banks are serving the vast majority of the German online banking market.

Process

Giropay offers merchants a real-time payment method (publicized as virtually risk-free) to accept internet payments. For customers, Giropay uses the same environment as their banks' online banking sites. The level of security depends on the participating bank. Some German Banks offer two-factor authentication (2FA), such as a challenge-response access token based on the chip embedded in the debit card or ATM card. Others, however, offer simpler PIN and TAN based online banking services. No sensitive information is being shared with the merchant, such as credit card or Giro account numbers. There is no chargeback right however, which can be considered a disadvantage for the consumer using this payment method. This is considered an advantage to the merchants.

Giropay works as follows:

- Merchant offers Giropay as payment method, often in addition to the regular credit card payment options

- Consumer selects Giropay and selects his bank

- Consumer is redirected to his bank's login page

- Participating bank displays transaction data

- Customer enters account number, PIN, and either:

    o A remittance slip is sent to the customer for confirming the transaction, containing a TAN (transaction number). The customer enters this number to confirm the transaction.

    o The customer signs the transaction digitally using a 2FA token (if their bank offers that service)

- Bank authorizes transaction in real-time, deducting the amount directly from the consumer's account (if there is not enough balance, the transaction will be refused)

- Merchant received real-time confirmation of the payment by the bank

- Consumer is redirected back to the merchant page with a confirmation that the payment has been successful

Payments are guaranteed for amounts up to 5000 euros.

Costs

Costs are calculated on a per transaction basis and decrease with transaction volume or value. The NetBanx payment gateway quotes figures from 1.2% to 0.9%, plus 8c euro per transaction.

eFaktura

eFaktura is a Norwegian electronic billing system issued by Nets Branch Norway AS (Nets). The system involves both business-to-customer (B2C) systems, branded as eFaktura, and business-to-business (B2B) branded as eFaktura B2B. The system is built upon the bankgiro system used for online banking.

Use of eFaktura require the customer to use an online banking system from a Norwegian bank. Because all banks are connected to BBS, there is no discrimination between customers of different banks. Any company or organisation can sign an eFaktura agreement with their bank (though usually for a typically five-digit NOK startup fee) and send electronic bills to any client as long as they have a Norwegian online banking account. There is no requirement for the two to use the same bank. The ordinary eFaktura includes a specification of the bill, and the entire bill or invoice can be seen in the online banking system, and printed if so desired. eFaktura was launched in 2000.

For companies the eFaktura B2B has been developed. Companies using electronic billing need to be able to import the invoice directly into the accounting software of the company. Nets offers services to send out paper bills to any company not able to receive electronic billing. eFaktura B2B was launched in 2006.

Micropayment

A micropayment is a financial transaction involving a very small sum of money and usually one that occurs online. A number of micropayment systems were proposed and developed in the mid-to-late 1990s, all of which were ultimately unsuccessful. A second generation of micropayment systems emerged in the 2010s.

While micropayments were originally envisioned to involve very small sums of money, practical systems to allow transactions of less than 1 USD have seen little success. One problem that has prevented the emergence of micropayment systems is a need to keep costs for individual transactions low, which is impractical when transacting such small sums even if the transaction fee is just a few cents.

Definition

There are a number of different definitions of what constitutes a micropayment. PayPal defines a micropayment as a transaction of less than £5 while Visa defines it as a transaction under 20 Australian dollars.

History

Micropayments were initially devised as a way of allowing the sale of online content and as a way to pay for very low cost network services. They were envisioned to involve small fractions of a cent, as little as US$0.0001 to a few cents. Micropayments would enable people to sell content on the Internet and would be an alternative to advertising revenue.

During the late 1990s, there was a movement to create microtransaction standards, and the World Wide Web Consortium (W3C) worked on incorporating micropayments into HTML even going as far as to suggest the embedding of payment-request information in HTTP error codes. The W3C has since stopped its efforts in this area, and micropayments have not become a widely used method of selling content over the Internet.

Early Research and Systems

In the late 1990s, established companies like IBM and Compaq had microtransaction divisions, and research on micropayments and micropayment standards was performed at Carnegie Mellon and by the World Wide Web Consortium.

IBM Micro Payments

IBM's Micro Payments was established c. 1999, and were it to have become operational would have "allowed vendors and merchants to sell content, information, and services over the Internet for amounts as low as one cent".

iPIN

An early attempt at making micropayments work, iPIN was a 1998 venture-capital-funded startup that provided services that allowed purchasers to add incremental micropayment charges to their existing bill for Internet services. Debuting in 1999, its service was never widely adopted.

Millicent

Millicent, originally a project of Digital Equipment Corporation, was a micropayment system that was to support transactions from as small as 1/10 of a cent up to $5.00. It grew out of The Millicent Protocol for Inexpensive Electronic Commerce, which was presented at the 1995 World Wide Web Conference in Boston, but the project became associated with Compaq after that company purchased Digital Equipment Corporation. The payment system employed symmetric cryptography.

NetBill

The NetBill electronic commerce project at Carnegie Mellon university researched distributed transaction processing systems and developed protocols and software to support payment for goods and services over the Internet. It featured pre-paid accounts from which micropayment charges could be drawn. NetBill was initially absorbed by CyberCash in 1997 and ultimately taken over by PayPal.

Online Gaming

The term micropayment or microtransaction is sometimes used to the sale of virtual goods in online games, most commonly involving an in game currency or service bought with real world money and only available within the online game.

Recent Micropayment Systems

Current systems either allow many micropayments but charge the user's phone bill one lump sum or use funded wallets.

Flattr

Flattr is a micropayment system (more specifically, a microdonation system) which launched in August, 2010. Actual bank transactions and overhead costs are involved only on funds withdrawn from the recipient's accounts.

M-Coin

A service provided by TIMWE, M-Coin allows users to make micropayments on the Internet. The user's phone bill is then charged by the mobile network operator.

PayPal

PayPal MicroPayments is a micropayment system that charges payments to user's PayPal account and allows transactions of less than US$12 to take place. As of 2013, the service is offered in selected currencies only.

SatoshiPay

SatoshiPay is a micropayment processing platform for online media. The service allows websites to monetize content through single click or automatic payments and removes friction associated with existing paywall solutions by operating without signup or software download for the end user. Transaction amounts down to US$0.01 or less, which the company calls "nanopayments", are enabled by the use of smart contracts and blockchain technology.

Swish

Swish is a payment system between bank accounts in Sweden. It is designed for use when private people pay each other instead of using cash (cash has become fairly little used in Sweden after 2010), but also sports clubs etc who don't want take the cost of a credit card reader is using it. The cell phone number is used as user number, which must have been registered in the internet bank. A smartphone app is used to send money, but any cell phone can be used as receiver. The lowest payment is 1 SEK (around €0,11) and the highest 10,000, although 150,000 SEK can be paid if the transaction is preregistered in the internet bank. The fee is in general zero, but the banks have hinted a future fee of 1 SEK. Is has become popular with 50 % of the Swedish population as users in 2016.

Zong

Zong mobile payments was a micropayment system that charged payments to users' mobile phone bills. The company was acquired by eBay and integrated with PayPal in 2011.

Transaction Processing

In computer science, transaction processing is information processing that is divided into individual, indivisible operations called *transactions*. Each transaction must succeed or fail as a complete unit; it can never be only partially complete.

For example, when you purchase a book from an online bookstore, you exchange money (in the form of credit) for a book. If your credit is good, a series of related operations ensures that you get the book and the bookstore gets your money. However, if a single operation in the series fails during the exchange, the entire exchange fails. You do not get the book and the bookstore does not get your money. The technology responsible for making the exchange balanced and predictable is called transaction processing. Transactions ensure that data-oriented resources are not permanently updated unless all operations within the transactional unit complete successfully. By combining a set of related operations into a unit that either completely succeeds or completely fails, one can simplify error recovery and make one's application more reliable.

Transaction processing systems consist of computer hardware and software hosting a transaction-oriented application that performs the routine transactions necessary to conduct business. Examples include systems that manage sales order entry, airline reservations, payroll, employee records, manufacturing, and shipping.

Since most, though not necessarily all, transaction processing today is interactive the term is often treated as synonymous with *online transaction processing*.

Description

Transaction processing is designed to maintain a system's Integrity (typically a database or some modern filesystems) in a known, consistent state, by ensuring that interdependent operations on the system are either all completed successfully or all canceled successfully.

For example, consider a typical banking transaction that involves moving $700 from a customer's savings account to a customer's checking account. This transaction involves at least two separate operations in computer terms: debiting the savings account by $700, and crediting the checking account by $700. If one operation succeeds but the other does not, the books of the bank will not balance at the end of the day. There must therefore be a way to ensure that either both operations succeed or both fail, so that there is never any inconsistency in the bank's database as a whole.

Transaction processing links multiple individual operations in a single, indivisible transaction, and ensures that either all operations in a transaction are completed without error, or none of them are. If some of the operations are completed but errors occur when the others are attempted, the transaction-processing system "rolls back" all of the operations of the transaction (including the successful ones), thereby erasing all traces of the transaction and restoring the system to the consistent, known state that it was in before processing of the transaction began. If all operations of a transaction are completed successfully, the transaction is committed by the system, and all changes to the database are made permanent; the transaction cannot be rolled back once this is done.

Transaction processing guards against hardware and software errors that might leave a transaction partially completed. If the computer system crashes in the middle of a transaction, the transaction processing system guarantees that all operations in any uncommitted transactions are cancelled.

Generally, transactions are issued concurrently. If they overlap (i.e. need to touch the same portion of the database), this can create conflicts. For example, if the customer mentioned in the example above has $150 in his savings account and attempts to transfer $100 to a different person while at the same time moving $100 to the checking account, only one of them can succeed. However, forcing transactions to be processed sequentially is inefficient. Therefore, concurrent implementations of transaction processing is programmed to guarantee that the end result reflects a conflict-free outcome, the same as could be reached if executing the transactions sequentially in any order (a property called serializability). In our example, this means that no matter which transaction was issued first, either the transfer to a different person or the move to the checking account succeeds, while the other one fails.

Methodology

The basic principles of all transaction-processing systems are the same. However, the terminology may vary from one transaction-processing system to another, and the terms used below are not necessarily universal.

Rollback

Transaction-processing systems ensure database integrity by recording intermediate states of the database as it is modified, then using these records to restore the database to a known state if a transaction cannot be committed. For example, copies of information on the database *prior* to its modification by a transaction are set aside by the system before the transaction can make any modifications (this is sometimes called a *before image*). If any part of the transaction fails before it is committed, these copies are used to restore the database to the state it was in before the transaction began.

Rollforward

It is also possible to keep a separate journal of all modifications to a database management system. (sometimes called *after images*). This is not required for rollback of failed transactions but it is useful for updating the database management system in the event of a database failure, so some transaction-processing systems provide it. If the database management system fails entirely, it must be restored from the most recent back-up. The back-up will not reflect transactions committed since the back-up was made. However, once the database management system is restored, the journal of after images can be applied to the database (*rollforward*) to bring the database management system up to date. Any transactions in progress at the time of the failure can then be rolled back. The result is a database in a consistent, known state that includes the results of all transactions committed up to the moment of failure.

Deadlocks

In some cases, two transactions may, in the course of their processing, attempt to access the same portion of a database at the same time, in a way that prevents them from proceeding. For example, transaction A may access portion X of the database, and transaction B may access portion Y of the database. If, at that point, transaction A then tries to access portion Y of the database while transaction B tries to access portion X, a *deadlock* occurs, and neither transaction can move forward. Transaction-processing systems are designed to detect these deadlocks when they occur. Typically both transactions will be cancelled and rolled back, and then they will be started again in a different order, automatically, so that the deadlock doesn't occur again. Or sometimes, just one of the deadlocked transactions will be cancelled, rolled back, and automatically restarted after a short delay.

Deadlocks can also occur among three or more transactions. The more transactions involved, the more difficult they are to detect, to the point that transaction processing systems find there is a practical limit to the deadlocks they can detect.

Compensating Transaction

In systems where commit and rollback mechanisms are not available or undesirable, a compensating transaction is often used to undo failed transactions and restore the system to a previous state.

ACID Criteria

Jim Gray defined properties of a reliable transaction system in the late 1970s under the acronym *ACID* — atomicity, consistency, isolation, and durability.

Atomicity

A transaction's changes to the state are atomic: either all happen or none happen. These changes include database changes, messages, and actions on transducers.

Consistency

Consistency: A transaction is a correct transformation of the state. The actions taken as a group do not violate any of the integrity constraints associated with the state.

Isolation

Even though transactions execute concurrently, it appears to each transaction T, that others executed either before T or after T, but not both.

Durability

Once a transaction completes successfully (commits), its changes to the state survive failures and retain its changes

Benefits

Transaction processing has these benefits:

- It allows sharing of computer resources among many users

- It shifts the time of job processing to when the computing resources are less busy

- It avoids idling the computing resources without minute-by-minute human interaction and supervision

- It is used on expensive classes of computers to help amortize the cost by keeping high rates of utilization of those expensive resources

Implementations

Standard transaction-processing software, notably IBM's Information Management System, was first developed in the 1960s, and was often closely coupled to particular database management systems. Client–server computing implemented similar principles in the 1980s with mixed success. However, in more recent years, the distributed client–server model has become considerably more difficult to maintain. As the number of transactions grew in response to various online services (especially the Web), a single distributed database was not a practical solution. In addition, most online systems consist of a whole suite of programs operating together, as opposed to a strict client–server model where the single server could handle the transaction processing. Today a number of transaction processing systems are available that work at the inter-program level and which scale to large systems, including mainframes.

One well-known (and open) industry standard is the X/Open Distributed Transaction Processing (DTP). However, proprietary transaction-processing environments such as IBM's CICS are still very popular, although CICS has evolved to include open industry standards as well.

The term 'Extreme Transaction Processing' (XTP) has been used to describe transaction processing systems with uncommonly challenging requirements, particularly throughput requirements (transactions per second). Such systems may be implemented via distributed or cluster style architectures.

Online Transaction Processing

Online transaction processing, or OLTP, is a class of information systems that facilitate and manage transaction-oriented applications, typically for data entry and retrieval transaction processing.

The term is somewhat ambiguous; some understand a "transaction" in the context of computer or database transactions, while others (such as the Transaction Processing Performance Council) define it in terms of business or commercial transactions. OLTP has also been used to refer to processing in which the system responds immediately to user requests. An automated teller machine (ATM) for a bank is an example of a commercial transaction processing application. Online transaction processing applications are high throughout and insert or update-intensive in database management. These applications are used concurrently by hundreds of users. The key goals of OLTP applications are availability, speed, concurrency and recoverability. Reduced paper trails and the faster, more accurate forecast for revenues and expenses are both examples of how OLTP makes things simpler for businesses. However, like many modern online information technology solutions, some systems require offline maintenance, which further affects the cost–benefit analysis of on line transaction processing system.

OLTP is typically contrasted to OLAP (online analytical processing), which is generally characterized by much more complex queries, in a smaller volume, for the purpose of business intelligence or reporting rather than to process transactions. Whereas OLTP systems process all kinds of queries (read, insert, update and delete), OLAP is generally optimized for read only and might not even support other kinds of queries.

Overview

OLTP system is a popular data processing system in today's enterprises. Some examples of OLTP systems include order entry, retail sales, and financial transaction systems. On line transaction processing system increasingly requires support for transactions that span a network and may include more than one company. For this reason, modern on line transaction processing software use client or server processing and brokering software that allows transactions to run on different computer platforms in a network.

In large applications, efficient OLTP may depend on sophisticated transaction management software (such as CICS) and/or database optimization tactics to facilitate the processing of large numbers of concurrent updates to an OLTP-oriented database.

For even more demanding decentralized database systems, OLTP brokering programs can distribute transaction processing among multiple computers on a network. OLTP is often integrated into service-oriented architecture (SOA) and Web services.

On line transaction processing (OLTP) involves gathering input information, processing the information and updating existing information to reflect the gathered and processed information. As of today, most organizations use a database management system to support OLTP. OLTP is carried in a client server system.

On line transaction process concerns about concurrency and atomicity. Concurrency controls guarantee that two users accessing the same data in the database system will not be able to change that data or the user has to wait until the other user has finished processing, before changing that piece of data. Atomicity controls guarantee that all the steps in transaction are completed successfully as a group. That is, if any steps between the transaction fail, all other steps must fail also.

Systems Design

To build an OLTP system, a designer must know that the large number of concurrent users does not interfere with the system's performance. To increase the performance of OLTP system, designer must avoid the excessive use of indexes and clusters.

The following elements are crucial for the performance of OLTP systems:

- Rollback segments

  Rollback segments are the portions of database that record the actions of transactions in the event that a transaction is rolled back. Rollback segments provide read consistency, roll back transactions, and recover the database.

- Clusters

  A cluster is a schema that contains one or more tables that have one or more columns in common. Clustering tables in database improves the performance of join operation.

- Discrete transactions

  All changes to the data are deferred until the transaction commits during a discrete transaction. It can improve the performance of short, non-distributed transaction.

- Block (data storage) size

  The data block size should be a multiple of the operating system's block size within the maximum limit to avoid unnecessary I/O.

- Buffer cache size

  To avoid unnecessary resource consumption, tune SQL statements to use the database buffer cache.

- Dynamic allocation of space to tables and rollback segments

- Transaction processing monitors and the multi-threaded server

  A transaction processing monitor is used for coordination of services. It is like an operating system and does the coordination at a high level of granularity and can span multiple computing devices.

- Partition (database)

  Partition increases performance for sites that have regular transactions while still maintain availability and security.

- Database tuning

With database tuning, OLTP system can maximize its performance as efficiently and rapidly as possible.

Contrasted to

- Batch processing

- Grid computing

Peer-to-peer Banking

Peer-to-peer banking is an online system that allows individual members to complete financial transactions with one another by using an auction style process that lets members offer loans for a specific amount and at a specific rate.

Operation

Buyers have the option to look for an amount and rate of interest that meets their needs. All members are categorized by their risk level. Members can browse for other people based on various demographic information.

Since P2P banking does not use third party banking institution intermediaries the rates and terms are often much more favourable for the members.

Unlike conventional banking where the spread between deposit rates and lending rates are consumed to finance the bank's administrative and logistic expenses, both lenders and borrowers get to save such costs, while paying certain commission to the P2P portal provider and/or the credit rating agency.

P2P banking and financing has been proposed as a method to accelerate the development renewable energy projects while more equitably distributing the return on investment. These concepts have now been instituted by Energy in Common and Kiva in their green fund.

Models of P2P Banking

The following two pictures show the difference between the peer to peer banking approach and the normal way with a financial institute.

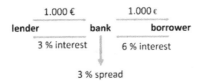

Traditional banking model (simplified)

Peer to peer banking model (simplified)

Google Wallet

Google Wallet is a peer-to-peer payments service developed by Google that allows people to send and receive money from a mobile device or desktop computer at no cost to either sender or receiver. When set up, a Google Wallet account must be linked to an existing debit card or bank account in the United States. Google Wallet can be used through the Google Wallet app, Gmail and the Google Wallet Card. The app is available for Android devices running Android 4.0 and above, and for iOS devices running iOS 7.0 and above. Google Wallet also had NFC payment capabilities, until the creation of Android Pay

The physical Google Wallet Card was an optional addition to the app which allowed users to make purchases at point-of-sale (in stores or online) drawing from funds in their Google Wallet account, attached debit card account, or bank account. The card could also be used to withdraw cash at ATMs with no Google-associated fee, and could be used like a debit card for virtually any purpose, including such things as renting a car. It was discontinued on June 30, 2016.

Service

Google Wallet is structured to allow its patrons to send money to each other. To send money, a Google Wallet user enters the email address or phone number of the recipient. The recipient must then link that phone number or email address to a bank account in order to access those funds. If the recipient also has a Google Wallet account, the funds will post to that account directly.

Users can link up to two U.S. bank accounts when the Wallet account is created. Received money goes to the Google Wallet Balance and stays there until the user decides to cash out to a linked account, or spend it directly from there using a Google Wallet Card.

The Google Wallet app is available for free from either Google Play or the App Store. After downloading the app, the user creates a four-digit personal identification number (PIN) for managing everything within their Google Wallet account. The PIN verifies access to the Wallet app on the user's mobile device.

Before it was discontinued on June 30, 2016, the Google Wallet Card was recognized by the Cirrus network operated by MasterCard (rather than the Plus network operated by Visa).

History

Early History

The Google Wallet card

Google demonstrated the original version of the service at a press conference on May 26, 2011. The first app was released in the US only on September 19, 2011.

On May 15, 2013, Google announced the integration of Google Wallet and Gmail, allowing users to send money through Gmail attachments. While Google Wallet is available only in the United States, the Gmail integration is currently available in the U.S. and the United Kingdom.

The original version of Google Wallet allowed users to make point-of-sale purchases with their mobile devices using near-field communication (NFC) technology. As of September 2015, however, Google dropped NFC from Google Wallet, offering the technology only through Android Pay, which is a separate application available only to Android users. As a result, any gift cards, loyalty programs, and promotional offers stored in an older version of Google Wallet could no longer be used. For Android users, those outstanding offers and gift cards were automatically transferred to Android Pay. For iOS users, instructions were provided to export the offers for alternative use. There were no reported security problems with the NFC technology.

On March 31, 2016, Google announced that it was dropping support for the Google Wallet Card as of June 30, 2016.

Distinction from Android Pay

On February 23, 2015, Google announced that it would acquire the intellectual property of the carrier-backed competitor Softcard and integrate it into Google Wallet, and that AT&T Mobility, T-Mobile US, and Verizon Wireless would bundle the Google Wallet app on their compatible devices. The effective merger resulted in the new service known as Android Pay, a competitor to Apple Pay and similar NFC mobile payment service.

Separate from Android Pay, Google Wallet now allows peer-to-peer transactions for cases such as when people want to split the cost of shared expenses, reimburse each other, keep track of joint spending, or give money as a gift or loan.

While Android Pay is only available to Android users, Google Wallet is available on iOS and via Gmail as well. For those using Android, the two products together (Android Pay and Google Wallet) offer a comprehensive payments management system, a "tool for staying in charge of the bank account." Users can link their bank accounts or debit cards to Android Pay and to their Google Wallet app. With this approach, users can manage their money from one source, with the ability to:

- Pay at point-of-sale by tapping their phone (via Android Pay)

- Send and receive money to other individuals for free (via the Google Wallet app)

- Keep track of spending (through the optional Google Wallet Card)

Business Model

Google does not charge users for access to Google Wallet. Sending and receiving money is free, as is adding money to a Wallet Card through a linked bank account. There are limits on how much money users can add to their Wallet Balance, withdraw from the linked account or card, or send and receive to other individuals. These limits are set per transaction and within certain time periods. Previously, a 2.9% fee applied to funds added via debit card, although Google dropped that ability as of May 2, 2016.

Funds sent from a Wallet balance, debit card, or linked bank account are generally available to the recipient immediately, and if the recipient has his or her own Wallet account and card, he or she can make an immediate withdrawal of those funds from an ATM. If the funds are drawn on the sender's Wallet balance, the balance will also reflect this change immediately. Any portion of funds drawn via a linked bank account will take two or three days to actually post to that account, though these funds will show as "pending" withdrawals on that account within 24 hours.

While Google does not have revenue coming in from the Wallet ecosystem (the web service, app, and the Wallet Card), the product is part of a larger suite of e-commerce products, including Android Pay, which integrates loyalty programs and promotions from other businesses.

Security

Google Wallet protects payment credentials by storing user data on secure servers and encrypting all payment information with industry-standard SSL (secure socket layer) technology. Full credit and debit card information is never shown in the app. All Google Wallet users are also required to have a PIN to protect access to their Wallet account. The payments PIN is used for:

- Gaining access to the Google Wallet app on a mobile device

- Making point-of-sale purchases with a Google Wallet Card

- Withdrawing cash with a Google Wallet Card at an ATM

Google also recommends having a general passcode on mobile devices for additional security.

In some cases, users have to verify their identity in order to make certain transactions. If prompted to do so, the user will visit the Wallet website and follow steps to ensure their accurate identity. This is in adherence with US Federal Deposit Insurance Corporation financial regulations that require payment providers to ensure customer identity.

If a Google Wallet Card is lost or stolen, users can immediately cancel access to it by signing into myaccount.google.com. Google also offers the additional flexibility of temporarily locking the card if a user suspects that the card has simply been misplaced. In the event of unauthorized transactions, Google Wallet Fraud Protection covers 100% of verified unauthorized transactions made in the US reported within 120 days of the transaction. Only US residents who have Wallet accounts associated with a US address are eligible for coverage under this policy.

Criticism

Regarding an earlier version of Google Wallet (in 2012), an analysis by security company NowSecure revealed that some card information stored by Google Wallet was accessible outside of the application. It is suggested that hackers could create a way to intercept data by eavesdropping on Google Analytics, which monitors apps used on the Android OS. A previous analysis by the same firm revealed a number of other exploits that have since been fixed.

Privacy

Privacy concerns include the storing of data regarding payment information, transaction details, payment attempts and other information stored by Google indefinitely. The privacy policy for Google Wallet, called the Google Payments Privacy Notice, indicates that much of the data is stored but may not be shared outside Google except under certain circumstances. Information that may be collected upon signing up includes credit or debit card number and expiration date, address, phone number, date of birth, social security number, or taxpayer ID number. Information that may be collected about a transaction made through Google Wallet includes date, time, and amount of transaction, merchant's location and description, a description of goods or services purchased, any photo the user associates with the transaction, the names and email addresses of sender and recipient, the type of payment method used, and a description of the reason for the transaction if included.

The storage of such personal information about users' transactions is of significant financial value to a company that earns much of its revenue from data, but may be controversial to users aware of the policies. Information collected is shared with Google's affiliates, meaning other companies owned and controlled by Google Inc., which can be used for their everyday business purposes. They provide the option to opt out of certain sharing capacities with these affiliates. Google states that it will only share personal information with other companies or individuals outside of Google in the following circumstances:

- As permitted under the Google Privacy Policy

- As necessary to process your transaction and maintain your account

- To complete your registration for a service provided by a third party

PayPal Lawsuit

Shortly after the launch of Google Wallet's first iteration in 2011, PayPal filed a lawsuit against Google and two former employees of PayPal – Osama Bedier and Stephanie Tilenius. The complaint alleges "misappropriation of trade secrets" and "breach of fiduciary duty". The lawsuit reveals that Google was negotiating with PayPal for two years to power payments on mobile devices. But just as the deal was about to be signed, Google backed off and instead hired the PayPal executive negotiating the deal, Bedier. The lawsuit notes that Bedier knew all of PayPal's future plans for mobile payments, as well as an internal detailed analysis of Google's weaknesses in the area. Not only that, it accuses him of storing "confidential information in locations such as his non-PayPal computers, non-PayPal e-mail account, and an account on the remote computing service called 'Dropbox.'"

Google ran a competitor to PayPal, Google Checkout, from 2006 to 2013. In 2011, Google Wallet replaced Checkout's services, and development on Checkout was discontinued in 2013.

Comparison of Payment systems

Comparison of payment systems (also known as comparison of payment processing services, comparison of payment processors, or comparison of merchant services) is a list displaying comparative information and fee rates on various payment systems (also payment processing services, payment processor, or merchant services). Information such as these are compared and shown: seller's/merchant's fees, buyer's fees, banking transfer fees, clearing-house fees, interchange fees, chargeback/return fees, currency conversion fees, monthly fees, usage, verification time, deposit time, technology support, customer-service quality, etc.

There are too many payment systems and services providers to list in detail or in brief all on the same page. This article will focus mainly on the payment/merchant systems and services that are the most popular among majority of sellers and buyers, have comparatively lowest fee rate or free options, and which have comparatively most features for sellers/merchants and buyers, lowest cost or free payment receiving (card readers, PT, POS) & printing equipments, and which have good or better track record, (good or better) customer service quality, etc according to BBB and similar credible rating services.

Displayed fees and rates can change anytime. Displayed fee-data and rate info may not be actual fee or rate in use currently right now. Fee-rates also vary, based on volumes/quantities of sale, for different seller/business, i.e. sellers/merchants can negotiate with payment-system or merchant-service provider to obtain a comparatively lower & better rate, when their selling volume is comparatively very high. When this page is edited by Wikipedia editors, then they will usually add at-that-moment minimum-fee or flat-rate info, for the section which they are editing. Visit payment-system's referenced linked webpage (shown at bottom-side), for payment service provider's current information.

General Comparison Information

To find the definition of an unknown abbreviation, please press Ctrl+F (or Cmd+F) and then type in that abbreviation and press the ">" or "<" button to find the location where it is shown in full.

Payment System Name: brief comparative, key-points & highlighted description. Y = Yes. N = No. I = Incomplete. P = Partial. aka = also known as, aka Alias. Vsa = Visa. Ds = Discover. AmEx = American Express. MC = MasterCard. Dn = Diner. TR / Tx = Transaction. TX = Transmit/Send. RCV / RX = Receive. RCVd / RXd = Received. POS = Point of Sale. PT = Payment Terminal, aka POS. NFC = Near Field Communicator. HCE = Host Card Emulation. MS / MSC = Magnetic Stripe card. MST = Magnetic Secure Transmission (used to emulate MSC). EMVCo / EMV = Europay, MasterCard, and Visa (cards with electronic IC/Chip). ACH = Automated Clearing House. Crd / Cr = Credit, Credit Card. Dbt / Db = Debit, Debit Card. ETF = Early Termination Fee. PTF / PTC = Minimum Per Transaction Fee (aka, Per Transaction Cost). BBB = Better Business Bureau. M.Phn.App / M.App = Mobile Phone/Device App. Bnk = Bank. Acnt / Accnt = Account. Chk = Checking, Checking/Deposit acnt. Sav = Savings, Savings acnt. Thru = Through. Frm = From. Pswrd = Password. KB / kB = KiloBytes (equals to 1024 Bytes). BTC = XBT = ฿ = ฿ = bitcoin (virtual currency, aka, virtual commodity). DOSP = Depends On Service Provider. DD / DC = Direct Deposit (aka Direct Credit, aka ACH, aka Giro, aka Direct Entry). DW = Direct Debit aka Direct Withdrawal, aka ACH, aka PAD, aka PAP. Tech = Technology.	Retail Shopping Centers /Markets POS Support	Online Shopping Carts Support Tech
Monthly Fee. Yearly Fee / Vsa/MC/Ds Swipe Fee / AmEx Fee / Keyed-In Fee / Free Equipment / ACH/ DW/ DC/ chk Fee / ETF		-
Amazon Local Register (ALR): no chargeback/return fees, no international fees. A $10 card-reader device purchase is necessary, (and a free App from Apple app-store or Android play-store), to attach with seller's own (non-rooted or non-jailbroken)	Y	Y

mobile device, and then Amazon gives credit of $10 into seller's accnt (after opening account), so card-reader is free (but this policy may have been changed currently by Amazon, so inquire on this before proceeding). Fees which are charged to sellers/ merchants are shown in below table-row. Next-day deposit. Bank statement (as PDF file) is required to be submitted to ALR to verify bnk acnt, or bnk-acnt password is needed to be shared with ALR, (change pswrd after they verified bnk acnt, or change pswrd 1st to something temporary but not too easy, and then share it to verify bnk acnt). Keyed-in TR may be kept on-hold for 7 to 14 days. ALR m.app forcefully requires GPS geo-location access.   **Y**   **MSC**

| N. N | Vsa/MC/Ds Swipe: 2.5% | AmEx: 2.5% | Keyed-In: 2.99% | Free Equipment: Yes | | ETF: No | |

Apple Pay: it is used, for example in iTunes stores or in Apple Store, etc. Apple based services, products, and it is also supported by many retail shopping centers+markets & POS. Apple initially charged (or taken-away or cut) around 0.15%--0.30% fee from each payment TR paid by buyer (using their Crd/Dbt cards), and rest ended-up going into seller's hand. This was changed in Sept, 2015, Apple now charges around 15% + $0.15 from each payment TR, before giving rest of the amount to seller. And, banks take-away around 2% fee from Apple's portion for each (Apple Pay) TR. If seller's or merchant's PT/POS supports NFC, then it will also accept Apple Pay based payment. If NFC support is not present in PT/POS, then Apple Pay will not work.   **Y Y** / **Y NFC**

| N. N | Vsa/MC/Ds Swipe: 15% + $0.15 | AmEx: 15% + $0.15 | | Free Equipment: No | | ETF: No | |

Bitcoin Payment System: bitcoin transaction fees. Such payment processing services are used by bitcoin (virtual currency, aka virtual commodity) supporting trading services, products. It is supported by some retail shopping centers+markets & POS, and it is supported by many online (centralized+decentralized) shopping centers/ markets/stores. Usually btc transaction (TR/Tx) fee was ฿0 (zero), but changed into "Cost very little". To transfer bitcoin virtual-currency (aka, bitcoin virtual-commodity) from one bitcoin-wallet to another wallet, and to include that proof of transfer in Bitcoin blockchain (decentralized distributed database) and to receive verification (or proof, or confirmations) on that transfer very quickly (within 15 minutes or 1:30 hour:minutes), then there is a variable higher fee rate which is charged by bitcoin miners. But currently minimum fee for miners is close to or around ฿0.00001 btc per KB (kilobytes) of data/info for a confirmed btc transfer. A typical btc TR may contain around 0.5 KB (or 512 Bytes) of data. Some bitcoin mining service providers also support free or almost-free or very very low cost bitcoin-currency transfer (usually for a TR which has less than 1 KB data), though verification might be slightly delayed. For more info on such very-low cost or free confirmation, view: Free Tx Relay policy and Eligius mining pool. Sellers who cannot run their own btc mining hardware, bitcoin node, etc to include a Tx into the blockchain, or sellers who cannot integrate plugin/addon into their shopping-cart for connecting with their own btc mining & related servers/nodes, for receiving btc-Tx verification (aka, confirmations), for a sale/purchase, then such sellers have to use 3rd-party services from other btc exchange or other btc merchant service processor, etc and their processing fees are much higher. Seller/Merchant should not ship-out or deliver products or services, before receiving sufficient number of confirmations (>3) on a BTC/XBT payment.   **Y Y** / **Y DOSP**

N (DOSP). N (DOSP)	Vsa/MC/Ds Swipe: DOSP	AmEx: DOSP	Keyed-In: DOSP	Free Equipment: DOSP	ACH/ DW/ DC/ chk: DOSP	ETF: DOSP	
Capital One Merchant Services (Spark Pay): it has a no monthly-fee plan: Go plan. Fees which are charged to Go-Plan sellers/merchants, are shown below in table-row. Minimum PTF is $0.05. No minimum number of TR requirement. Mobile card reader device is included for free (it needs to be attached with Seller's own mobile device). Receipt can be emailed or network printer can be used for printing the receipt when paper/hard-copy receipt is required. SparkPay m.app (v1.5.0) forcefully requires GPS geo-location access, (when this info was added here on July 2, 2016). Mobile card reader does not support EMV/IC-chip feature yet. As EMV cards also has magnetic-stripe, so SparkPay free card-reader can still charge such cards.						Y Y	Y MSC M.App
Go.Plan N. N	Vsa/MC/Ds Swipe: 2.65% + $0.05	AmEx: 3.7% + $0.05	Keyed-In: 3.7% + $0.05	Free Equipment: Yes (Card Reader)		ETF: No	
Google Pay (aka, Google Wallet, upgraded into Android Pay): Google-Checkout was upgraded into Google-Wallet, then Google-Wallet was upgraded into Android-Pay (also known as Google-Pay). Android Pay (or Google Wallet) is used by Google based services, products, and supported by many retail shopping centers+markets & POS. Google Wallet allows users to send money from Wallet to other users, relatives, etc via their Android or iOS based phone, it also allows to receive money. Android Pay (GAP) is used by buyers for purchasing, and available mostly on Google Android OS based phone. Google charges sellers/merchants (or takes-away) around 30% fee from each payment TR what buyer pays. Google Wallet charged 2.9% fee to users when a fund was added (into Wallet) from Debit-card, but changed policy on May 2, 2016 that fund addition into Wallet is not allowed anymore from bnk-acnt or Dbt-card (after May 1, 2016), fund must be RCVd from another Wallet account or RCVd from another (Android Pay) user, and, fee for receiving fund is $0 (zero). Google Wallet (v15.0-R265-v4) and Android Pay (v1.4.125363284) m.apps both forcefully require access to GPS geo-location, (when this info was added here on July 2, 2016), Google Wallet (GW) even reads contacts-list, modify systems settings, etc. Such app need to ask user, before each access, and single contact needs to be copied out of user's Contacts-List and pasted manually into GW when needed. Usually Android v4.4 (KitKat) Phones & above, have NFC & HCE feature, which are needed for initiating payment from Google-Pay/Android-Pay supported devices. If seller's or merchant's PT/POS supports NFC, then it will also accept Google Pay based payments. If NFC support is not present in PT/POS then Google Pay will not work.						Y Y	Y NFC HCE M.App
N. N	Vsa/MC/Ds Swipe: 30%	AmEx: 30%	Keyed-In: 30%	Free Equipment: No		ETF: No	
Payment System Name: brief comparative, key-points & highlighted description. Y = Yes. N = No. I = Incomplete. P = Partial. aka = also known as, aka Alias. Vsa = Visa. Ds = Discover. AmEx = American Express. MC = MasterCard. Dn = Diner. TR / Tx = Transaction. TX = Transmit/Send. RCV / RX = Receive. RCVd / RXd = Received. POS = Point of Sale. PT = Payment Terminal, aka POS. NFC = Near Field Communicator. HCE = Host Card Emulation. MS / MSC = Magnetic Stripe card. MST = Magnetic Secure Transmission (used to emulate MSC). EMVCo / EMV = Europay, MasterCard, and Visa (cards with electronic IC/Chip). ACH = Automated Clearing House. Crd / Cr = Credit, Credit Card. Dbt / Db = Debit, Debit Card. ETF = Early Termination Fee. PTF / PTC = Minimum Per Transaction Fee (aka, Per Transaction Cost). BBB = Better Business Bureau. M.Phn.App / M.App = Mobile Phone/Device App. Bnk = Bank. Acnt / Accnt = Account. Chk = Checking, Checking/Deposit acnt.						Retail Shopping Centers /Markets POS Support	Online Shopping Carts Support Tech

Sav = Savings, Savings acnt. Thru = Through. Frm = From. Pswrd = Password. KB / kB = KiloBytes (equals to 1024 Bytes). BTC = XBT = ฿ = ฿ = bitcoin (virtual currency, aka, virtual commodity). DOSP = Depends On Service Provider. DD / DC = Direct Deposit (aka Direct Credit, aka ACH, aka Giro, aka Direct Entry). DW = Direct Debit aka Direct Withdrawal, aka ACH, aka PAD, aka PAP. Tech = Technology.

Monthly Fee. Yearly Fee	Vsa/MC/Ds Swipe Fee	AmEx Fee	Keyed-In Fee	Free Equipment	ACH/ DW/ DC/ chk Fee	ETF	-
National Processing (NP): it has low monthly fee. No long term contracts. Crd/Dbtcard processing service fees which are charged to sellers/merchants are shown in below table-row. Per return fee $2.00. Communicate early & make sure that your contract/agreement includes clause for No-ETF, if you obtained PT/POS.						Y / Y	Y / MSC
Y ($2.00 /month). N.	Vsa/MC/Ds Swipe: 2.7% + $0.20	AmEx: 2.7% + $0.20	Keyed-In: 2.7% + $0.20	Free Equipment: No	ACH/ DW/ DC/ chk: $15/ month + $0.24/ TR	ETF: No	
North American Bancard (NAB): per TR fees charged to sellers/merchants are shown in below table-row. Month-to-month contract. No Startup fees. Gateway/Virtual-Terminal: Authorize.Net. Communicate early & make sure that your contract/agreement includes clause for No-ETF, if you obtained PT/POS.						Y / Y	Y / MSC EMV NFC Tablet M.App
N. N	Vsa/MC/Ds Swipe: 0.29%	AmEx: 0.29%	Keyed-In: 0.29%	Free Equipment: Yes (Virtual Terminal App)		ETF: No	
PayPal: fees charged to sellers/merchants for each TR by the PayPal is shown in below table-row. PayPal payment system can be integrated with other shopping cart systems, which enables individual website, retail+online shopping centers/markets or POS to accept payments on their own. And PayPal can also be used by any individuals for TX/RX (send/receive) personal payments. PayPal m.app v6.3.5 forcefully requires GPS geo-location, reads contacts-list, (when these info were added here on July 2, 2016). "PayPal Here" (PPH) service can allow sellers/merchants to receive payment on their own mobile devices with a free magnetic-stripe (MS) card-reader (a 2nd card-reader is $14), or with a $149 EMV(IC-chip)+MS card-reader from PayPal. Fees charged to sellers/merchants are shown in below table-row. PPH charges sellers/merchants 2.9% + $0.30 for any invoiced TR. PayPal-Here m.app (v2.6.2) forcefully collects list of all running apps, and reads sensitive log data from all apps, and forcefully accesses GPS based geo-location, reads contacts-list, (when these info were added here on July 2, 2016), so m.app very likely violating seller/merchant's Privacy-Rights.						Y / Y	Y / MSC M.App

PayPal: N. N	Vsa/MC/Ds Swipe: 2.90% + $0.30	AmEx: 2.90% + $0.30	Keyed-In: 2.90% + $0.30	Free Equipment: No		ETF: No	
PayPal Here: N. N	2.70%	2.70%	3.50% + $0.15	Yes (Card Reader)		No	

	Y	Y
Samsung Pay: it is used by Samsung-based services, products, and supported by many retail shopping centers/markets & POS. When Samsung Pay is used via Samsung smartphone devices, then fee for buyer is $0.000 (zero), and fee for seller is also $0.000 (zero). In S. Korea (home/origin nation of Samsung) it is already free even for non-Samsung devices. According to a March, 2015 report, when Samsung Pay is used via other non-Samsung devices then Samsung may charge seller or may take-away 0.015% fee from each payment TR. But according to a later April, 2015 report, Samsung indicated this 0.015% fee per-TR policy for sellers/merchants, may be changed into "free" per transaction, when the service will be finalized for US & other countries. Then according to a June, 2016 report, Samsung Pay is now totally free, (zero) $0.00 fee, for any TR, for both sellers/merchants and buyers. Mobile phone users (buyers) in US (and other countries) need to use specific series of Samsung mobile phones, for Samsung Pay based buying+payment to work. If seller's or merchant's PT/POS already supports NFC, then it can also accept Samsung Pay based payments easily. Many (or most) sellers/merchants are still using magnetic-stripe (MS) card reader based PT/POS. Most of such PT/POS will still work with Samsung Pay supported payment devices, but some PT/POS may need a software update, or a plugin/addon software tool can be loaded into the PT/POS to enable MST support. Even when a PT/POS does not support NFC, but if it supports regular magnetic-stripe (MS) payment cards, then Samsung Pay based payments can still work.	Y	MSC MST NFC EMV M.App

N. N	Vsa/MC/Ds Swipe: 0.000% + $0.000	AmEx: 0.000% + $0.000	Keyed-In: 0.000% + $0.000	Free Equipment: No		ETF: No	

	Y	Y
Stripe: Stripe charges sellers/merchants fees, which are shown in below table-row. Each ACH TR has a max-fee, capped-at max-$5, (when buyer used their bank's chk acnt for sending payment). Stripe charges seller ฿0.50% from bitcoin based payment. Each chargeback/return fee includes $15 fee. Stripe payment system can be integrated with other shopping cart systems, which enables individual website, retail+online shopping centers+markets & POS to accept payments on their own. Does not require a Merchant-Account.	Y	MSC

N. N	Vsa/MC/Ds Swipe: 2.90% + $0.30	AmEx: 2.90% + $0.30	Keyed-In: 2.90% + $0.30	Free Equipment: No	ACH/ DW/ DC/ chk: 0.8% + $0.30

	Y	Y
Total Merchant Services (TMS): No long-term contracts. Month-to-month contract. Recently they may be offering free equipment, (must be returned when service is cancelled), inquire on this before proceeding. Free online marketing tool. 2 days deposit. Cr/Db goes thru Global Payments. Groovv POS Terminal for retail outlets. Communicate early & make sure your contract/agreement clearly includes clause for No-ETF, and also make sure No-ETF exists for "Global Payments" too.	Y	MSC NFC EMV

N. N				Virtual Terminal web app is free. USB Reader is free. Mobile PaymentJack rent is $5/month	ETF: No	
Payment System Name: brief comparative, key-points & highlighted description. Y = Yes. N = No. I = Incomplete. P = Partial. aka = also known as, aka Alias. Vsa = Visa. Ds = Discover. AmEx = American Express. MC = MasterCard. Dn = Diner. TR / Tx = Transaction. TX = Transmit/Send. RCV / RX = Receive. RCVd / RXd = Received. POS = Point of Sale. PT = Payment Terminal, aka POS. NFC = Near Field Communicator. HCE = Host Card Emulation. MS / MSC = Magnetic Stripe card. MST = Magnetic Secure Transmission (used to emulate MSC). EMVCo / EMV = Europay, MasterCard, and Visa (cards with electronic IC/Chip). ACH = Automated Clearing House. Crd / Cr = Credit, Credit Card. Dbt / Db = Debit, Debit Card. ETF = Early Termination Fee. PTF / PTC = Minimum Per Transaction Fee (aka, Per Transaction Cost). BBB = Better Business Bureau. M.Phn.App / M.App = Mobile Phone/Device App. Bnk = Bank. Acnt / Accnt = Account. Chk = Checking, Checking/Deposit acnt. Sav = Savings, Savings acnt. Thru = Through. Frm = From. Pswrd = Password. KB / kB = KiloBytes (equals to 1024 Bytes). BTC = XBT = ฿ = ฿ = bitcoin (virtual currency, aka, virtual commodity). DOSP = Depends On Service Provider. DD / DC = Direct Deposit (aka Direct Credit, aka ACH, aka Giro, aka Direct Entry). DW = Direct Debit aka Direct Withdrawal, aka ACH, aka PAD, aka PAP. Tech = Technology.					Retail Shopping Centers /Markets / POS Support	Online Shopping Carts Support / Tech
Monthly Fee. Yearly Fee	Vsa/MC/Ds Swipe Fee	AmEx Fee	Keyed-In Fee	Free Equipment	ACH/ DW/ DC/ chk Fee	ETF	-

References

- Degeler, Andrii (25 February 2016). "The future of media monetization: Cryptocurrencies and micropayments". The Next Web. Retrieved 2016-05-24.

- Allison, Ian (1 February 2016). "Blockchain innovator SatoshiPay offers alternative to advertising for web publishers". International Business Times. Retrieved 2016-05-24.

- UTC, Christina Warren2011-05-26 12:00:29. "Google Reveals Mobile Payment System: Google Wallet". Mashable. Retrieved 2016-02-08.

- Olivarez-Giles, Nathan (2015-09-10). "Android Pay Goes Live, Google Wallet Becomes Cash Swap App". WSJ Blogs - Personal Tech News. Retrieved 2016-02-08.

- "What is a Payment System?" (PDF). Federal Reserve Bank of New York. 13 Oc 2000. Retrieved 23 July 2015.

- Rao, Leena (October 26, 2010). "PayPal Unveils Micropayments For Digital Goods, Facebook Signs Up". techcrunch.com. AOL. Retrieved November 23, 2012.

- Gray, Jim; Reuter, Andreas. "Transaction Processing - Concepts and Techniques (Powerpoint)". Retrieved Nov 12, 2012.

- Kevin Fogarty, Even after rewrites, Google Wallet retains gaping security holes, mainly due to Android, itworld, February 10, 2012.

- "MCoin Product Lines - Mobile Marketing magazine". Mobile Marketing Magazine. 2011-06-30. Retrieved 2011-07-02.

- McMahan, Ty (July 7, 2011). "EBay's Zong Deal: Mobile Payments Are All Fun & Games". WSJ Blogs: Venture Capital Dispatch

- K. Branker, E. Shackles, J. M. Pearce, "Peer-to-Peer Financing Mechanisms to Accelerate Renewable Energy Deployment" The Journal of Sustainable Finance & Investment 1(2), pp. 138- 155 (2011).

- "China's 'Super Online Banking System' Launches on Monday". Business China. August 30, 2010. Retrieved September 3, 2010.

- O'Hear, Steve (August 12, 2010). "Flattr opens to the public, now anybody can 'Like' a site with real money". TechCrunch Europe. Retrieved August 13, 2010.

Permissions

All chapters in this book are published with permission under the Creative Commons Attribution Share Alike License or equivalent. Every chapter published in this book has been scrutinized by our experts. Their significance has been extensively debated. The topics covered herein carry significant information for a comprehensive understanding. They may even be implemented as practical applications or may be referred to as a beginning point for further studies.

We would like to thank the editorial team for lending their expertise to make the book truly unique. They have played a crucial role in the development of this book. Without their invaluable contributions this book wouldn't have been possible. They have made vital efforts to compile up to date information on the varied aspects of this subject to make this book a valuable addition to the collection of many professionals and students.

This book was conceptualized with the vision of imparting up-to-date and integrated information in this field. To ensure the same, a matchless editorial board was set up. Every individual on the board went through rigorous rounds of assessment to prove their worth. After which they invested a large part of their time researching and compiling the most relevant data for our readers.

The editorial board has been involved in producing this book since its inception. They have spent rigorous hours researching and exploring the diverse topics which have resulted in the successful publishing of this book. They have passed on their knowledge of decades through this book. To expedite this challenging task, the publisher supported the team at every step. A small team of assistant editors was also appointed to further simplify the editing procedure and attain best results for the readers.

Apart from the editorial board, the designing team has also invested a significant amount of their time in understanding the subject and creating the most relevant covers. They scrutinized every image to scout for the most suitable representation of the subject and create an appropriate cover for the book.

The publishing team has been an ardent support to the editorial, designing and production team. Their endless efforts to recruit the best for this project, has resulted in the accomplishment of this book. They are a veteran in the field of academics and their pool of knowledge is as vast as their experience in printing. Their expertise and guidance has proved useful at every step. Their uncompromising quality standards have made this book an exceptional effort. Their encouragement from time to time has been an inspiration for everyone.

The publisher and the editorial board hope that this book will prove to be a valuable piece of knowledge for students, practitioners and scholars across the globe.

Index

CPSIA information can be obtained
at www.ICGtesting.com
Printed in the USA
BVOW07*2334010218
506942BV00004BA/210/P

9 781635 490534